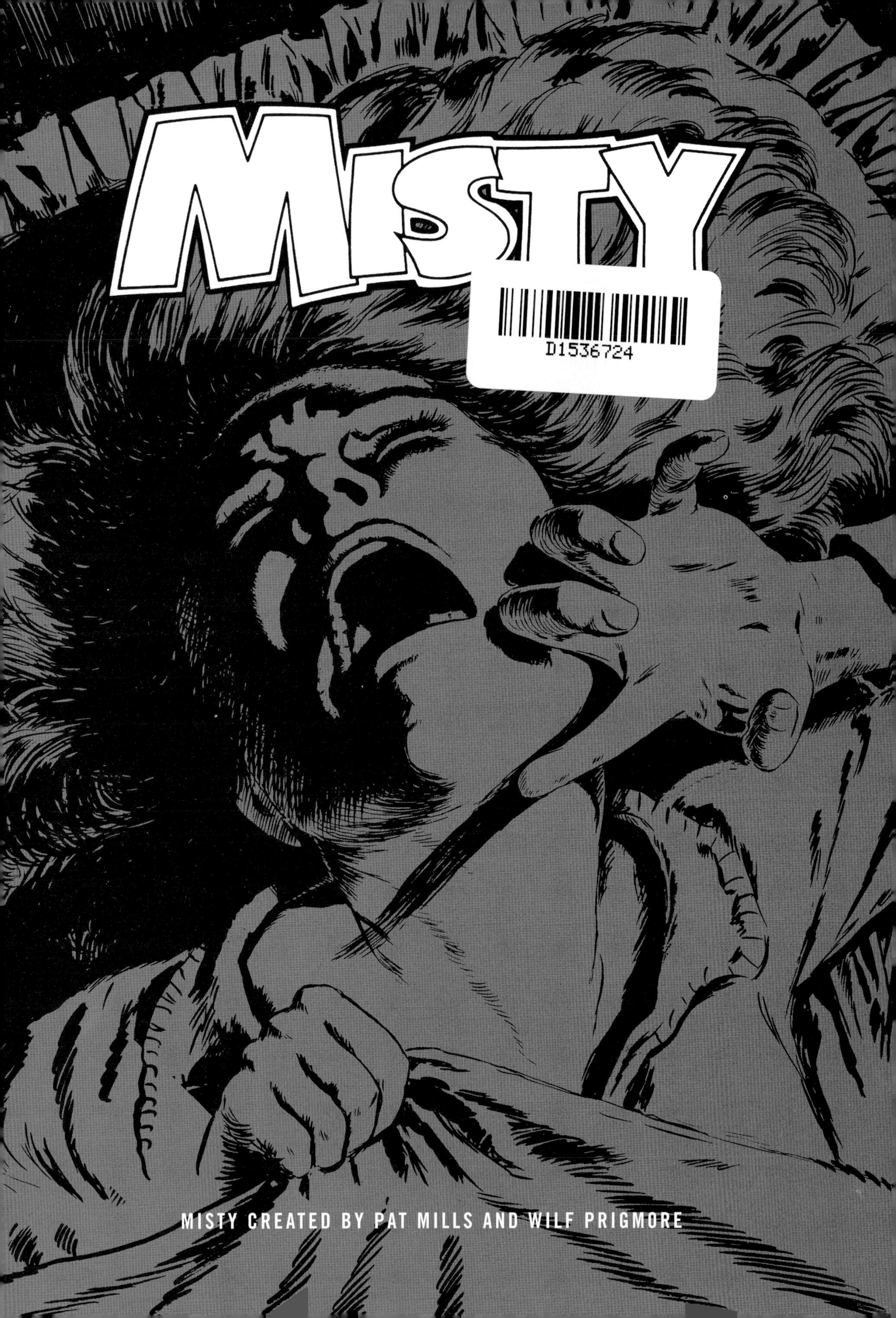
MISTY
MISTY CREATED BY PAT MILLS AND WILF PRIGMORE

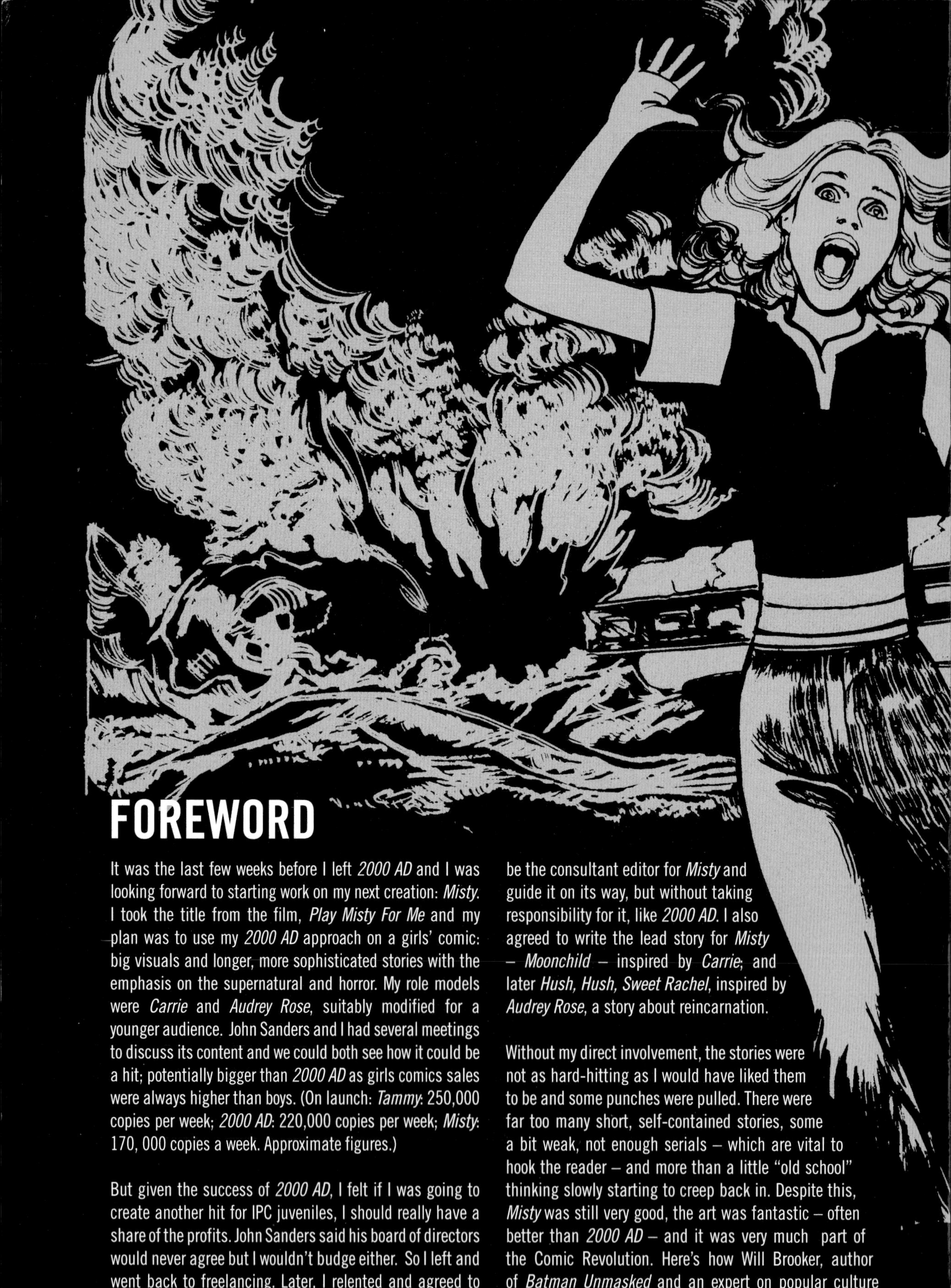

# FOREWORD

It was the last few weeks before I left *2000 AD* and I was looking forward to starting work on my next creation: *Misty*. I took the title from the film, *Play Misty For Me* and my plan was to use my *2000 AD* approach on a girls' comic: big visuals and longer, more sophisticated stories with the emphasis on the supernatural and horror. My role models were *Carrie* and *Audrey Rose*, suitably modified for a younger audience. John Sanders and I had several meetings to discuss its content and we could both see how it could be a hit; potentially bigger than *2000 AD* as girls comics sales were always higher than boys. (On launch: *Tammy*: 250,000 copies per week; *2000 AD*: 220,000 copies per week; *Misty*: 170, 000 copies a week. Approximate figures.)

But given the success of *2000 AD*, I felt if I was going to create another hit for IPC juveniles, I should really have a share of the profits. John Sanders said his board of directors would never agree but I wouldn't budge either. So I left and went back to freelancing. Later, I relented and agreed to be the consultant editor for *Misty* and guide it on its way, but without taking responsibility for it, like *2000 AD*. I also agreed to write the lead story for *Misty* – *Moonchild* – inspired by *Carrie*; and later *Hush, Hush, Sweet Rachel*, inspired by *Audrey Rose*, a story about reincarnation.

Without my direct involvement, the stories were not as hard-hitting as I would have liked them to be and some punches were pulled. There were far too many short, self-contained stories, some a bit weak, not enough serials – which are vital to hook the reader – and more than a little "old school" thinking slowly starting to creep back in. Despite this, *Misty* was still very good, the art was fantastic – often better than *2000 AD* – and it was very much part of the Comic Revolution. Here's how Will Brooker, author of *Batman Unmasked* and an expert on popular culture

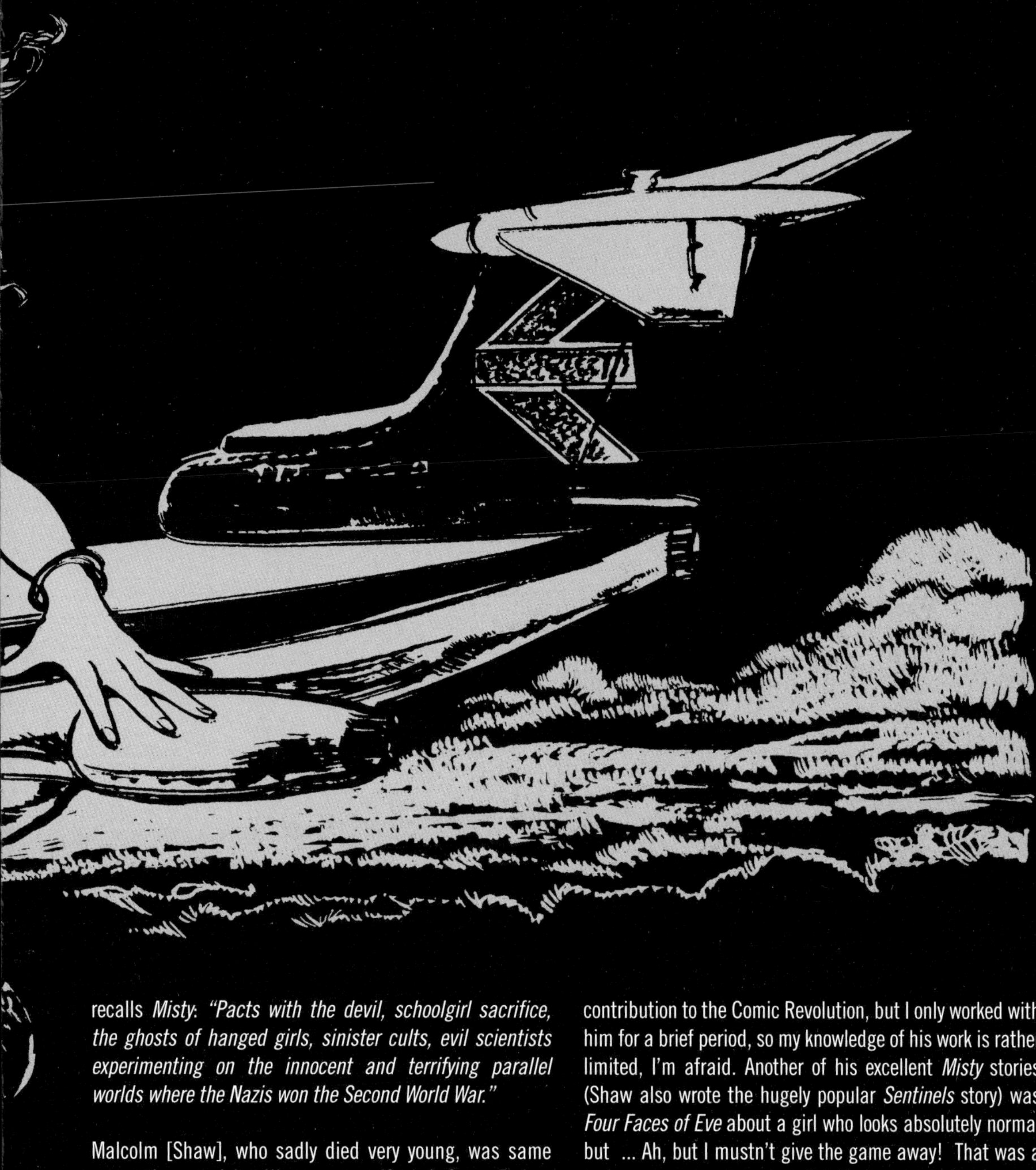

recalls *Misty*: *"Pacts with the devil, schoolgirl sacrifice, the ghosts of hanged girls, sinister cults, evil scientists experimenting on the innocent and terrifying parallel worlds where the Nazis won the Second World War."*

Malcolm [Shaw], who sadly died very young, was same generation as John Wagner, myself and Gerry Finley-Day (creator of *Tammy*). Why was it mainly guys on girls comics, I hear you ask? Answer: because all the younger female magazine journalists looked down on girls comics and didn't want to write or edit them, aspiring to teenage and women's glossy magazines instead.

Malcolm was a brilliant writer of girls comics and also some early *Judge Dredds*. We started *Jinty* together, dreaming up a selection of stories, before Mavis Miller (previously editor of *June*) was appointed editor and turned it into a very successful comic with a strong science fiction edge. Malcolm really deserves a separate article on his important contribution to the Comic Revolution, but I only worked with him for a brief period, so my knowledge of his work is rather limited, I'm afraid. Another of his excellent *Misty* stories (Shaw also wrote the hugely popular *Sentinels* story) was *Four Faces of Eve* about a girl who looks absolutely normal but ... Ah, but I mustn't give the game away! That was a truly awesome and scary serial. That was a truly awesome and scary serial with great art by Brian Delaney.

I've always regretted not creating *Misty* the way I created *2000 AD*. I've little doubt if I had, it would still be around today and it could have changed the British comics landscape for the better. Alas, *Misty* eventually died, but it's still well-thought of to this day. Many of us hope it could be reprinted with collected stories, just as *2000 AD* stories have been successfully collected. And here they finally are!

**Pat Mills**
**2012 & June 2016**

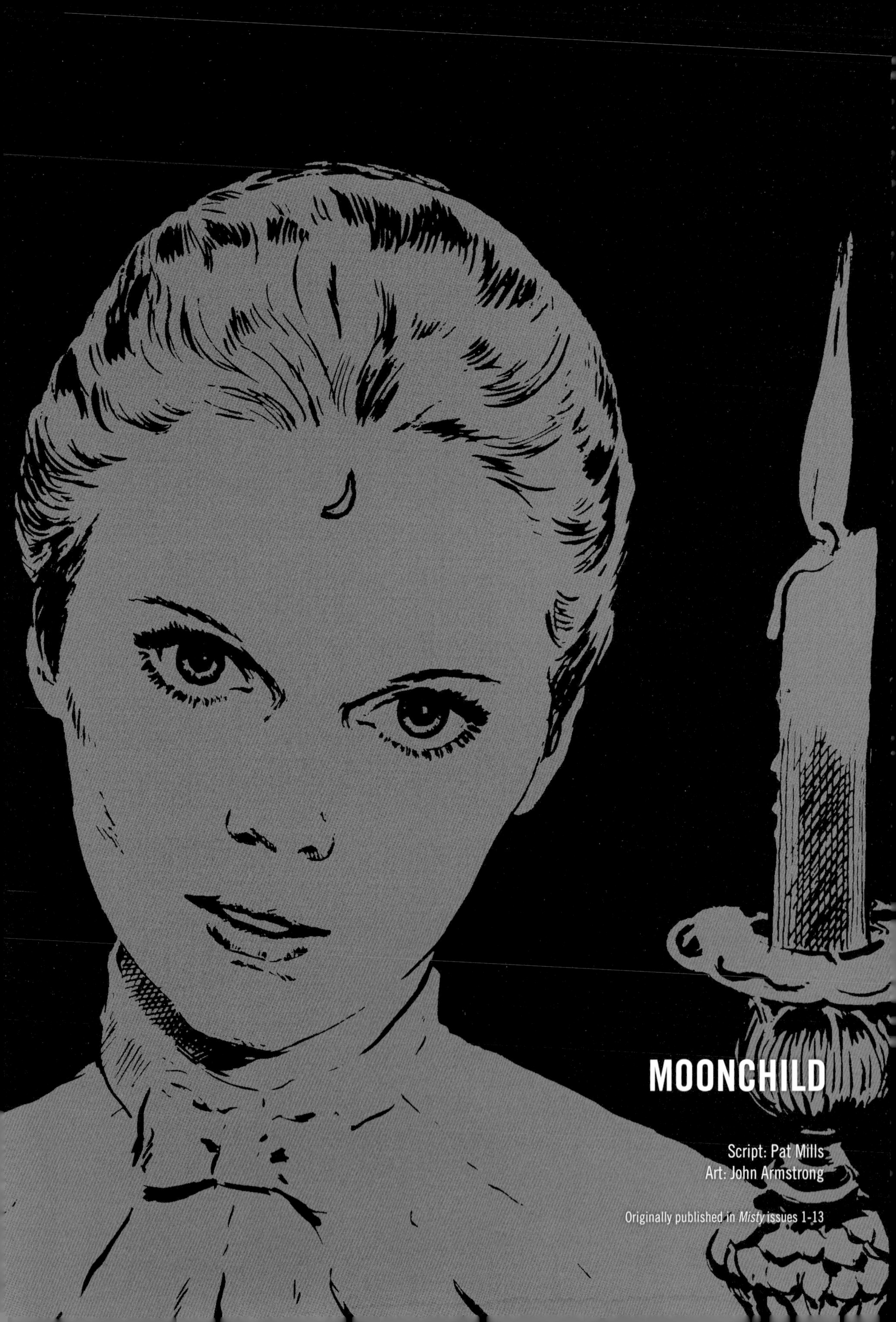

# MOONCHILD

Script: Pat Mills
Art: John Armstrong

Originally published in *Misty* issues 1-13

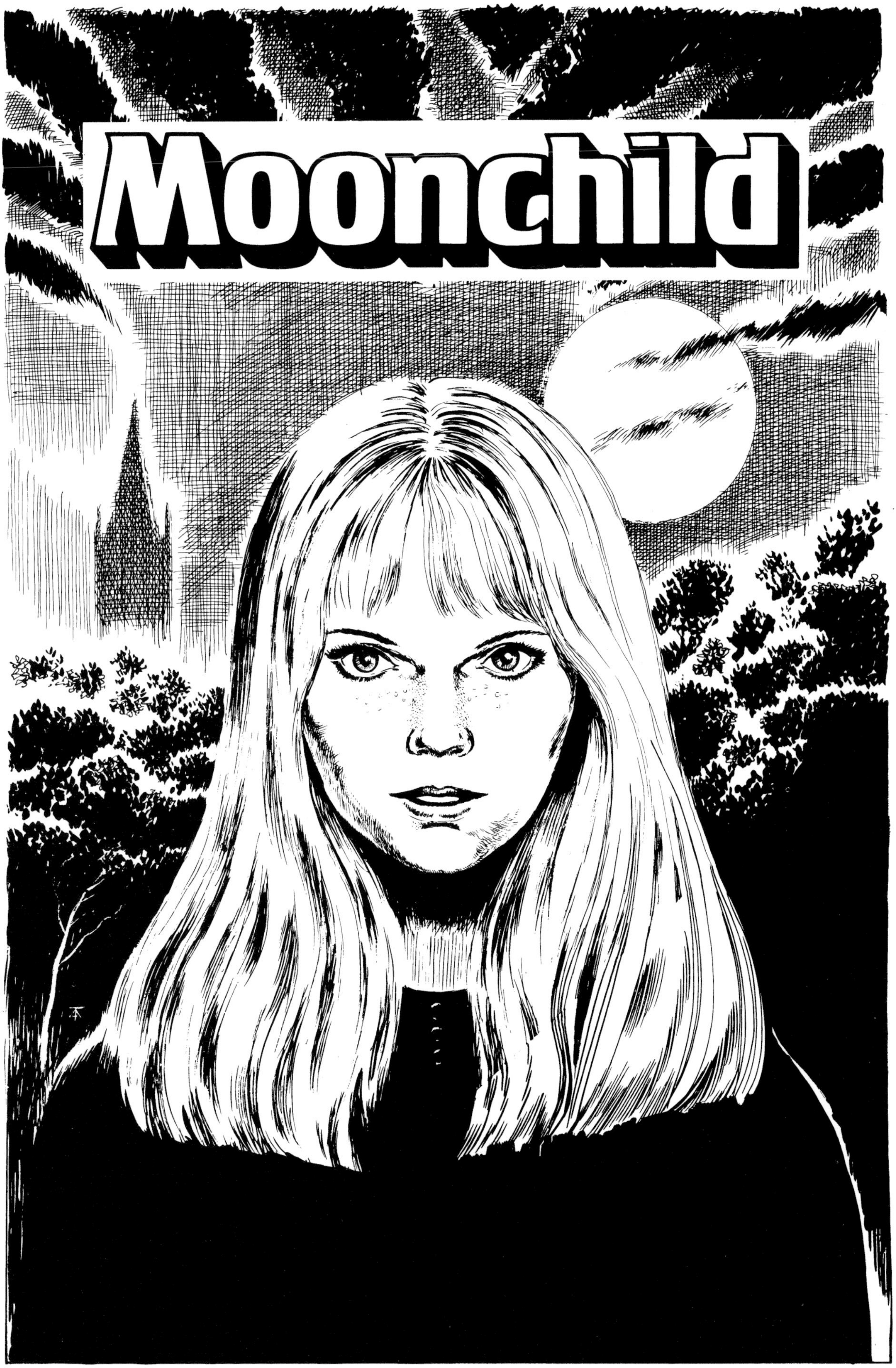
Moonchild

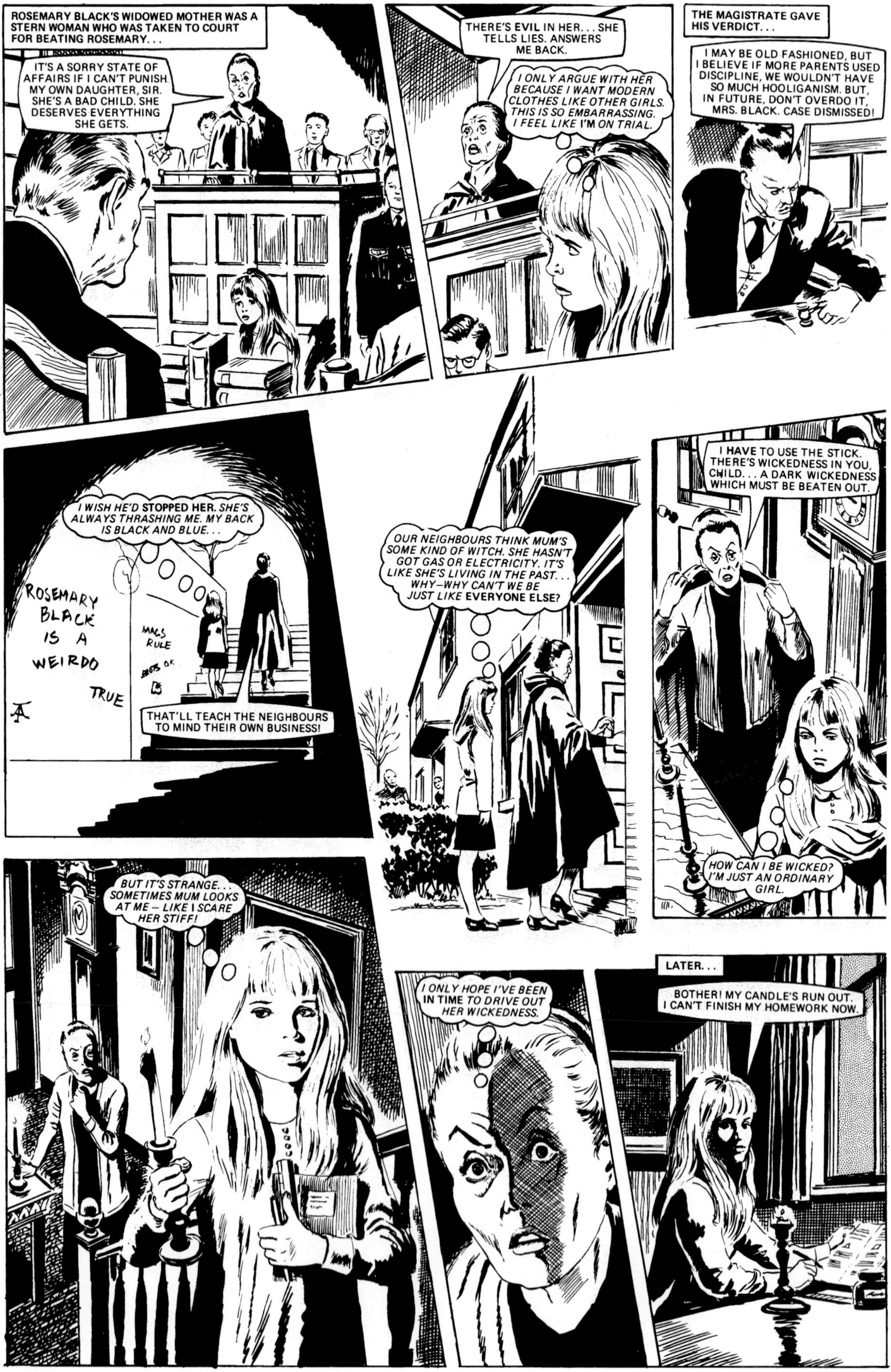

ROSEMARY BLACK'S WIDOWED MOTHER WAS A STERN WOMAN WHO WAS TAKEN TO COURT FOR BEATING ROSEMARY...
IT'S A SORRY STATE OF AFFAIRS IF I CAN'T PUNISH MY OWN DAUGHTER, SIR. SHE'S A BAD CHILD. SHE DESERVES EVERYTHING SHE GETS.
THERE'S EVIL IN HER... SHE TELLS LIES. ANSWERS ME BACK.
I ONLY ARGUE WITH HER BECAUSE I WANT MODERN CLOTHES LIKE OTHER GIRLS. THIS IS SO EMBARRASSING. I FEEL LIKE I'M ON TRIAL.
THE MAGISTRATE GAVE HIS VERDICT...
I MAY BE OLD FASHIONED, BUT I BELIEVE IF MORE PARENTS USED DISCIPLINE, WE WOULDN'T HAVE SO MUCH HOOLIGANISM. BUT, IN FUTURE, DON'T OVERDO IT, MRS. BLACK. CASE DISMISSED!
I WISH HE'D STOPPED HER. SHE'S ALWAYS THRASHING ME. MY BACK IS BLACK AND BLUE...
ROSEMARY BLACK IS A WEIRDO
TRUE
MAGS RULE
THAT'LL TEACH THE NEIGHBOURS TO MIND THEIR OWN BUSINESS!
OUR NEIGHBOURS THINK MUM'S SOME KIND OF WITCH. SHE HASN'T GOT GAS OR ELECTRICITY. IT'S LIKE SHE'S LIVING IN THE PAST... WHY—WHY CAN'T WE BE JUST LIKE EVERYONE ELSE?
I HAVE TO USE THE STICK. THERE'S WICKEDNESS IN YOU, CHILD... A DARK WICKEDNESS WHICH MUST BE BEATEN OUT.
HOW CAN I BE WICKED? I'M JUST AN ORDINARY GIRL.
BUT IT'S STRANGE... SOMETIMES MUM LOOKS AT ME — LIKE I SCARE HER STIFF!
I ONLY HOPE I'VE BEEN IN TIME TO DRIVE OUT HER WICKEDNESS.
LATER...
BOTHER! MY CANDLE'S RUN OUT. I CAN'T FINISH MY HOMEWORK NOW.

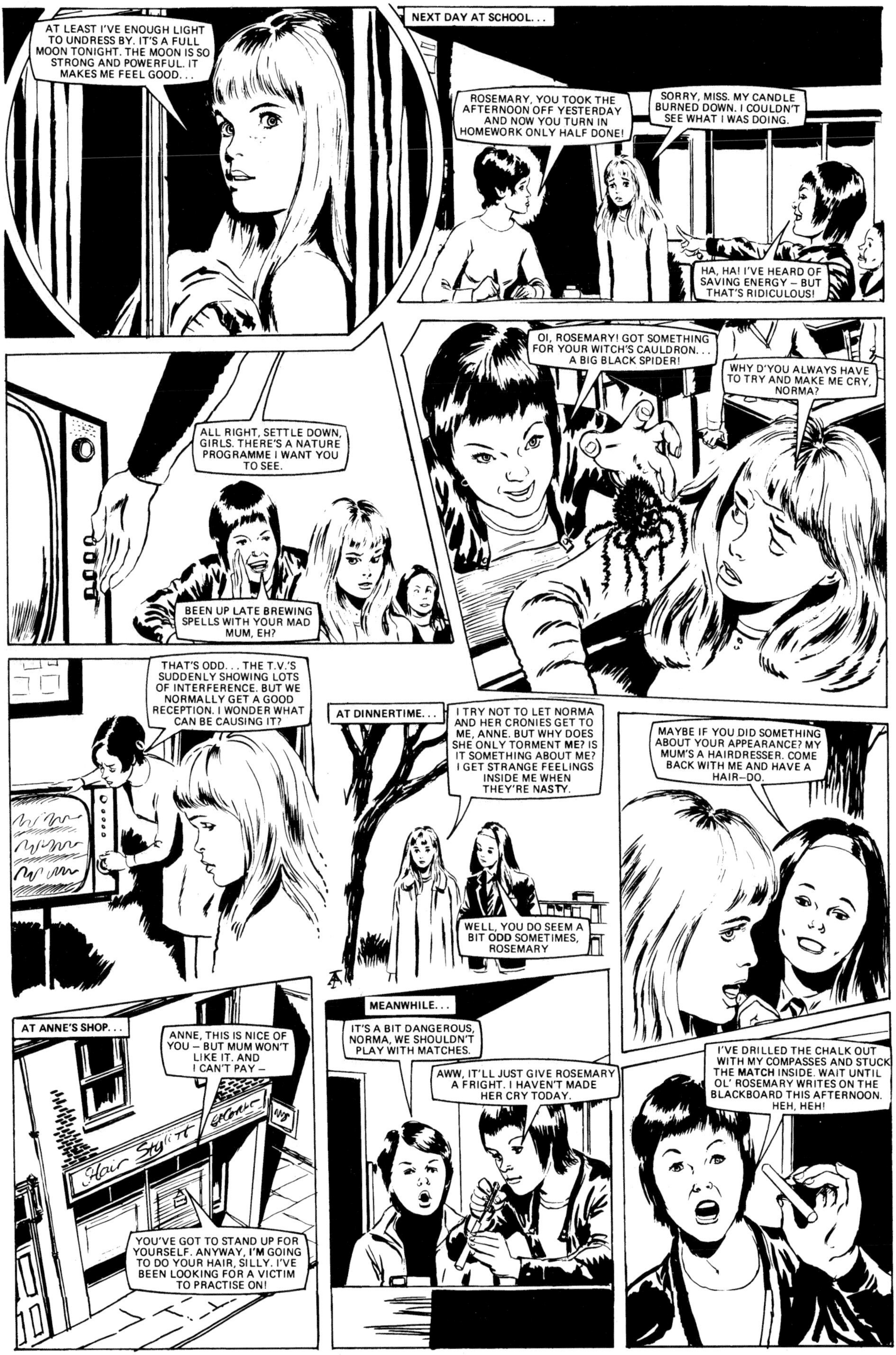
AT LEAST I'VE ENOUGH LIGHT TO UNDRESS BY. IT'S A FULL MOON TONIGHT. THE MOON IS SO STRONG AND POWERFUL. IT MAKES ME FEEL GOOD. . .
NEXT DAY AT SCHOOL. . .
ROSEMARY, YOU TOOK THE AFTERNOON OFF YESTERDAY AND NOW YOU TURN IN HOMEWORK ONLY HALF DONE!
SORRY, MISS. MY CANDLE BURNED DOWN. I COULDN'T SEE WHAT I WAS DOING.
HA, HA! I'VE HEARD OF SAVING ENERGY – BUT THAT'S RIDICULOUS!
ALL RIGHT, SETTLE DOWN, GIRLS. THERE'S A NATURE PROGRAMME I WANT YOU TO SEE.
BEEN UP LATE BREWING SPELLS WITH YOUR MAD MUM, EH?
OI, ROSEMARY! GOT SOMETHING FOR YOUR WITCH'S CAULDRON. . . A BIG BLACK SPIDER!
WHY D'YOU ALWAYS HAVE TO TRY AND MAKE ME CRY, NORMA?
THAT'S ODD. . . THE T.V.'S SUDDENLY SHOWING LOTS OF INTERFERENCE. BUT WE NORMALLY GET A GOOD RECEPTION. I WONDER WHAT CAN BE CAUSING IT?
AT DINNERTIME. . .
I TRY NOT TO LET NORMA AND HER CRONIES GET TO ME, ANNE. BUT WHY DOES SHE ONLY TORMENT ME? IS IT SOMETHING ABOUT ME? I GET STRANGE FEELINGS INSIDE ME WHEN THEY'RE NASTY.
WELL, YOU DO SEEM A BIT ODD SOMETIMES, ROSEMARY
MAYBE IF YOU DID SOMETHING ABOUT YOUR APPEARANCE? MY MUM'S A HAIRDRESSER. COME BACK WITH ME AND HAVE A HAIR–DO.
AT ANNE'S SHOP. . .
ANNE, THIS IS NICE OF YOU – BUT MUM WON'T LIKE IT. AND I CAN'T PAY –
YOU'VE GOT TO STAND UP FOR YOURSELF. ANYWAY, I'M GOING TO DO YOUR HAIR, SILLY. I'VE BEEN LOOKING FOR A VICTIM TO PRACTISE ON!
MEANWHILE. . .
IT'S A BIT DANGEROUS, NORMA, WE SHOULDN'T PLAY WITH MATCHES.
AWW, IT'LL JUST GIVE ROSEMARY A FRIGHT. I HAVEN'T MADE HER CRY TODAY.
I'VE DRILLED THE CHALK OUT WITH MY COMPASSES AND STUCK THE MATCH INSIDE. WAIT UNTIL OL' ROSEMARY WRITES ON THE BLACKBOARD THIS AFTERNOON. HEH, HEH!

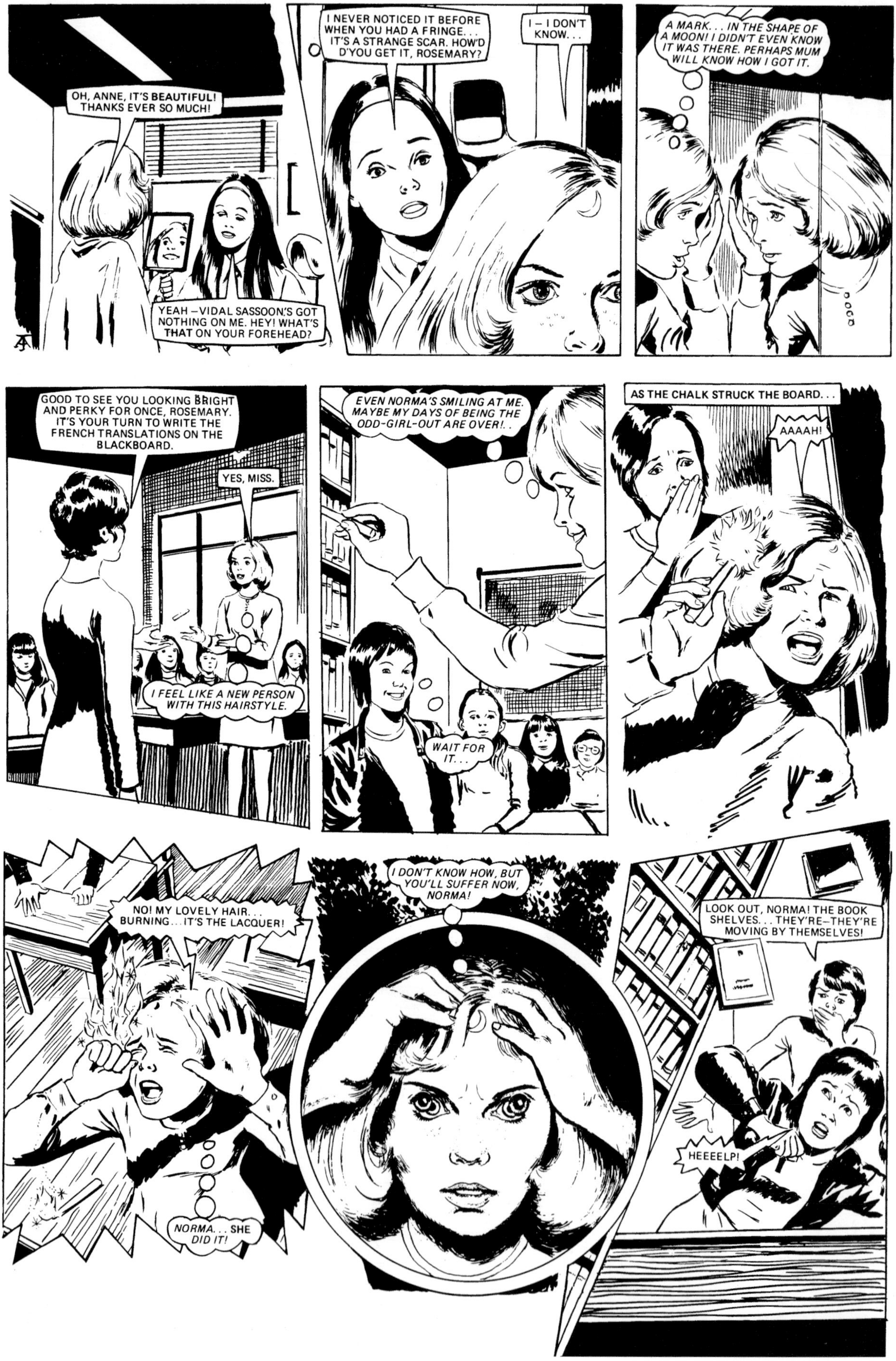

OH, ANNE, IT'S BEAUTIFUL! THANKS EVER SO MUCH!
YEAH – VIDAL SASSOON'S GOT NOTHING ON ME. HEY! WHAT'S THAT ON YOUR FOREHEAD?
I NEVER NOTICED IT BEFORE WHEN YOU HAD A FRINGE... IT'S A STRANGE SCAR. HOW'D D'YOU GET IT, ROSEMARY?
I – I DON'T KNOW...
A MARK... IN THE SHAPE OF A MOON! I DIDN'T EVEN KNOW IT WAS THERE. PERHAPS MUM WILL KNOW HOW I GOT IT.
GOOD TO SEE YOU LOOKING BRIGHT AND PERKY FOR ONCE, ROSEMARY. IT'S YOUR TURN TO WRITE THE FRENCH TRANSLATIONS ON THE BLACKBOARD.
YES, MISS.
I FEEL LIKE A NEW PERSON WITH THIS HAIRSTYLE.
EVEN NORMA'S SMILING AT ME. MAYBE MY DAYS OF BEING THE ODD-GIRL-OUT ARE OVER!..
WAIT FOR IT...
AS THE CHALK STRUCK THE BOARD...
AAAAH!
NO! MY LOVELY HAIR... BURNING... IT'S THE LACQUER!
NORMA... SHE DID IT!
I DON'T KNOW HOW, BUT YOU'LL SUFFER NOW, NORMA!
LOOK OUT, NORMA! THE BOOK SHELVES... THEY'RE – THEY'RE MOVING BY THEMSELVES!
HEEEELP!

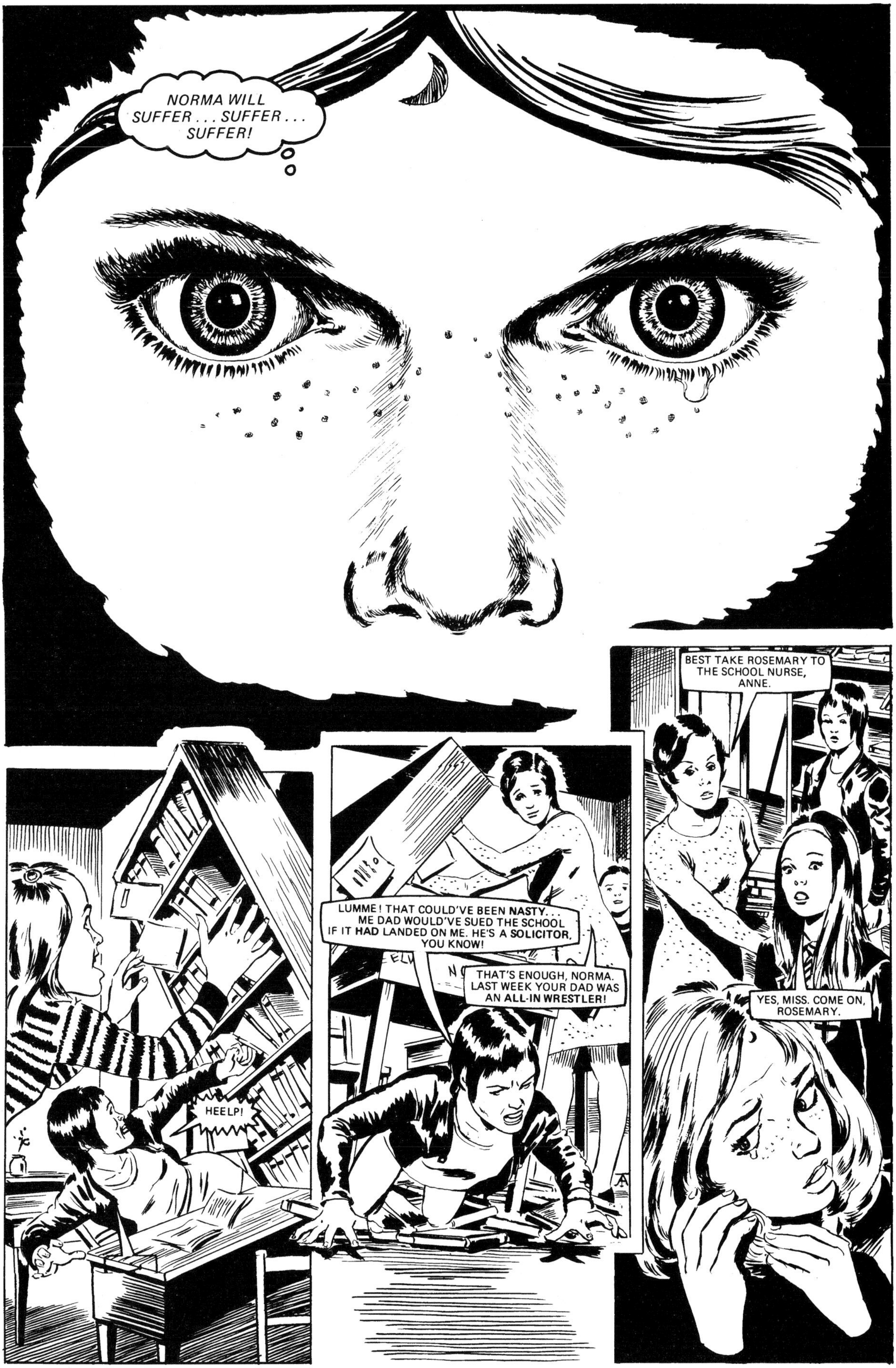

NORMA WILL SUFFER . . . SUFFER . . . SUFFER!
HEELP!
LUMME! THAT COULD'VE BEEN NASTY. . . ME DAD WOULD'VE SUED THE SCHOOL IF IT HAD LANDED ON ME. HE'S A SOLICITOR, YOU KNOW!
THAT'S ENOUGH, NORMA. LAST WEEK YOUR DAD WAS AN ALL-IN WRESTLER!
BEST TAKE ROSEMARY TO THE SCHOOL NURSE, ANNE.
YES, MISS. COME ON, ROSEMARY.

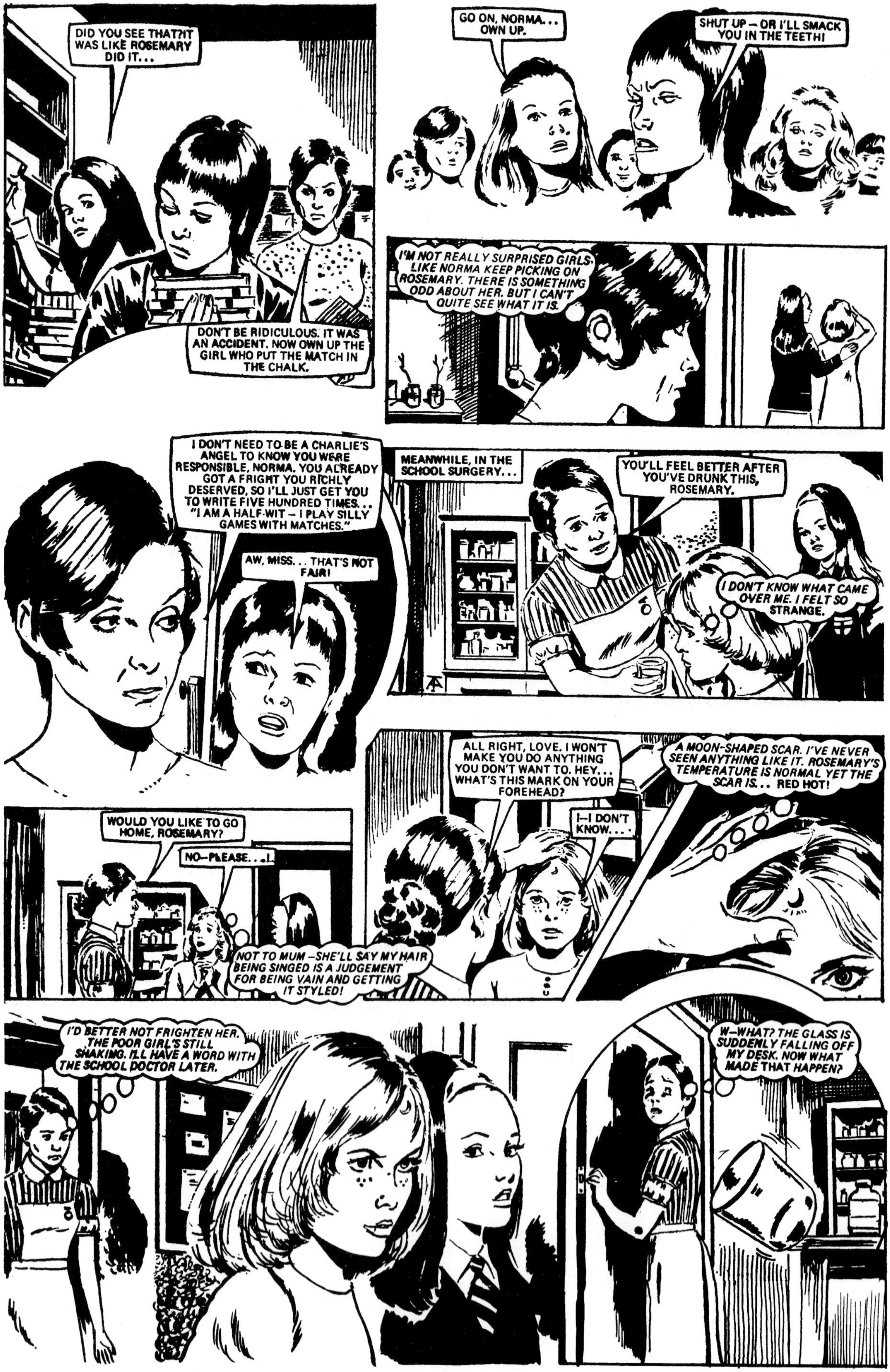

DID YOU SEE THAT?IT WAS LIKE ROSEMARY DID IT...
DON'T BE RIDICULOUS. IT WAS AN ACCIDENT. NOW OWN UP THE GIRL WHO PUT THE MATCH IN THE CHALK.
GO ON, NORMA... OWN UP.
SHUT UP – OR I'LL SMACK YOU IN THE TEETH!
I'M NOT REALLY SURPRISED GIRLS LIKE NORMA KEEP PICKING ON ROSEMARY. THERE IS SOMETHING ODD ABOUT HER. BUT I CAN'T QUITE SEE WHAT IT IS.
I DON'T NEED TO BE A CHARLIE'S ANGEL TO KNOW YOU WERE RESPONSIBLE, NORMA. YOU ALREADY GOT A FRIGHT YOU RICHLY DESERVED, SO I'LL JUST GET YOU TO WRITE FIVE HUNDRED TIMES... "I AM A HALF-WIT – I PLAY SILLY GAMES WITH MATCHES."
AW, MISS... THAT'S NOT FAIR!
MEANWHILE, IN THE SCHOOL SURGERY...
YOU'LL FEEL BETTER AFTER YOU'VE DRUNK THIS, ROSEMARY.
I DON'T KNOW WHAT CAME OVER ME. I FELT SO STRANGE.
WOULD YOU LIKE TO GO HOME, ROSEMARY?
NO–PLEASE...!
NOT TO MUM –SHE'LL SAY MY HAIR BEING SINGED IS A JUDGEMENT FOR BEING VAIN AND GETTING IT STYLED!
ALL RIGHT, LOVE. I WON'T MAKE YOU DO ANYTHING YOU DON'T WANT TO. HEY... WHAT'S THIS MARK ON YOUR FOREHEAD?
I–I DON'T KNOW...
A MOON-SHAPED SCAR. I'VE NEVER SEEN ANYTHING LIKE IT. ROSEMARY'S TEMPERATURE IS NORMAL YET THE SCAR IS... RED HOT!
I'D BETTER NOT FRIGHTEN HER. THE POOR GIRL'S STILL SHAKING. I'LL HAVE A WORD WITH THE SCHOOL DOCTOR LATER.
W–WHAT? THE GLASS IS SUDDENLY FALLING OFF MY DESK. NOW WHAT MADE THAT HAPPEN?

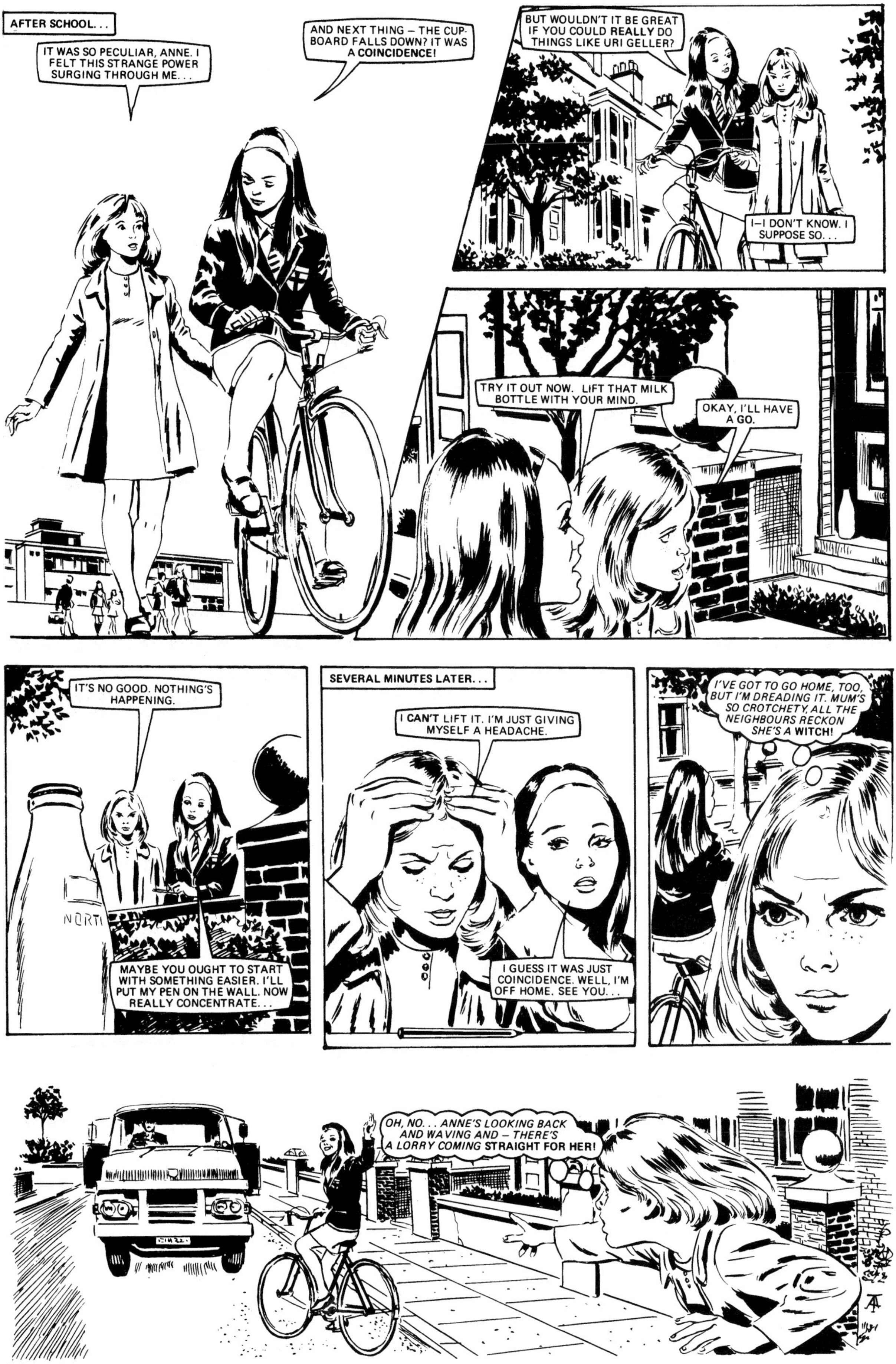

AFTER SCHOOL. . .
IT WAS SO PECULIAR, ANNE. I FELT THIS STRANGE POWER SURGING THROUGH ME. . .
AND NEXT THING – THE CUPBOARD FALLS DOWN? IT WAS A COINCIDENCE!
BUT WOULDN'T IT BE GREAT IF YOU COULD REALLY DO THINGS LIKE URI GELLER?
I–I DON'T KNOW. I SUPPOSE SO. . .
TRY IT OUT NOW. LIFT THAT MILK BOTTLE WITH YOUR MIND.
OKAY, I'LL HAVE A GO.
IT'S NO GOOD. NOTHING'S HAPPENING.
MAYBE YOU OUGHT TO START WITH SOMETHING EASIER. I'LL PUT MY PEN ON THE WALL. NOW REALLY CONCENTRATE. . .
SEVERAL MINUTES LATER. . .
I CAN'T LIFT IT. I'M JUST GIVING MYSELF A HEADACHE.
I GUESS IT WAS JUST COINCIDENCE. WELL, I'M OFF HOME. SEE YOU. . .
I'VE GOT TO GO HOME, TOO, BUT I'M DREADING IT. MUM'S SO CROTCHETY, ALL THE NEIGHBOURS RECKON SHE'S A WITCH!
OH, NO. . . ANNE'S LOOKING BACK AND WAVING AND – THERE'S A LORRY COMING STRAIGHT FOR HER!

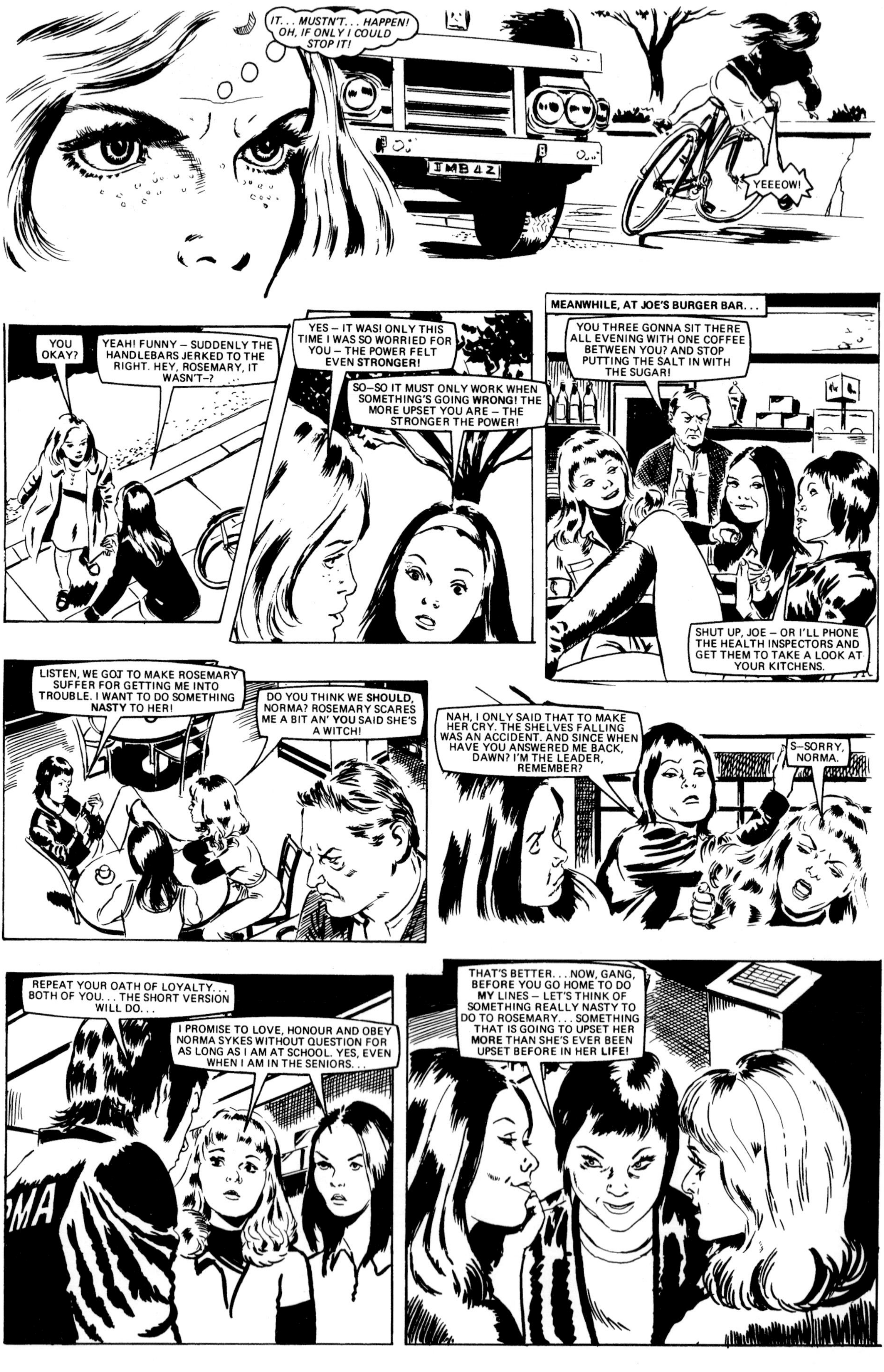
IT... MUSTN'T... HAPPEN! OH, IF ONLY I COULD STOP IT!
JMB 42
YEEEOW!
YOU OKAY?
YEAH! FUNNY – SUDDENLY THE HANDLEBARS JERKED TO THE RIGHT. HEY, ROSEMARY, IT WASN'T–?
YES – IT WAS! ONLY THIS TIME I WAS SO WORRIED FOR YOU – THE POWER FELT EVEN STRONGER!
SO–SO IT MUST ONLY WORK WHEN SOMETHING'S GOING WRONG! THE MORE UPSET YOU ARE – THE STRONGER THE POWER!
MEANWHILE, AT JOE'S BURGER BAR...
YOU THREE GONNA SIT THERE ALL EVENING WITH ONE COFFEE BETWEEN YOU? AND STOP PUTTING THE SALT IN WITH THE SUGAR!
SHUT UP, JOE – OR I'LL PHONE THE HEALTH INSPECTORS AND GET THEM TO TAKE A LOOK AT YOUR KITCHENS.
LISTEN, WE GOT TO MAKE ROSEMARY SUFFER FOR GETTING ME INTO TROUBLE. I WANT TO DO SOMETHING NASTY TO HER!
DO YOU THINK WE SHOULD, NORMA? ROSEMARY SCARES ME A BIT AN' YOU SAID SHE'S A WITCH!
NAH, I ONLY SAID THAT TO MAKE HER CRY. THE SHELVES FALLING WAS AN ACCIDENT. AND SINCE WHEN HAVE YOU ANSWERED ME BACK, DAWN? I'M THE LEADER, REMEMBER?
S–SORRY, NORMA.
REPEAT YOUR OATH OF LOYALTY... BOTH OF YOU... THE SHORT VERSION WILL DO...
I PROMISE TO LOVE, HONOUR AND OBEY NORMA SYKES WITHOUT QUESTION FOR AS LONG AS I AM AT SCHOOL. YES, EVEN WHEN I AM IN THE SENIORS...
THAT'S BETTER... NOW, GANG, BEFORE YOU GO HOME TO DO MY LINES – LET'S THINK OF SOMETHING REALLY NASTY TO DO TO ROSEMARY... SOMETHING THAT IS GOING TO UPSET HER MORE THAN SHE'S EVER BEEN UPSET BEFORE IN HER LIFE!

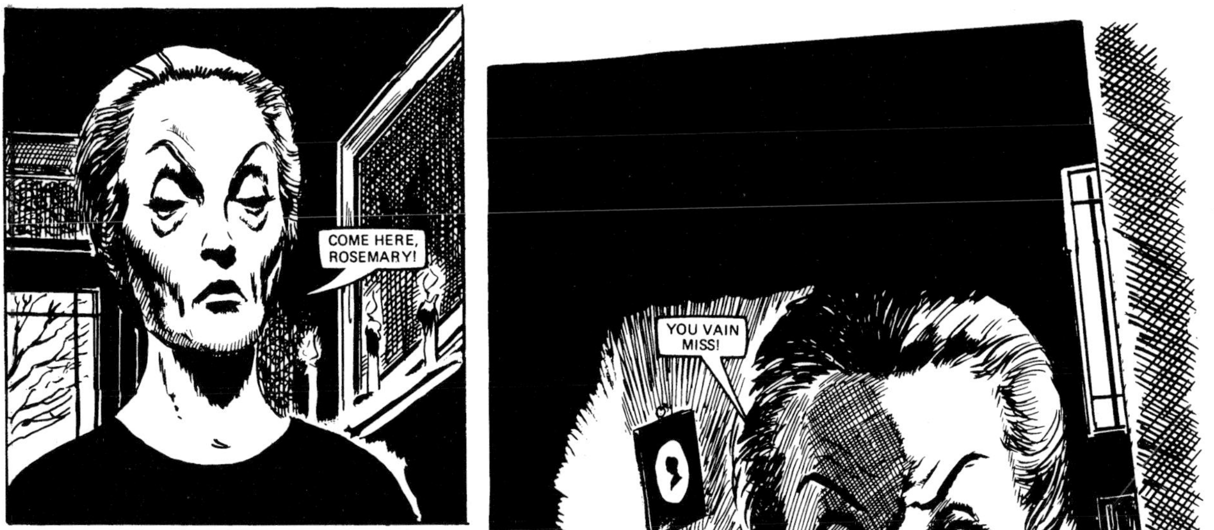
COME HERE, ROSEMARY!

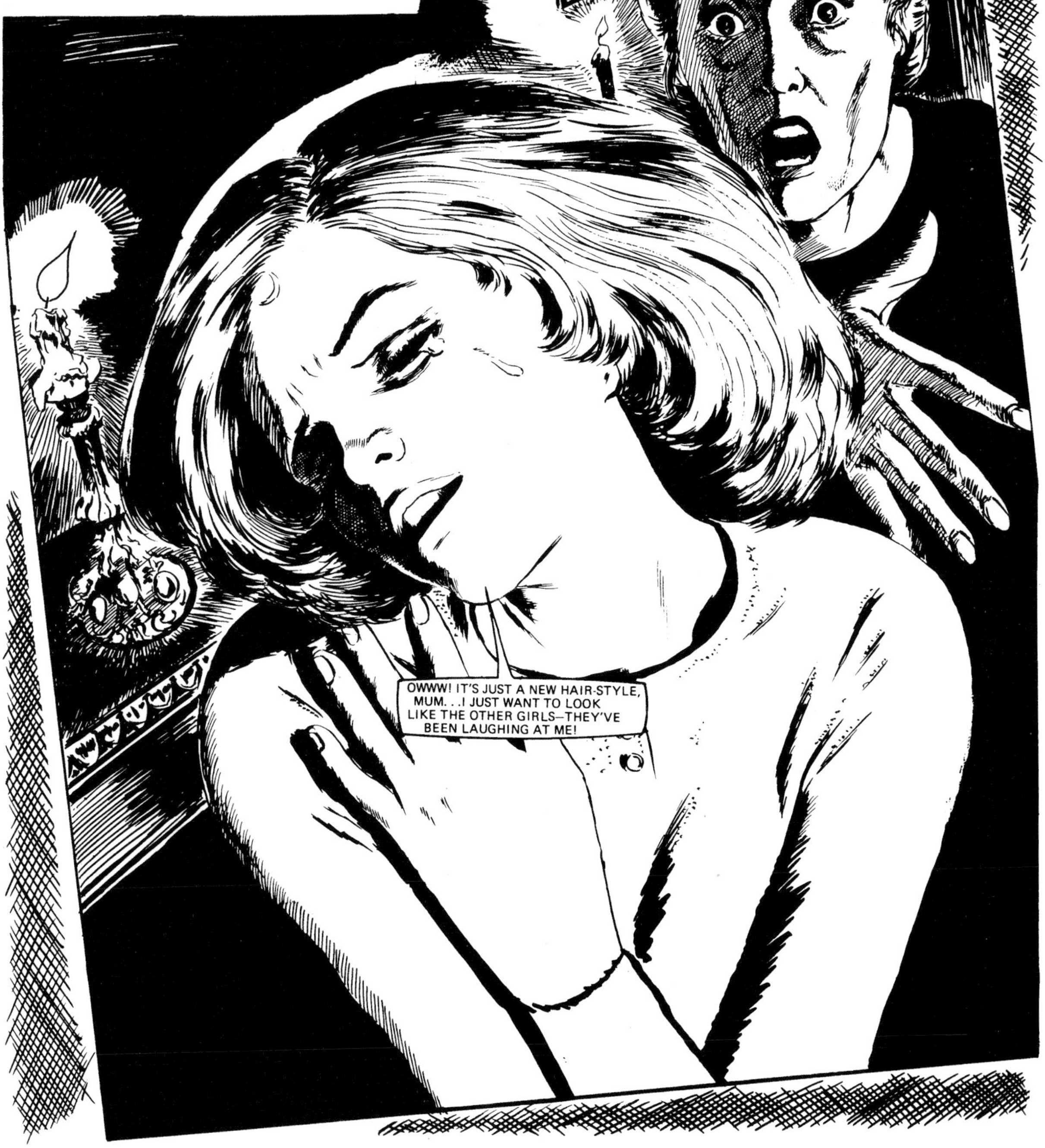
YOU VAIN MISS!
OWWW! IT'S JUST A NEW HAIR-STYLE, MUM. . .I JUST WANT TO LOOK LIKE THE OTHER GIRLS—THEY'VE BEEN LAUGHING AT ME!

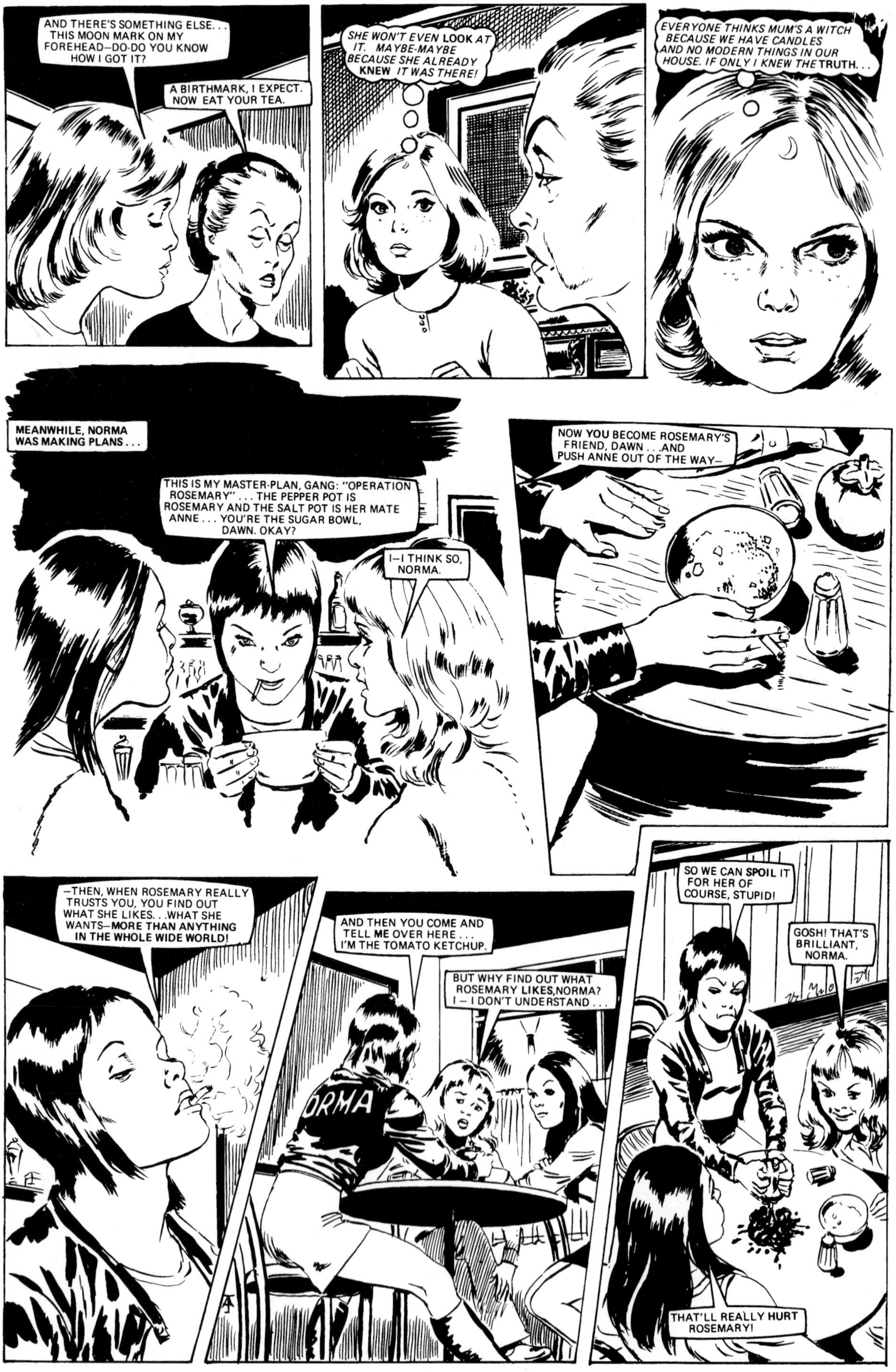
AND THERE'S SOMETHING ELSE... THIS MOON MARK ON MY FOREHEAD—DO-DO YOU KNOW HOW I GOT IT?
A BIRTHMARK, I EXPECT. NOW EAT YOUR TEA.
SHE WON'T EVEN LOOK AT IT. MAYBE-MAYBE BECAUSE SHE ALREADY KNEW IT WAS THERE!
EVERYONE THINKS MUM'S A WITCH BECAUSE WE HAVE CANDLES AND NO MODERN THINGS IN OUR HOUSE. IF ONLY I KNEW THE TRUTH...
MEANWHILE, NORMA WAS MAKING PLANS...
THIS IS MY MASTER-PLAN, GANG: "OPERATION ROSEMARY"... THE PEPPER POT IS ROSEMARY AND THE SALT POT IS HER MATE ANNE... YOU'RE THE SUGAR BOWL, DAWN. OKAY?
I—I THINK SO, NORMA.
NOW YOU BECOME ROSEMARY'S FRIEND, DAWN...AND PUSH ANNE OUT OF THE WAY—
—THEN, WHEN ROSEMARY REALLY TRUSTS YOU, YOU FIND OUT WHAT SHE LIKES...WHAT SHE WANTS—MORE THAN ANYTHING IN THE WHOLE WIDE WORLD!
AND THEN YOU COME AND TELL ME OVER HERE... I'M THE TOMATO KETCHUP.
BUT WHY FIND OUT WHAT ROSEMARY LIKES, NORMA? I—I DON'T UNDERSTAND...
SO WE CAN SPOIL IT FOR HER OF COURSE, STUPID!
GOSH! THAT'S BRILLIANT, NORMA.
THAT'LL REALLY HURT ROSEMARY!

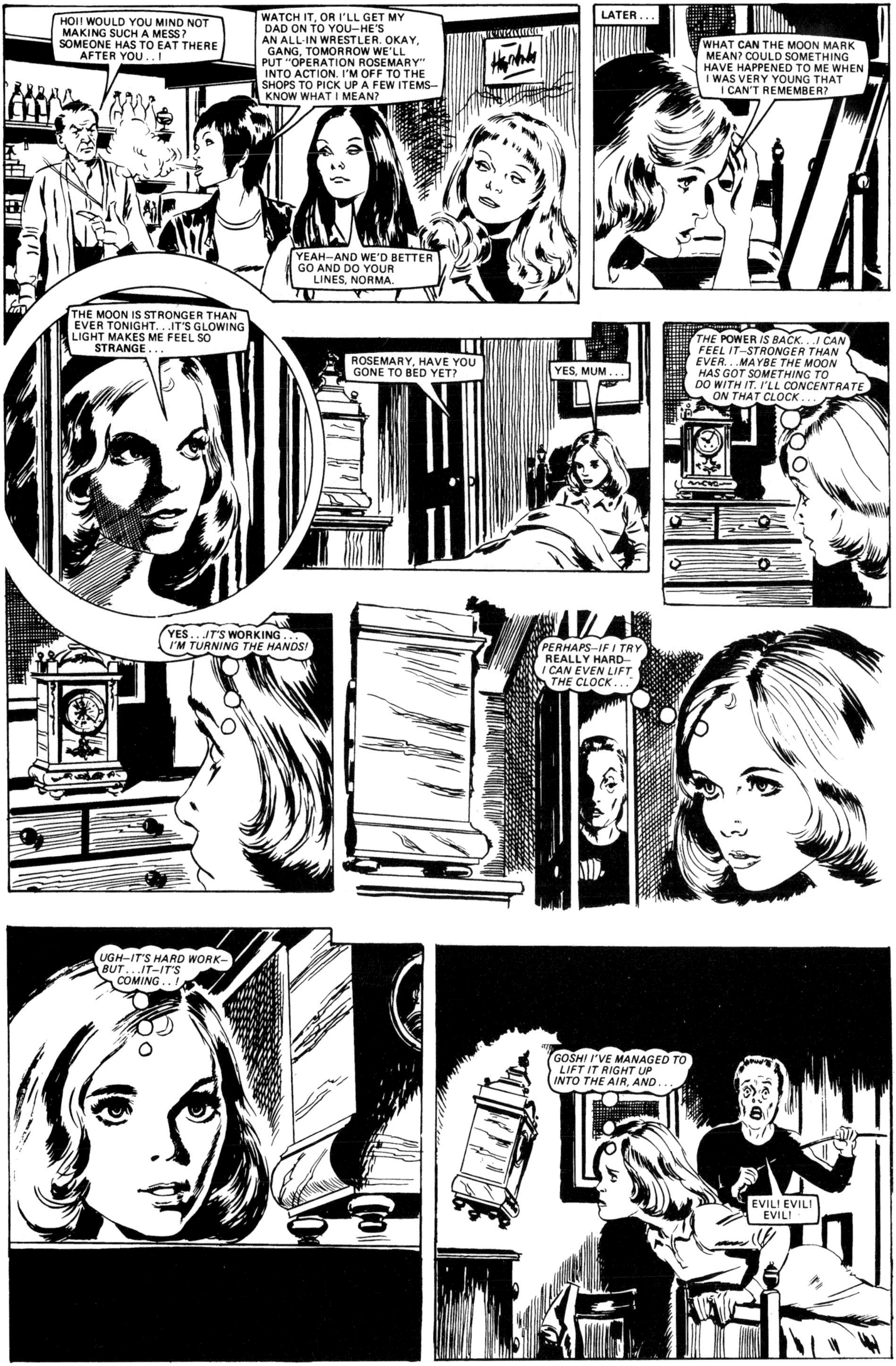

HOI! WOULD YOU MIND NOT MAKING SUCH A MESS? SOMEONE HAS TO EAT THERE AFTER YOU . . !
WATCH IT, OR I'LL GET MY DAD ON TO YOU—HE'S AN ALL-IN WRESTLER. OKAY, GANG, TOMORROW WE'LL PUT "OPERATION ROSEMARY" INTO ACTION. I'M OFF TO THE SHOPS TO PICK UP A FEW ITEMS—KNOW WHAT I MEAN?
YEAH—AND WE'D BETTER GO AND DO YOUR LINES, NORMA.
LATER . . .
WHAT CAN THE MOON MARK MEAN? COULD SOMETHING HAVE HAPPENED TO ME WHEN I WAS VERY YOUNG THAT I CAN'T REMEMBER?
THE MOON IS STRONGER THAN EVER TONIGHT. . .IT'S GLOWING LIGHT MAKES ME FEEL SO STRANGE . . .
ROSEMARY, HAVE YOU GONE TO BED YET?
YES, MUM . . .
THE POWER IS BACK. . .I CAN FEEL IT—STRONGER THAN EVER. . .MAYBE THE MOON HAS GOT SOMETHING TO DO WITH IT. I'LL CONCENTRATE ON THAT CLOCK . . .
YES . . .IT'S WORKING . . . I'M TURNING THE HANDS!
PERHAPS—IF I TRY REALLY HARD—I CAN EVEN LIFT THE CLOCK . . .
UGH—IT'S HARD WORK—BUT . . .IT—IT'S COMING . . !
GOSH! I'VE MANAGED TO LIFT IT RIGHT UP INTO THE AIR, AND . . .
EVIL! EVIL! EVIL!

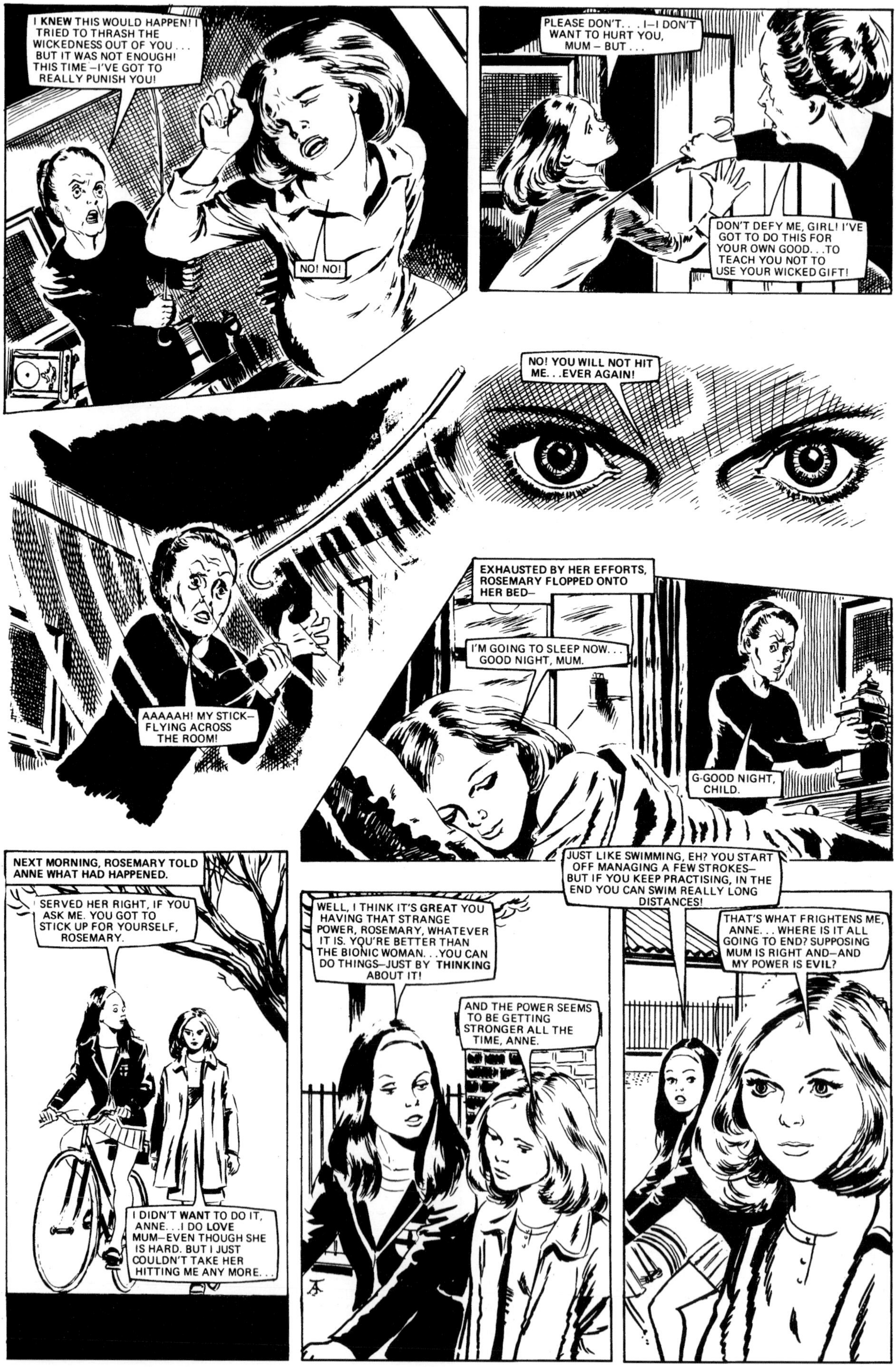
I KNEW THIS WOULD HAPPEN! I TRIED TO THRASH THE WICKEDNESS OUT OF YOU . . . BUT IT WAS NOT ENOUGH! THIS TIME—I'VE GOT TO REALLY PUNISH YOU!
NO! NO!
PLEASE DON'T. . . I—I DON'T WANT TO HURT YOU, MUM—BUT . . .
DON'T DEFY ME, GIRL! I'VE GOT TO DO THIS FOR YOUR OWN GOOD. . .TO TEACH YOU NOT TO USE YOUR WICKED GIFT!
NO! YOU WILL NOT HIT ME. . .EVER AGAIN!
AAAAAH! MY STICK—FLYING ACROSS THE ROOM!
EXHAUSTED BY HER EFFORTS, ROSEMARY FLOPPED ONTO HER BED—
I'M GOING TO SLEEP NOW. . . GOOD NIGHT, MUM.
G-GOOD NIGHT, CHILD.
NEXT MORNING, ROSEMARY TOLD ANNE WHAT HAD HAPPENED.
SERVED HER RIGHT, IF YOU ASK ME. YOU GOT TO STICK UP FOR YOURSELF, ROSEMARY.
I DIDN'T WANT TO DO IT, ANNE. . .I DO LOVE MUM—EVEN THOUGH SHE IS HARD. BUT I JUST COULDN'T TAKE HER HITTING ME ANY MORE. . .
WELL, I THINK IT'S GREAT YOU HAVING THAT STRANGE POWER, ROSEMARY, WHATEVER IT IS. YOU'RE BETTER THAN THE BIONIC WOMAN. . .YOU CAN DO THINGS—JUST BY THINKING ABOUT IT!
AND THE POWER SEEMS TO BE GETTING STRONGER ALL THE TIME, ANNE.
JUST LIKE SWIMMING, EH? YOU START OFF MANAGING A FEW STROKES—BUT IF YOU KEEP PRACTISING, IN THE END YOU CAN SWIM REALLY LONG DISTANCES!
THAT'S WHAT FRIGHTENS ME, ANNE. . . WHERE IS IT ALL GOING TO END? SUPPOSING MUM IS RIGHT AND—AND MY POWER IS EVIL?

# Moonchild

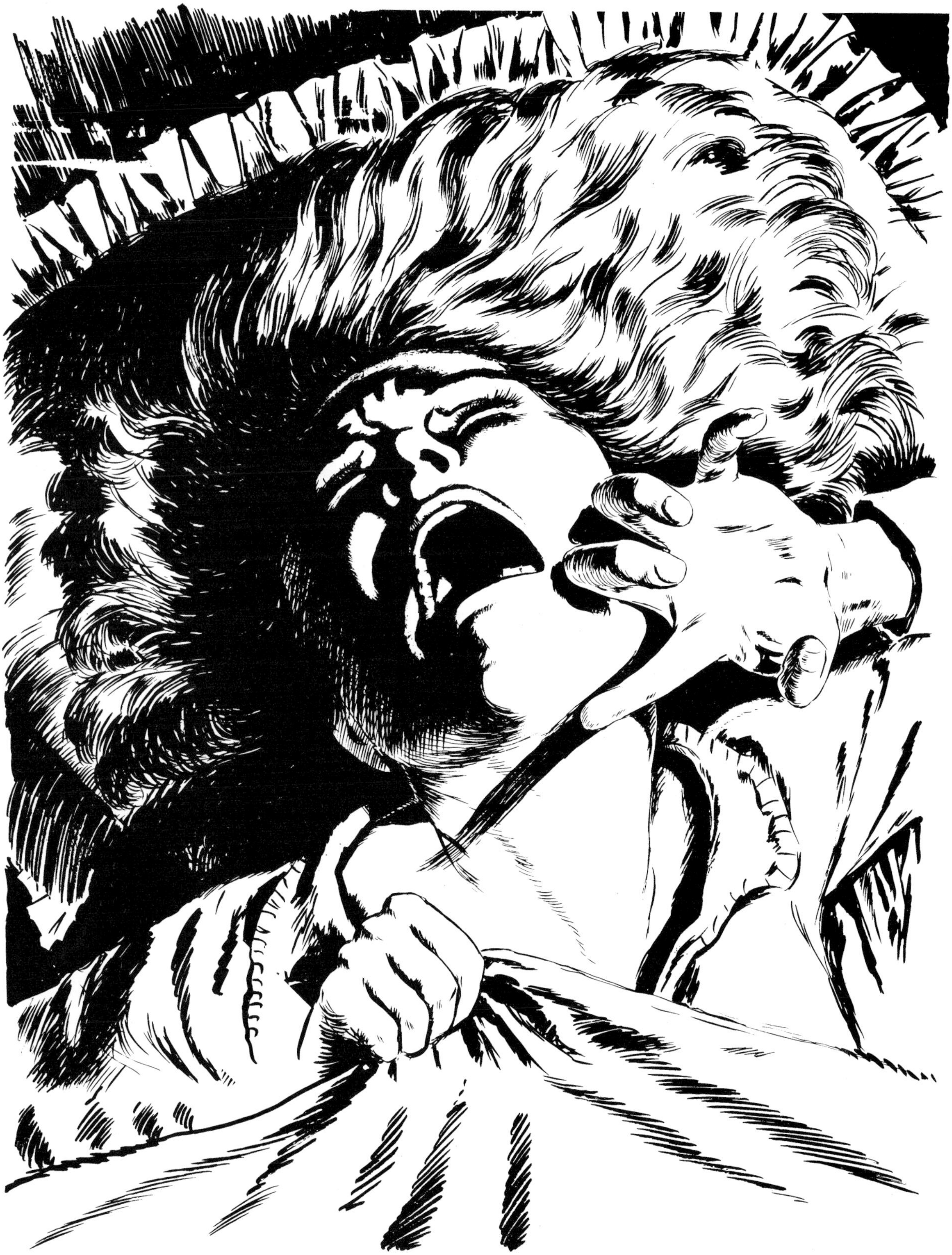

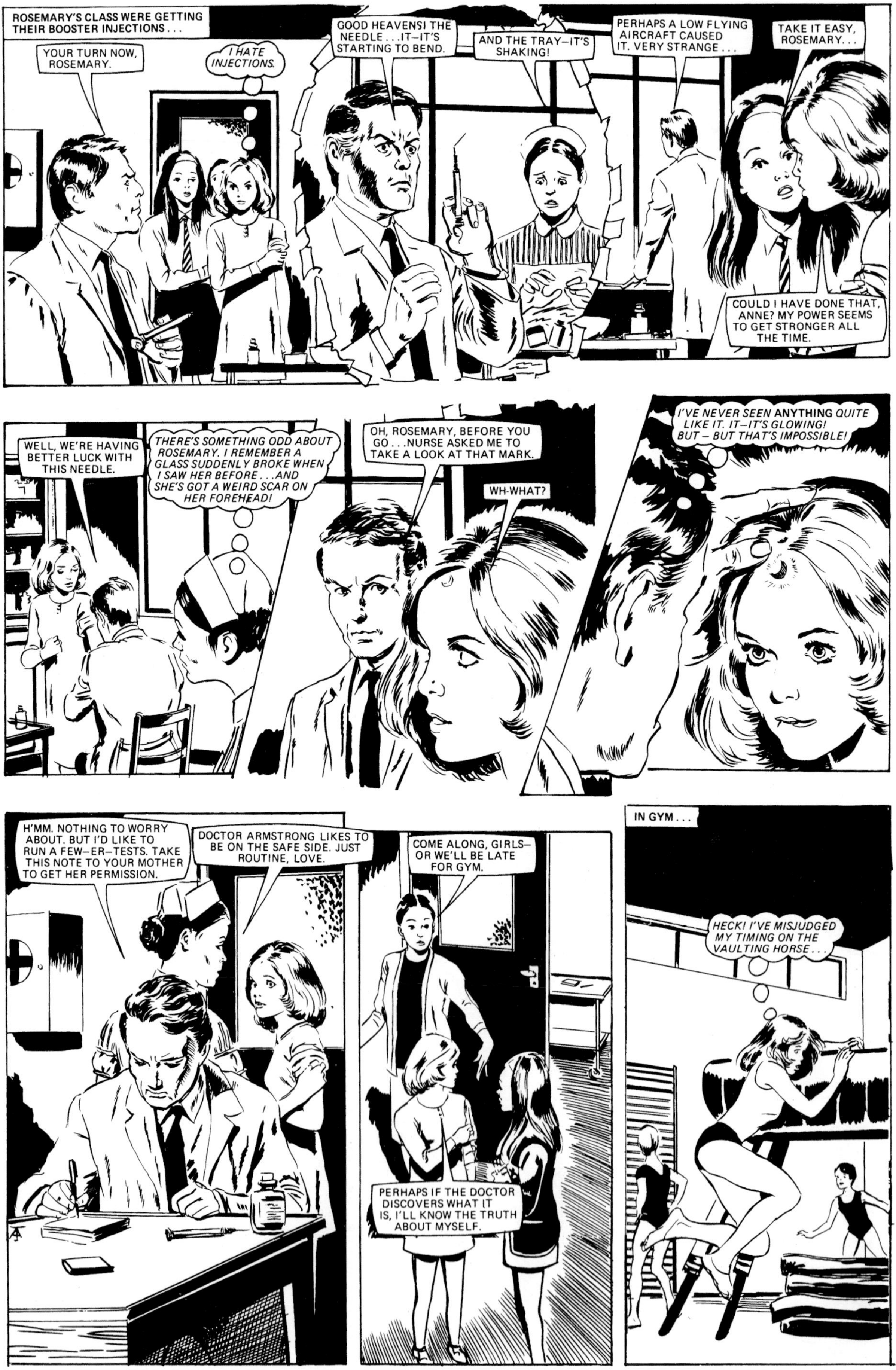
ROSEMARY'S CLASS WERE GETTING THEIR BOOSTER INJECTIONS . . .
YOUR TURN NOW, ROSEMARY.
I HATE INJECTIONS.
GOOD HEAVENS! THE NEEDLE . . . IT—IT'S STARTING TO BEND.
AND THE TRAY—IT'S SHAKING!
PERHAPS A LOW FLYING AIRCRAFT CAUSED IT. VERY STRANGE . . .
TAKE IT EASY, ROSEMARY . . .
COULD I HAVE DONE THAT, ANNE? MY POWER SEEMS TO GET STRONGER ALL THE TIME.
WELL, WE'RE HAVING BETTER LUCK WITH THIS NEEDLE.
THERE'S SOMETHING ODD ABOUT ROSEMARY. I REMEMBER A GLASS SUDDENLY BROKE WHEN I SAW HER BEFORE . . . AND SHE'S GOT A WEIRD SCAR ON HER FOREHEAD!
OH, ROSEMARY, BEFORE YOU GO . . . NURSE ASKED ME TO TAKE A LOOK AT THAT MARK.
WH-WHAT?
I'VE NEVER SEEN ANYTHING QUITE LIKE IT. IT—IT'S GLOWING! BUT — BUT THAT'S IMPOSSIBLE!
H'MM. NOTHING TO WORRY ABOUT. BUT I'D LIKE TO RUN A FEW—ER—TESTS. TAKE THIS NOTE TO YOUR MOTHER TO GET HER PERMISSION.
DOCTOR ARMSTRONG LIKES TO BE ON THE SAFE SIDE. JUST ROUTINE, LOVE.
COME ALONG, GIRLS—OR WE'LL BE LATE FOR GYM.
PERHAPS IF THE DOCTOR DISCOVERS WHAT IT IS, I'LL KNOW THE TRUTH ABOUT MYSELF.
IN GYM . . .
HECK! I'VE MISJUDGED MY TIMING ON THE VAULTING HORSE . . .

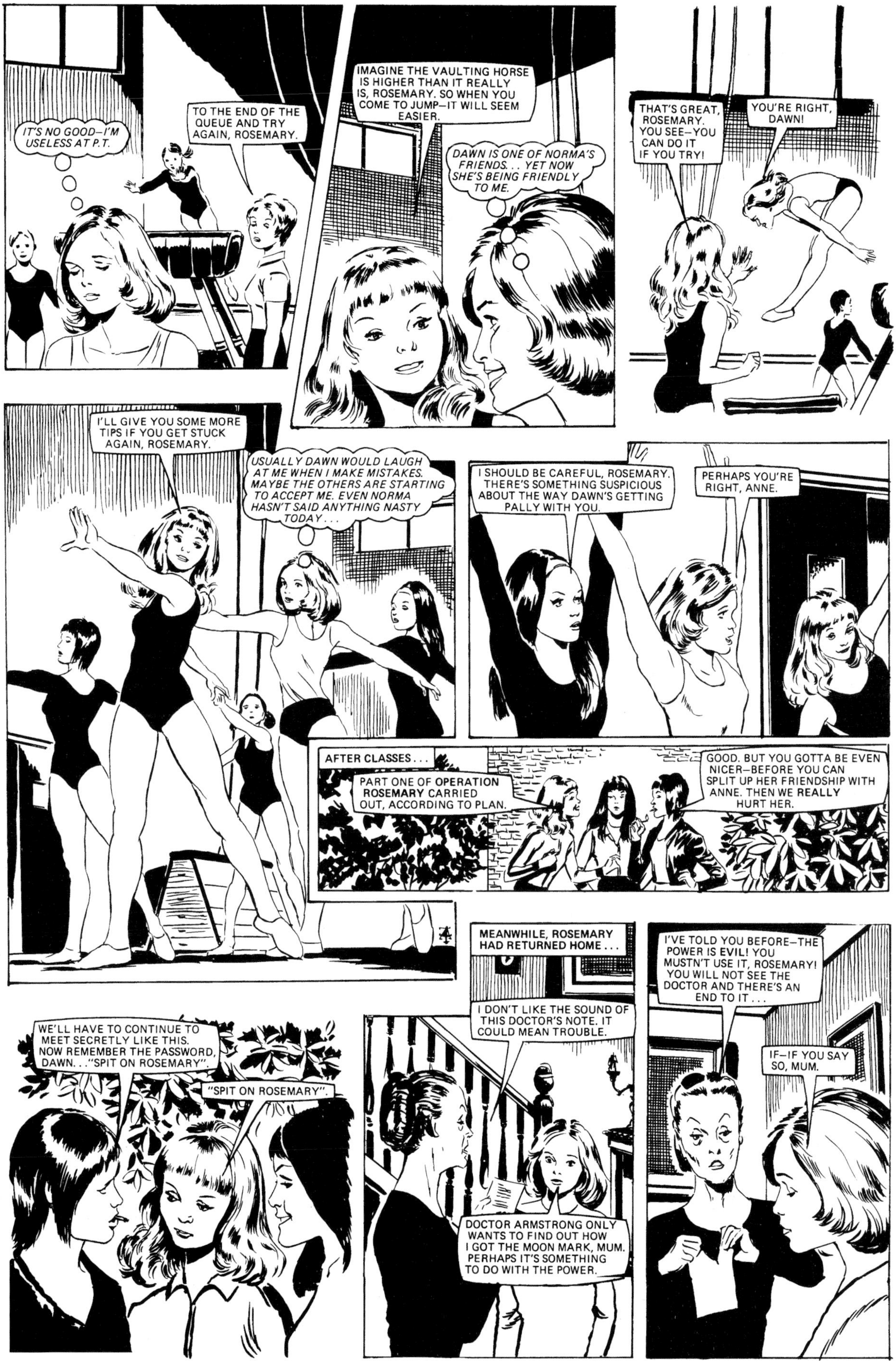
IT'S NO GOOD—I'M USELESS AT P.T.
TO THE END OF THE QUEUE AND TRY AGAIN, ROSEMARY.
IMAGINE THE VAULTING HORSE IS HIGHER THAN IT REALLY IS, ROSEMARY. SO WHEN YOU COME TO JUMP—IT WILL SEEM EASIER.
DAWN IS ONE OF NORMA'S FRIENDS. . . YET NOW SHE'S BEING FRIENDLY TO ME.
THAT'S GREAT, ROSEMARY. YOU SEE—YOU CAN DO IT IF YOU TRY!
YOU'RE RIGHT, DAWN!
I'LL GIVE YOU SOME MORE TIPS IF YOU GET STUCK AGAIN, ROSEMARY.
USUALLY DAWN WOULD LAUGH AT ME WHEN I MAKE MISTAKES. MAYBE THE OTHERS ARE STARTING TO ACCEPT ME. EVEN NORMA HASN'T SAID ANYTHING NASTY TODAY . . .
I SHOULD BE CAREFUL, ROSEMARY. THERE'S SOMETHING SUSPICIOUS ABOUT THE WAY DAWN'S GETTING PALLY WITH YOU.
PERHAPS YOU'RE RIGHT, ANNE.
AFTER CLASSES . . .
PART ONE OF OPERATION ROSEMARY CARRIED OUT, ACCORDING TO PLAN.
GOOD. BUT YOU GOTTA BE EVEN NICER—BEFORE YOU CAN SPLIT UP HER FRIENDSHIP WITH ANNE. THEN WE REALLY HURT HER.
WE'LL HAVE TO CONTINUE TO MEET SECRETLY LIKE THIS. NOW REMEMBER THE PASSWORD, DAWN. . . "SPIT ON ROSEMARY".
"SPIT ON ROSEMARY".
MEANWHILE, ROSEMARY HAD RETURNED HOME . . .
I DON'T LIKE THE SOUND OF THIS DOCTOR'S NOTE. IT COULD MEAN TROUBLE.
DOCTOR ARMSTRONG ONLY WANTS TO FIND OUT HOW I GOT THE MOON MARK, MUM. PERHAPS IT'S SOMETHING TO DO WITH THE POWER.
I'VE TOLD YOU BEFORE—THE POWER IS EVIL! YOU MUSTN'T USE IT, ROSEMARY! YOU WILL NOT SEE THE DOCTOR AND THERE'S AN END TO IT . . .
IF—IF YOU SAY SO, MUM.

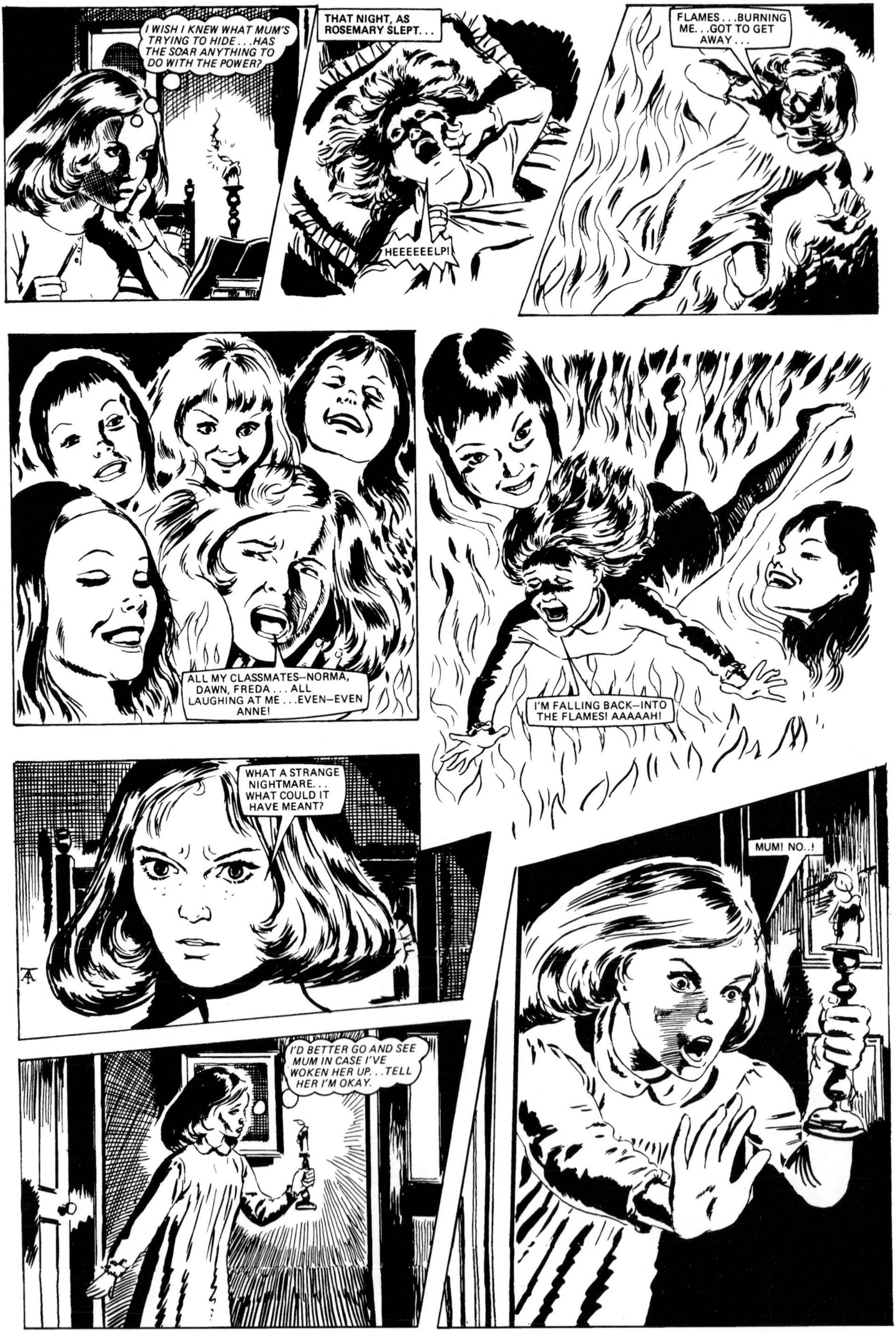
I WISH I KNEW WHAT MUM'S TRYING TO HIDE . . . HAS THE SCAR ANYTHING TO DO WITH THE POWER?
THAT NIGHT, AS ROSEMARY SLEPT . . .
HEEEEEELP!
FLAMES . . . BURNING ME. . . GOT TO GET AWAY . . .
ALL MY CLASSMATES—NORMA, DAWN, FREDA . . . ALL LAUGHING AT ME . . . EVEN—EVEN ANNE!
I'M FALLING BACK—INTO THE FLAMES! AAAAAH!
WHAT A STRANGE NIGHTMARE . . . WHAT COULD IT HAVE MEANT?
I'D BETTER GO AND SEE MUM IN CASE I'VE WOKEN HER UP . . . TELL HER I'M OKAY.
MUM! NO..!

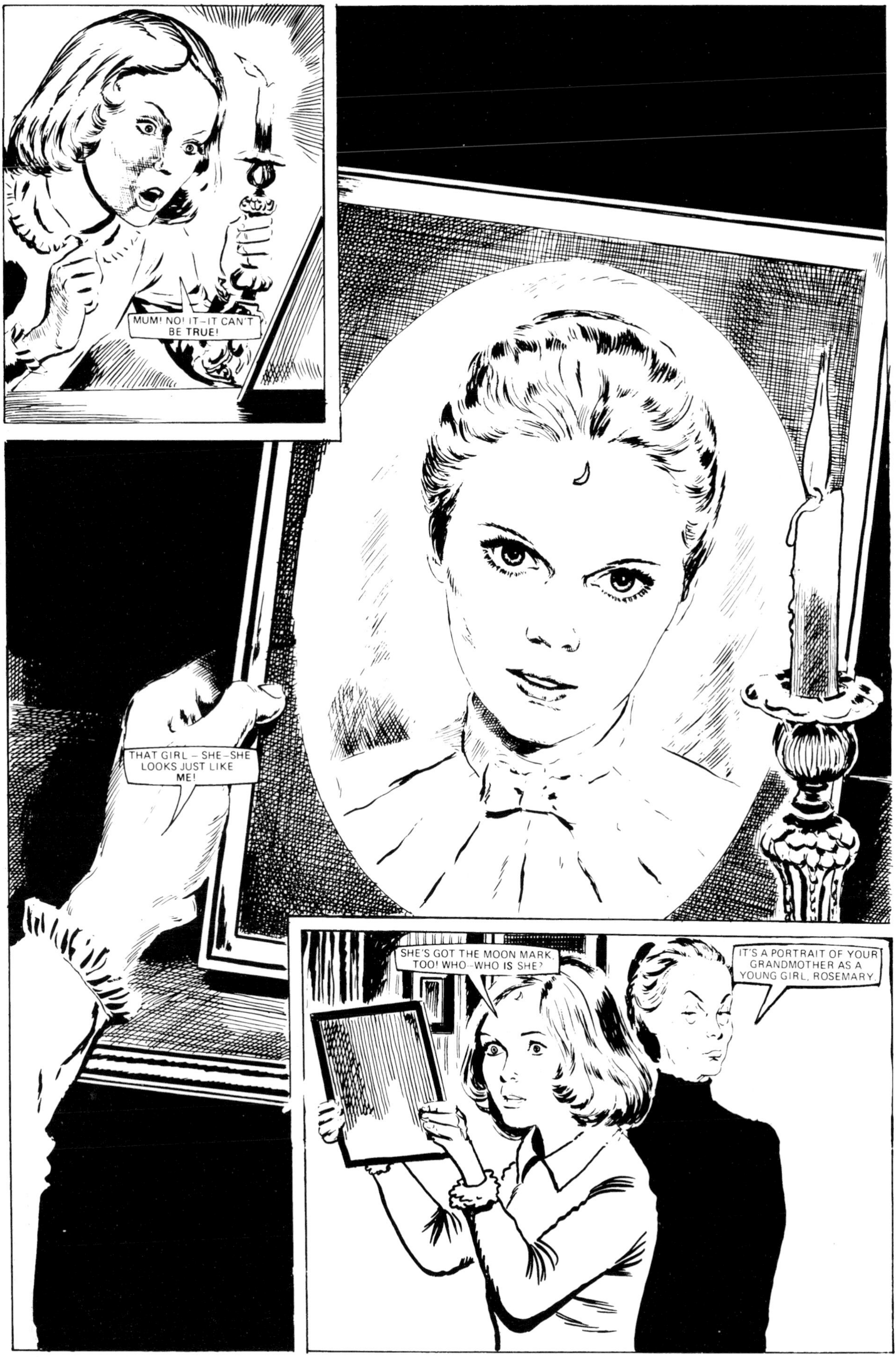
MUM! NO! IT—IT CAN'T BE TRUE!
THAT GIRL — SHE—SHE LOOKS JUST LIKE ME!
SHE'S GOT THE MOON MARK, TOO! WHO—WHO IS SHE?
IT'S A PORTRAIT OF YOUR GRANDMOTHER AS A YOUNG GIRL, ROSEMARY.

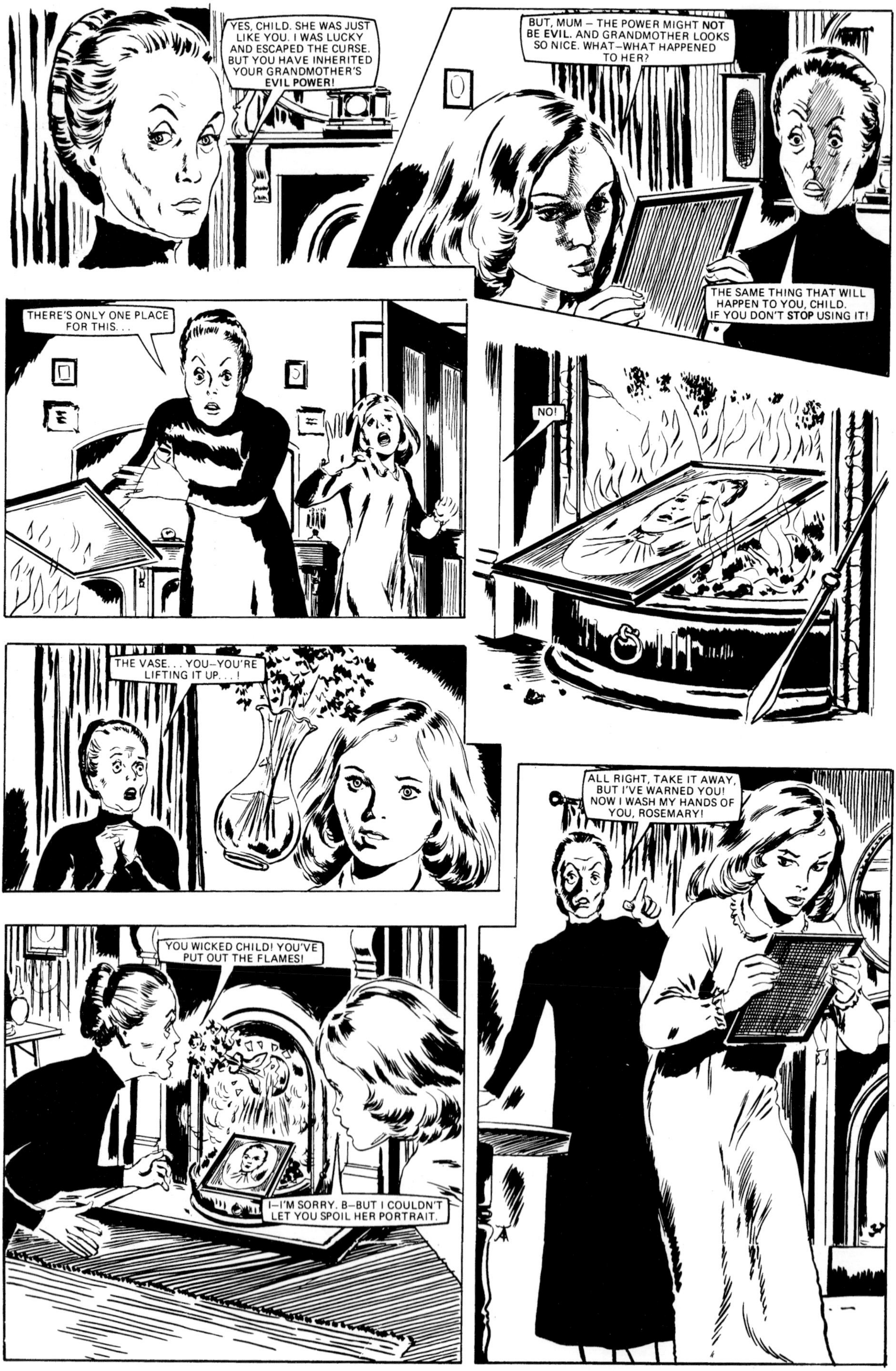
YES, CHILD. SHE WAS JUST LIKE YOU. I WAS LUCKY AND ESCAPED THE CURSE. BUT YOU HAVE INHERITED YOUR GRANDMOTHER'S EVIL POWER!
BUT, MUM – THE POWER MIGHT NOT BE EVIL. AND GRANDMOTHER LOOKS SO NICE. WHAT–WHAT HAPPENED TO HER?
THE SAME THING THAT WILL HAPPEN TO YOU, CHILD. IF YOU DON'T STOP USING IT!
THERE'S ONLY ONE PLACE FOR THIS. . .
NO!
THE VASE. . . YOU–YOU'RE LIFTING IT UP. . . !
ALL RIGHT, TAKE IT AWAY, BUT I'VE WARNED YOU! NOW I WASH MY HANDS OF YOU, ROSEMARY!
YOU WICKED CHILD! YOU'VE PUT OUT THE FLAMES!
I–I'M SORRY. B–BUT I COULDN'T LET YOU SPOIL HER PORTRAIT.

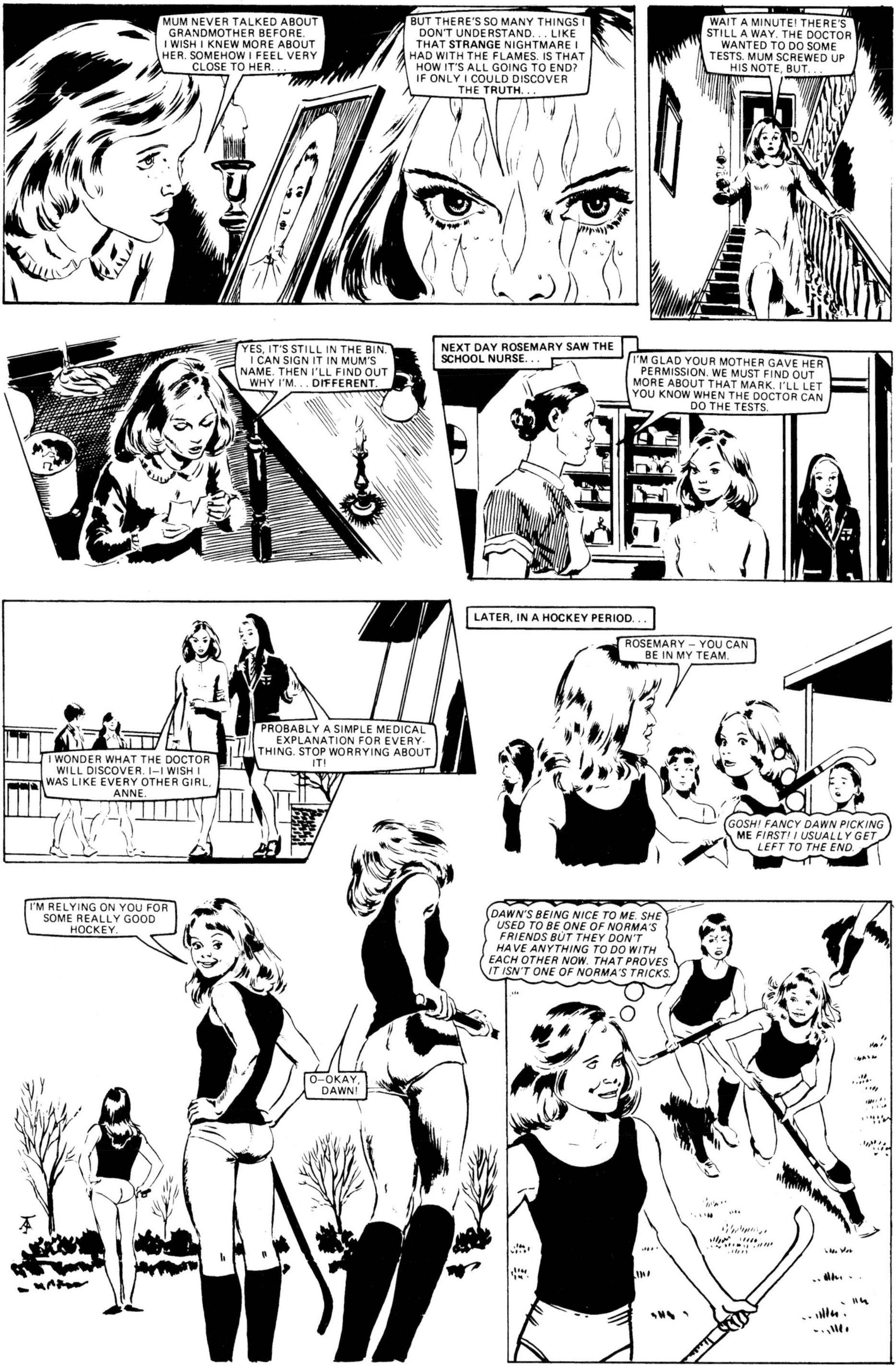
MUM NEVER TALKED ABOUT GRANDMOTHER BEFORE. I WISH I KNEW MORE ABOUT HER. SOMEHOW I FEEL VERY CLOSE TO HER...
BUT THERE'S SO MANY THINGS I DON'T UNDERSTAND... LIKE THAT STRANGE NIGHTMARE I HAD WITH THE FLAMES. IS THAT HOW IT'S ALL GOING TO END? IF ONLY I COULD DISCOVER THE TRUTH...
WAIT A MINUTE! THERE'S STILL A WAY. THE DOCTOR WANTED TO DO SOME TESTS. MUM SCREWED UP HIS NOTE, BUT...
YES, IT'S STILL IN THE BIN. I CAN SIGN IT IN MUM'S NAME. THEN I'LL FIND OUT WHY I'M... DIFFERENT.
NEXT DAY ROSEMARY SAW THE SCHOOL NURSE...
I'M GLAD YOUR MOTHER GAVE HER PERMISSION. WE MUST FIND OUT MORE ABOUT THAT MARK. I'LL LET YOU KNOW WHEN THE DOCTOR CAN DO THE TESTS.
I WONDER WHAT THE DOCTOR WILL DISCOVER. I—I WISH I WAS LIKE EVERY OTHER GIRL, ANNE.
PROBABLY A SIMPLE MEDICAL EXPLANATION FOR EVERYTHING. STOP WORRYING ABOUT IT!
LATER, IN A HOCKEY PERIOD...
ROSEMARY – YOU CAN BE IN MY TEAM.
GOSH! FANCY DAWN PICKING ME FIRST! I USUALLY GET LEFT TO THE END.
I'M RELYING ON YOU FOR SOME REALLY GOOD HOCKEY.
O–OKAY, DAWN!
DAWN'S BEING NICE TO ME. SHE USED TO BE ONE OF NORMA'S FRIENDS BUT THEY DON'T HAVE ANYTHING TO DO WITH EACH OTHER NOW. THAT PROVES IT ISN'T ONE OF NORMA'S TRICKS.

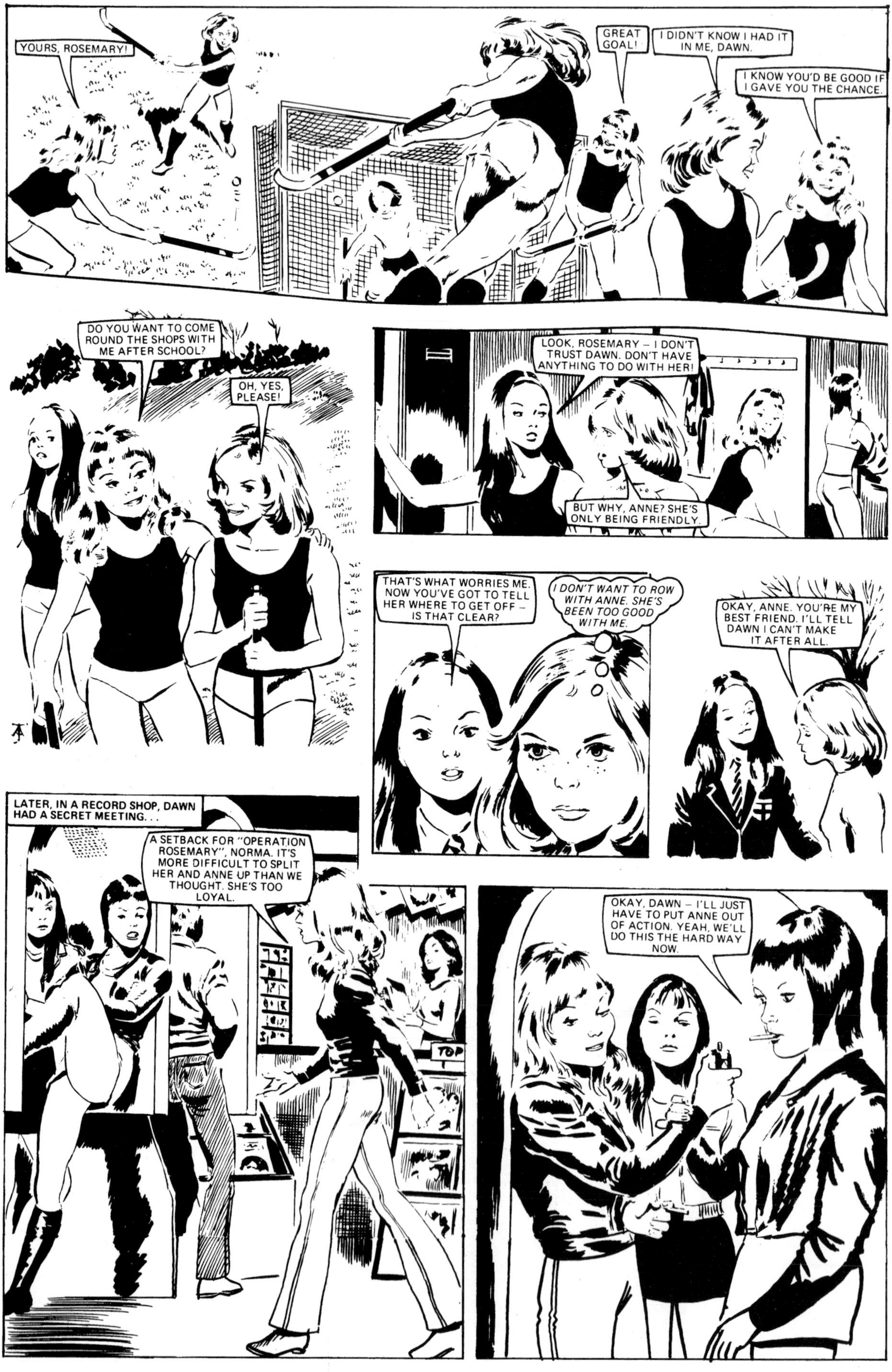

YOURS, ROSEMARY!
GREAT GOAL!
I DIDN'T KNOW I HAD IT IN ME, DAWN.
I KNOW YOU'D BE GOOD IF I GAVE YOU THE CHANCE.
DO YOU WANT TO COME ROUND THE SHOPS WITH ME AFTER SCHOOL?
OH, YES, PLEASE!
LOOK, ROSEMARY – I DON'T TRUST DAWN. DON'T HAVE ANYTHING TO DO WITH HER!
BUT WHY, ANNE? SHE'S ONLY BEING FRIENDLY.
THAT'S WHAT WORRIES ME. NOW YOU'VE GOT TO TELL HER WHERE TO GET OFF – IS THAT CLEAR?
I DON'T WANT TO ROW WITH ANNE. SHE'S BEEN TOO GOOD WITH ME.
OKAY, ANNE. YOU'RE MY BEST FRIEND. I'LL TELL DAWN I CAN'T MAKE IT AFTER ALL.
LATER, IN A RECORD SHOP, DAWN HAD A SECRET MEETING...
A SETBACK FOR "OPERATION ROSEMARY", NORMA. IT'S MORE DIFFICULT TO SPLIT HER AND ANNE UP THAN WE THOUGHT. SHE'S TOO LOYAL.
TOP
OKAY, DAWN – I'LL JUST HAVE TO PUT ANNE OUT OF ACTION. YEAH, WE'LL DO THIS THE HARD WAY NOW.

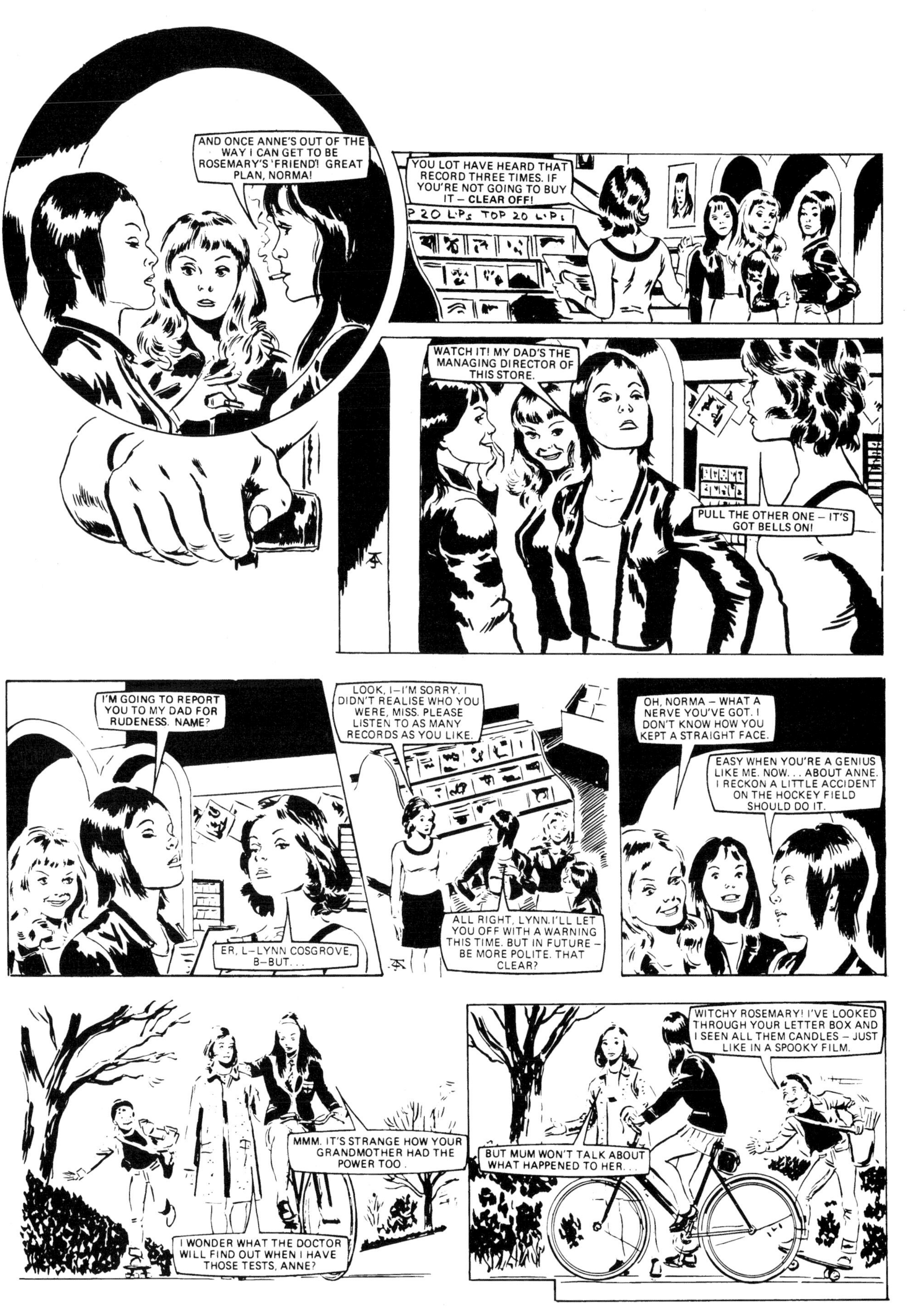
AND ONCE ANNE'S OUT OF THE WAY I CAN GET TO BE ROSEMARY'S 'FRIEND'! GREAT PLAN, NORMA!
YOU LOT HAVE HEARD THAT RECORD THREE TIMES. IF YOU'RE NOT GOING TO BUY IT – CLEAR OFF!
P 20 L.Ps TOP 20 L.P.
WATCH IT! MY DAD'S THE MANAGING DIRECTOR OF THIS STORE.
PULL THE OTHER ONE – IT'S GOT BELLS ON!
I'M GOING TO REPORT YOU TO MY DAD FOR RUDENESS. NAME?
ER, L–LYNN COSGROVE, B–BUT. . .
LOOK, I–I'M SORRY. I DIDN'T REALISE WHO YOU WERE, MISS. PLEASE LISTEN TO AS MANY RECORDS AS YOU LIKE.
ALL RIGHT, LYNN. I'LL LET YOU OFF WITH A WARNING THIS TIME. BUT IN FUTURE – BE MORE POLITE. THAT CLEAR?
OH, NORMA – WHAT A NERVE YOU'VE GOT. I DON'T KNOW HOW YOU KEPT A STRAIGHT FACE.
EASY WHEN YOU'RE A GENIUS LIKE ME. NOW. . . ABOUT ANNE. I RECKON A LITTLE ACCIDENT ON THE HOCKEY FIELD SHOULD DO IT.
I WONDER WHAT THE DOCTOR WILL FIND OUT WHEN I HAVE THOSE TESTS, ANNE?
MMM. IT'S STRANGE HOW YOUR GRANDMOTHER HAD THE POWER TOO .
BUT MUM WON'T TALK ABOUT WHAT HAPPENED TO HER. . .
WITCHY ROSEMARY! I'VE LOOKED THROUGH YOUR LETTER BOX AND I SEEN ALL THEM CANDLES – JUST LIKE IN A SPOOKY FILM.

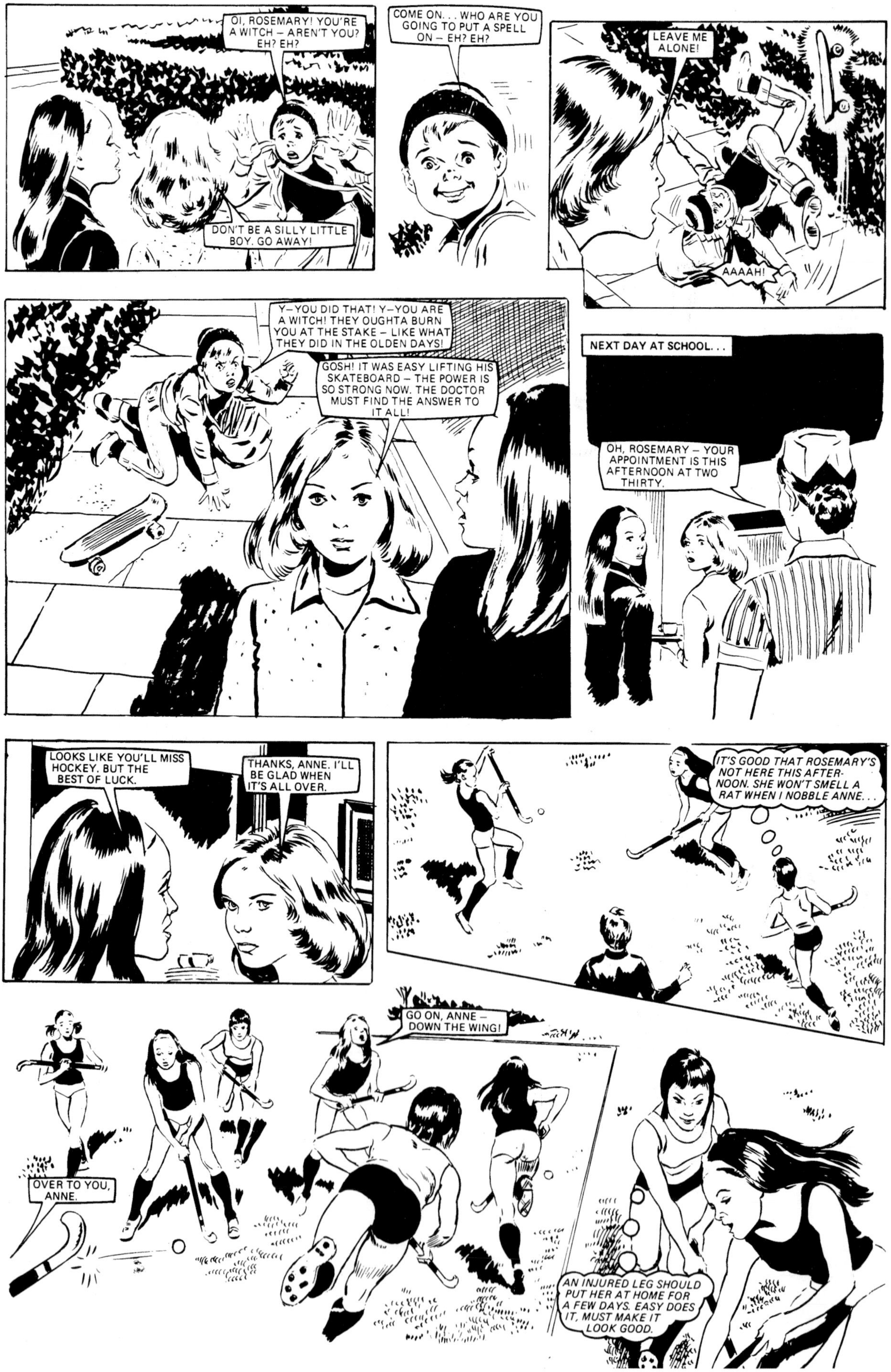

OI, ROSEMARY! YOU'RE A WITCH – AREN'T YOU? EH? EH?
DON'T BE A SILLY LITTLE BOY. GO AWAY!
COME ON... WHO ARE YOU GOING TO PUT A SPELL ON – EH? EH?
LEAVE ME ALONE!
AAAAH!
Y–YOU DID THAT! Y–YOU ARE A WITCH! THEY OUGHTA BURN YOU AT THE STAKE – LIKE WHAT THEY DID IN THE OLDEN DAYS!
GOSH! IT WAS EASY LIFTING HIS SKATEBOARD – THE POWER IS SO STRONG NOW. THE DOCTOR MUST FIND THE ANSWER TO IT ALL!
NEXT DAY AT SCHOOL...
OH, ROSEMARY – YOUR APPOINTMENT IS THIS AFTERNOON AT TWO THIRTY.
LOOKS LIKE YOU'LL MISS HOCKEY. BUT THE BEST OF LUCK.
THANKS, ANNE. I'LL BE GLAD WHEN IT'S ALL OVER.
IT'S GOOD THAT ROSEMARY'S NOT HERE THIS AFTERNOON. SHE WON'T SMELL A RAT WHEN I NOBBLE ANNE...
GO ON, ANNE – DOWN THE WING!
OVER TO YOU, ANNE.
AN INJURED LEG SHOULD PUT HER AT HOME FOR A FEW DAYS. EASY DOES IT, MUST MAKE IT LOOK GOOD.

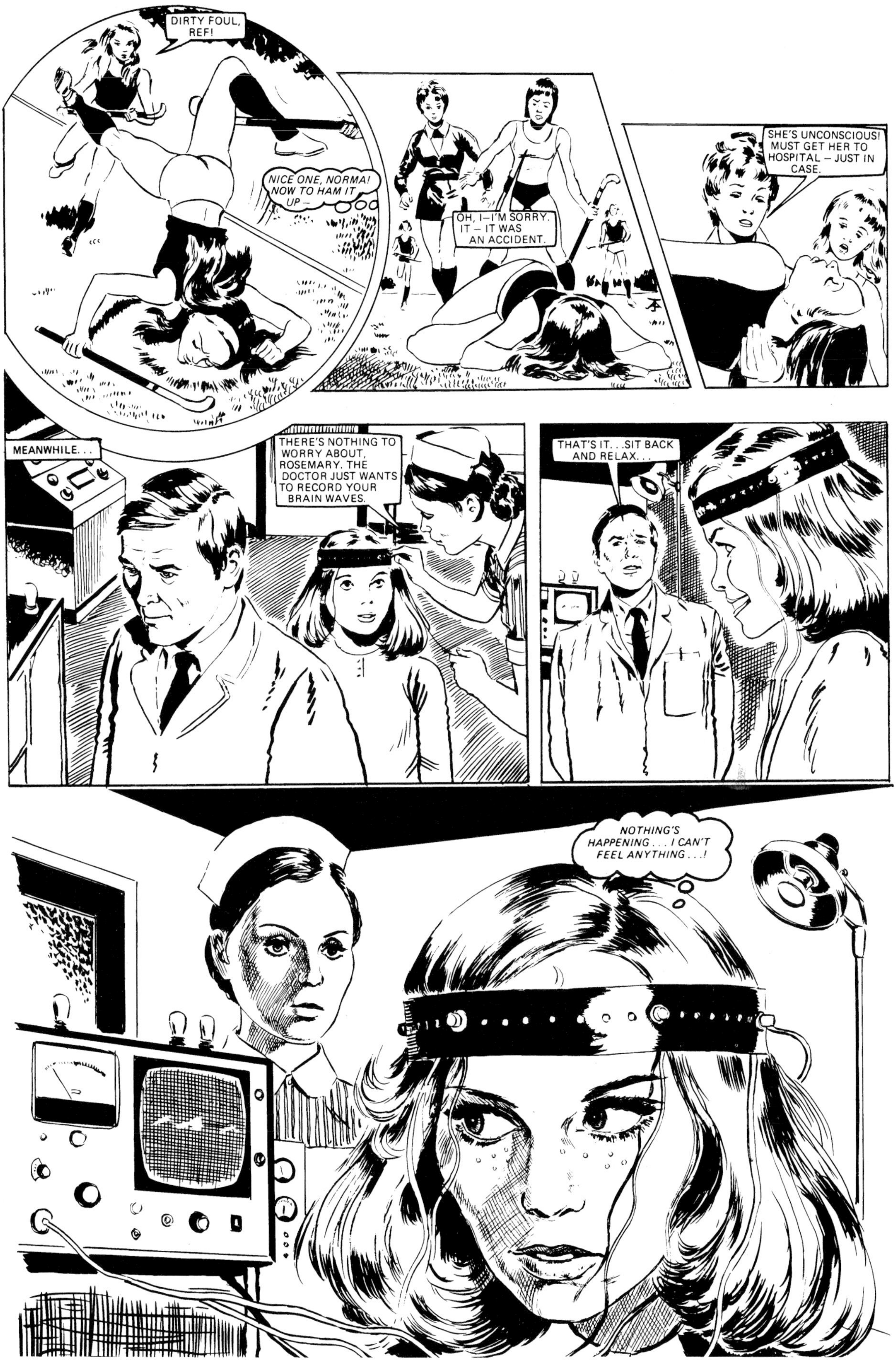
DIRTY FOUL, REF!
NICE ONE, NORMA! NOW TO HAM IT UP –
OH, I–I'M SORRY. IT – IT WAS AN ACCIDENT.
SHE'S UNCONSCIOUS! MUST GET HER TO HOSPITAL – JUST IN CASE.
MEANWHILE. . .
THERE'S NOTHING TO WORRY ABOUT, ROSEMARY. THE DOCTOR JUST WANTS TO RECORD YOUR BRAIN WAVES.
THAT'S IT. . .SIT BACK AND RELAX. . .
NOTHING'S HAPPENING . . . I CAN'T FEEL ANYTHING . . .!

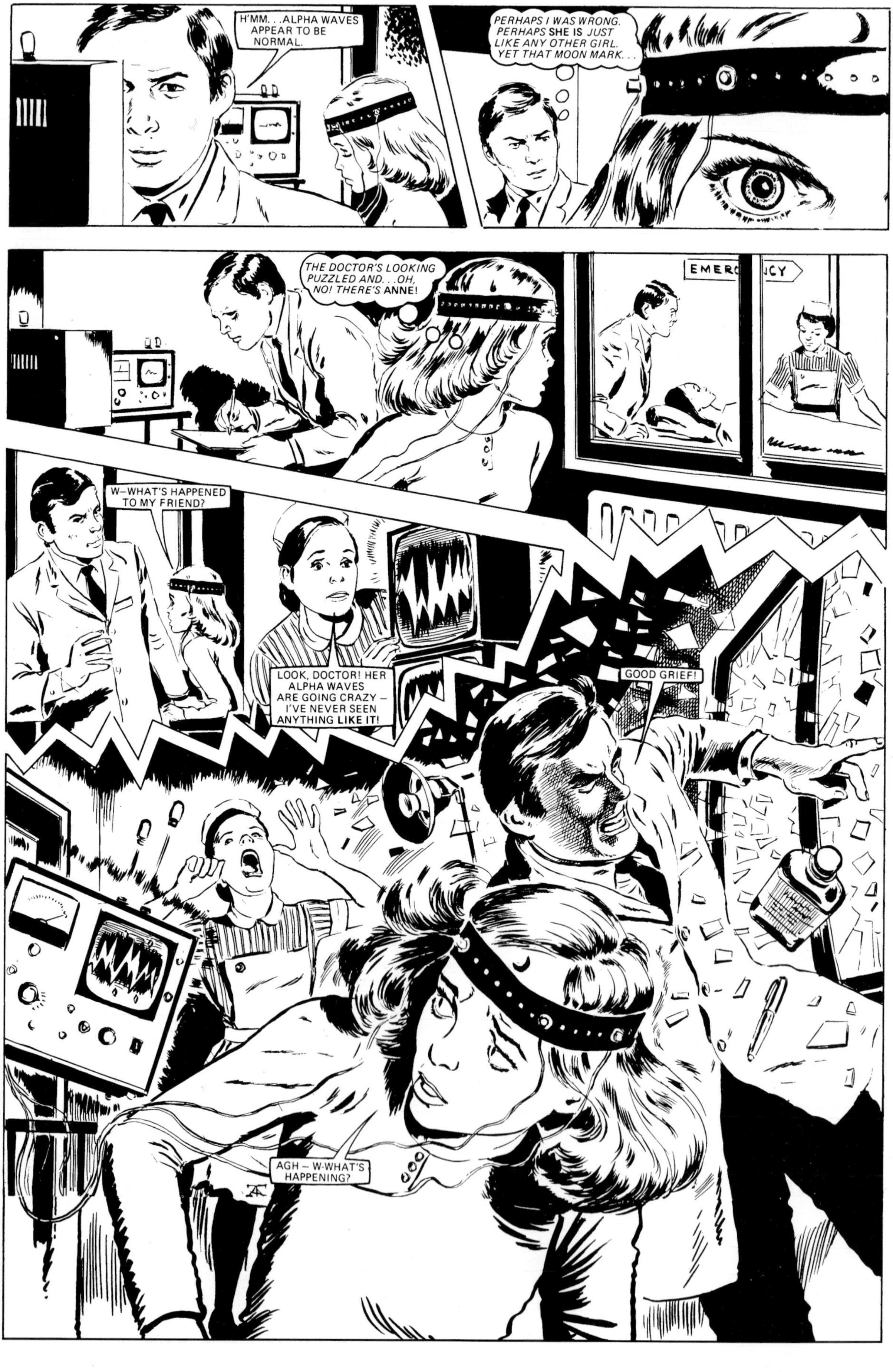

H'MM. . .ALPHA WAVES APPEAR TO BE NORMAL.
PERHAPS I WAS WRONG. PERHAPS SHE IS JUST LIKE ANY OTHER GIRL. YET THAT MOON MARK. . .
THE DOCTOR'S LOOKING PUZZLED AND. . .OH, NO! THERE'S ANNE!
W–WHAT'S HAPPENED TO MY FRIEND?
LOOK, DOCTOR! HER ALPHA WAVES ARE GOING CRAZY – I'VE NEVER SEEN ANYTHING LIKE IT!
GOOD GRIEF!
AGH – W-WHAT'S HAPPENING?

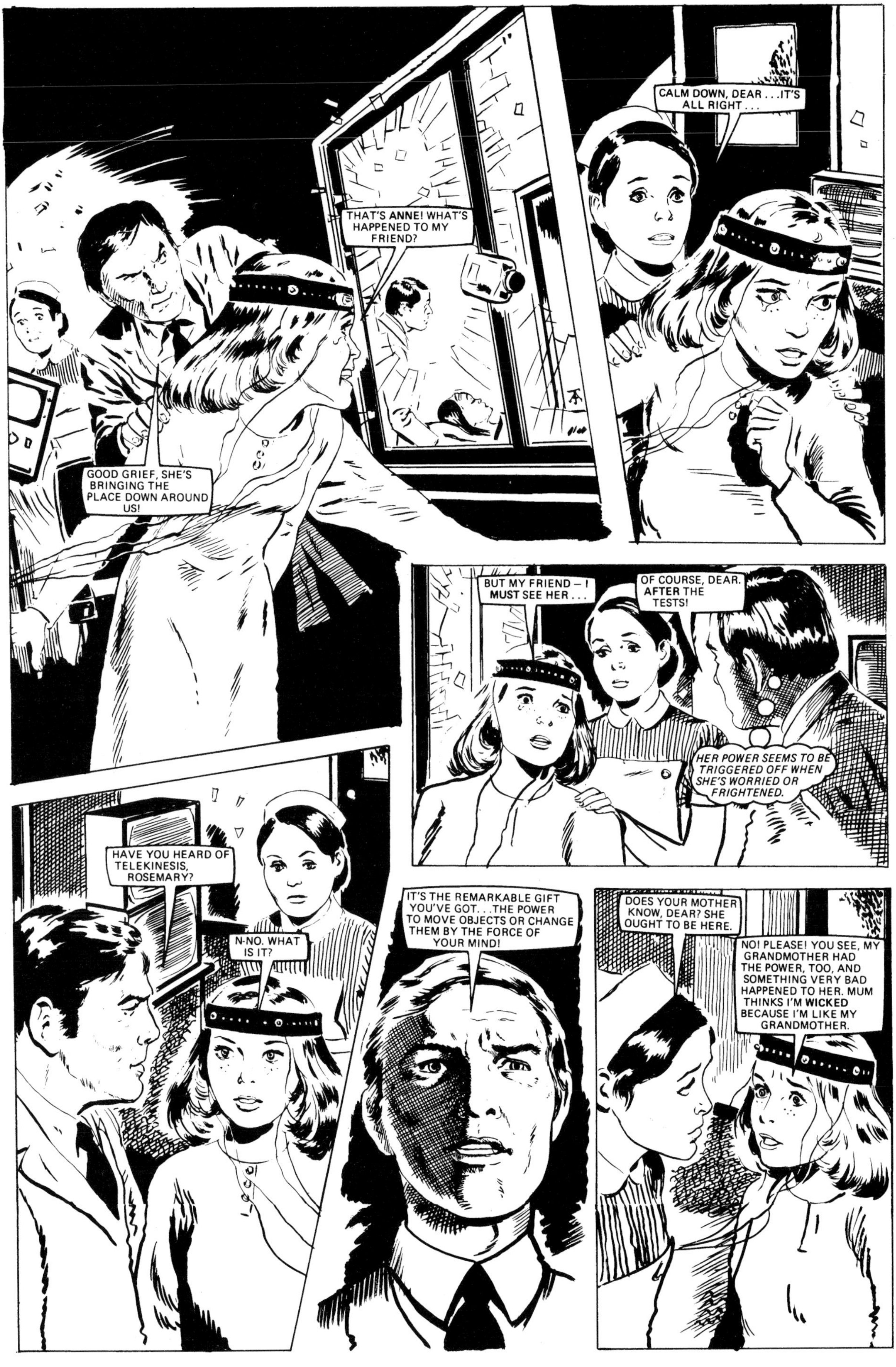
GOOD GRIEF, SHE'S BRINGING THE PLACE DOWN AROUND US!
THAT'S ANNE! WHAT'S HAPPENED TO MY FRIEND?
CALM DOWN, DEAR . . . IT'S ALL RIGHT . . .
BUT MY FRIEND – I MUST SEE HER . . .
OF COURSE, DEAR. AFTER THE TESTS!
HER POWER SEEMS TO BE TRIGGERED OFF WHEN SHE'S WORRIED OR FRIGHTENED.
HAVE YOU HEARD OF TELEKINESIS, ROSEMARY?
N-NO. WHAT IS IT?
IT'S THE REMARKABLE GIFT YOU'VE GOT. . . THE POWER TO MOVE OBJECTS OR CHANGE THEM BY THE FORCE OF YOUR MIND!
DOES YOUR MOTHER KNOW, DEAR? SHE OUGHT TO BE HERE.
NO! PLEASE! YOU SEE, MY GRANDMOTHER HAD THE POWER, TOO, AND SOMETHING VERY BAD HAPPENED TO HER. MUM THINKS I'M WICKED BECAUSE I'M LIKE MY GRANDMOTHER.

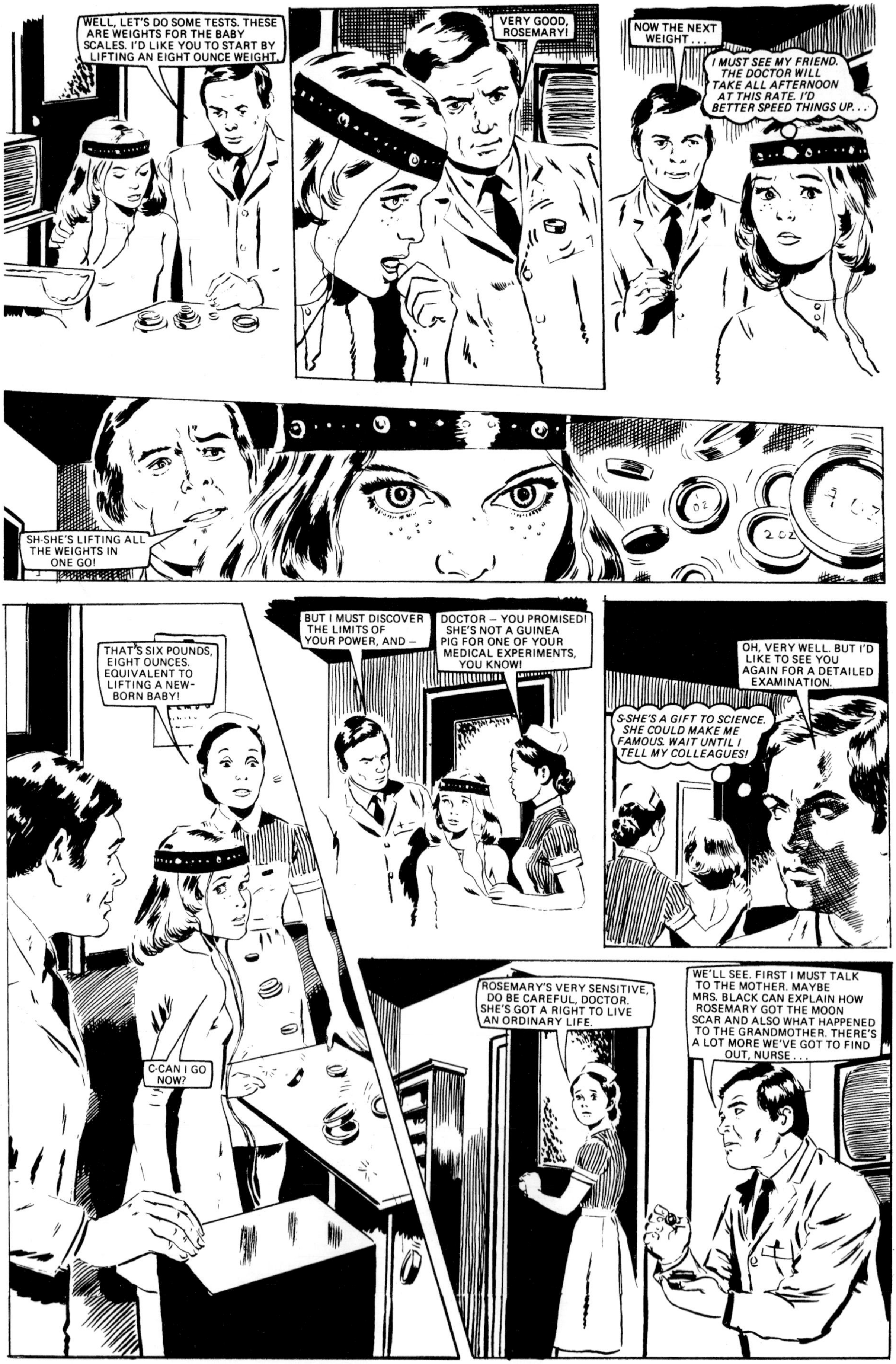
WELL, LET'S DO SOME TESTS. THESE ARE WEIGHTS FOR THE BABY SCALES. I'D LIKE YOU TO START BY LIFTING AN EIGHT OUNCE WEIGHT.
VERY GOOD, ROSEMARY!
NOW THE NEXT WEIGHT . . .
I MUST SEE MY FRIEND. THE DOCTOR WILL TAKE ALL AFTERNOON AT THIS RATE. I'D BETTER SPEED THINGS UP . . .
SH-SHE'S LIFTING ALL THE WEIGHTS IN ONE GO!
1 OZ
2 OZ
THAT'S SIX POUNDS, EIGHT OUNCES. EQUIVALENT TO LIFTING A NEW-BORN BABY!
C-CAN I GO NOW?
BUT I MUST DISCOVER THE LIMITS OF YOUR POWER, AND —
DOCTOR — YOU PROMISED! SHE'S NOT A GUINEA PIG FOR ONE OF YOUR MEDICAL EXPERIMENTS, YOU KNOW!
OH, VERY WELL. BUT I'D LIKE TO SEE YOU AGAIN FOR A DETAILED EXAMINATION.
S-SHE'S A GIFT TO SCIENCE. SHE COULD MAKE ME FAMOUS. WAIT UNTIL I TELL MY COLLEAGUES!
ROSEMARY'S VERY SENSITIVE, DO BE CAREFUL, DOCTOR. SHE'S GOT A RIGHT TO LIVE AN ORDINARY LIFE.
WE'LL SEE. FIRST I MUST TALK TO THE MOTHER. MAYBE MRS. BLACK CAN EXPLAIN HOW ROSEMARY GOT THE MOON SCAR AND ALSO WHAT HAPPENED TO THE GRANDMOTHER. THERE'S A LOT MORE WE'VE GOT TO FIND OUT, NURSE . . .

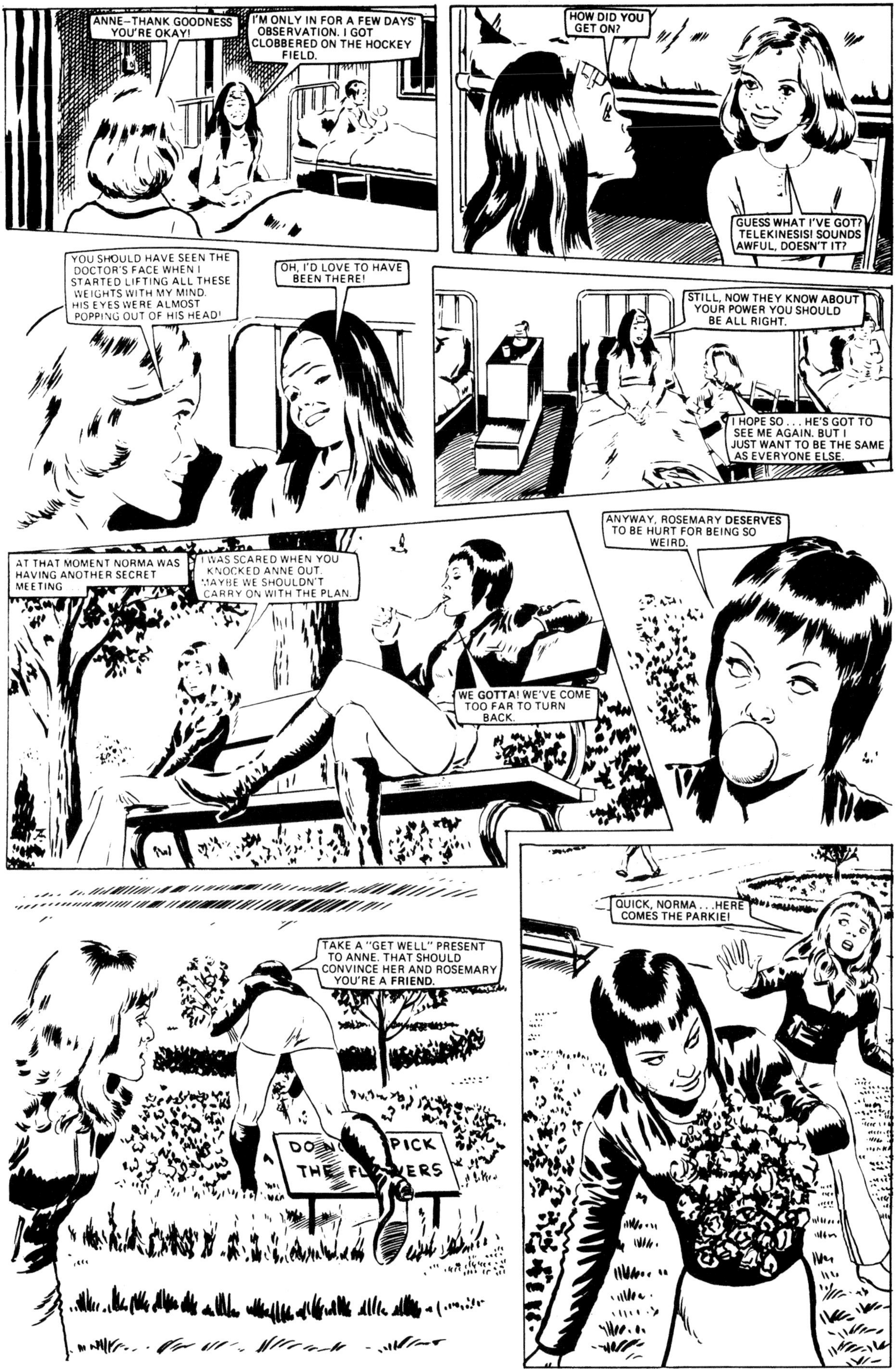
ANNE—THANK GOODNESS YOU'RE OKAY!
I'M ONLY IN FOR A FEW DAYS' OBSERVATION. I GOT CLOBBERED ON THE HOCKEY FIELD.
HOW DID YOU GET ON?
GUESS WHAT I'VE GOT? TELEKINESIS! SOUNDS AWFUL, DOESN'T IT?
YOU SHOULD HAVE SEEN THE DOCTOR'S FACE WHEN I STARTED LIFTING ALL THESE WEIGHTS WITH MY MIND. HIS EYES WERE ALMOST POPPING OUT OF HIS HEAD!
OH, I'D LOVE TO HAVE BEEN THERE!
STILL, NOW THEY KNOW ABOUT YOUR POWER YOU SHOULD BE ALL RIGHT.
I HOPE SO . . . HE'S GOT TO SEE ME AGAIN. BUT I JUST WANT TO BE THE SAME AS EVERYONE ELSE.
AT THAT MOMENT NORMA WAS HAVING ANOTHER SECRET MEETING . . .
I WAS SCARED WHEN YOU KNOCKED ANNE OUT. MAYBE WE SHOULDN'T CARRY ON WITH THE PLAN.
WE GOTTA! WE'VE COME TOO FAR TO TURN BACK.
ANYWAY, ROSEMARY DESERVES TO BE HURT FOR BEING SO WEIRD.
TAKE A "GET WELL" PRESENT TO ANNE. THAT SHOULD CONVINCE HER AND ROSEMARY YOU'RE A FRIEND.
QUICK, NORMA . . . HERE COMES THE PARKIE!

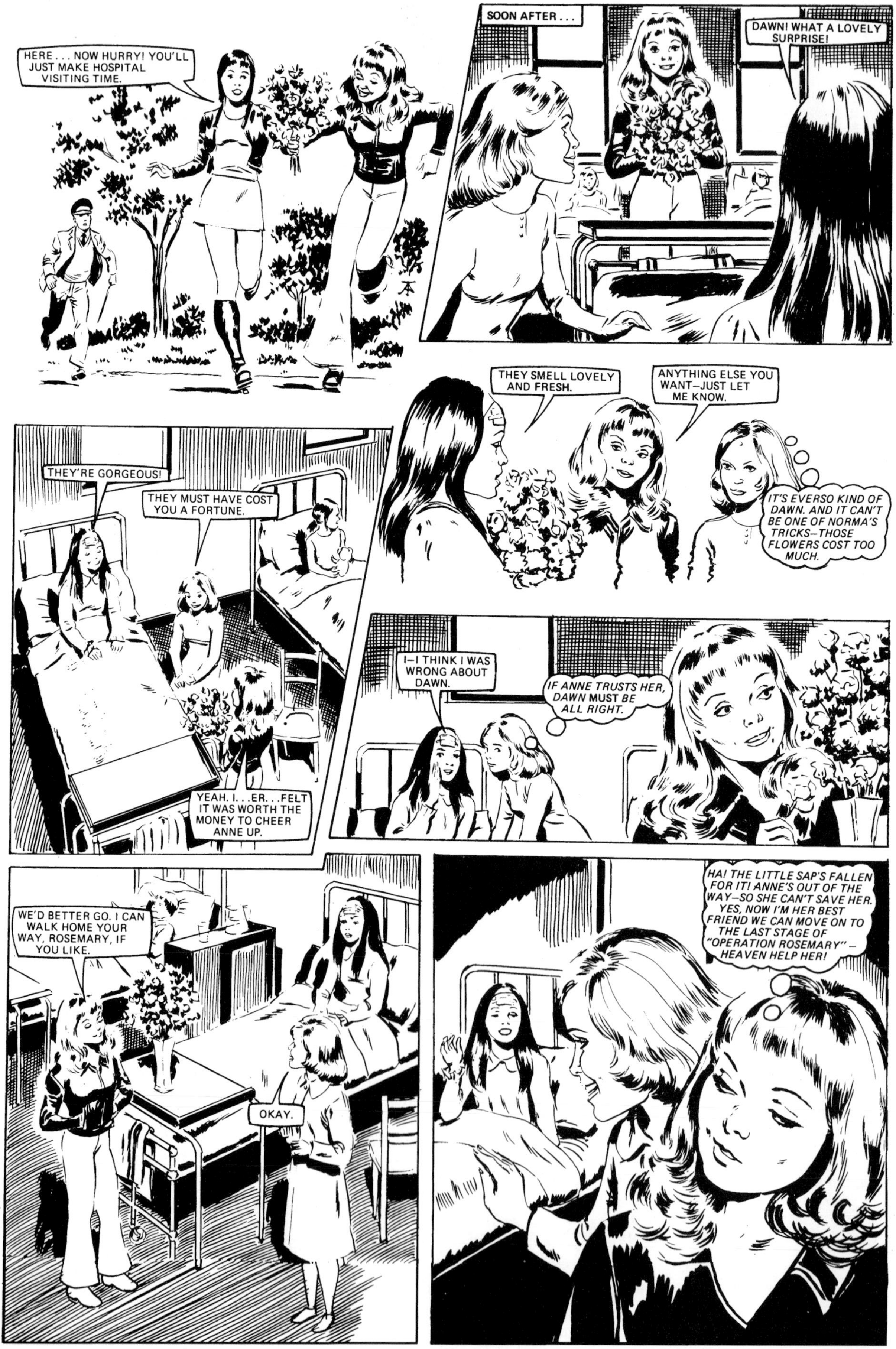

HERE . . . NOW HURRY! YOU'LL JUST MAKE HOSPITAL VISITING TIME.
SOON AFTER . . .
DAWN! WHAT A LOVELY SURPRISE!
THEY SMELL LOVELY AND FRESH.
ANYTHING ELSE YOU WANT—JUST LET ME KNOW.
IT'S EVERSO KIND OF DAWN. AND IT CAN'T BE ONE OF NORMA'S TRICKS—THOSE FLOWERS COST TOO MUCH.
THEY'RE GORGEOUS!
THEY MUST HAVE COST YOU A FORTUNE.
YEAH. I. . .ER. . .FELT IT WAS WORTH THE MONEY TO CHEER ANNE UP.
I—I THINK I WAS WRONG ABOUT DAWN.
IF ANNE TRUSTS HER, DAWN MUST BE ALL RIGHT.
WE'D BETTER GO. I CAN WALK HOME YOUR WAY, ROSEMARY, IF YOU LIKE.
OKAY.
HA! THE LITTLE SAP'S FALLEN FOR IT! ANNE'S OUT OF THE WAY—SO SHE CAN'T SAVE HER. YES, NOW I'M HER BEST FRIEND WE CAN MOVE ON TO THE LAST STAGE OF "OPERATION ROSEMARY"—HEAVEN HELP HER!

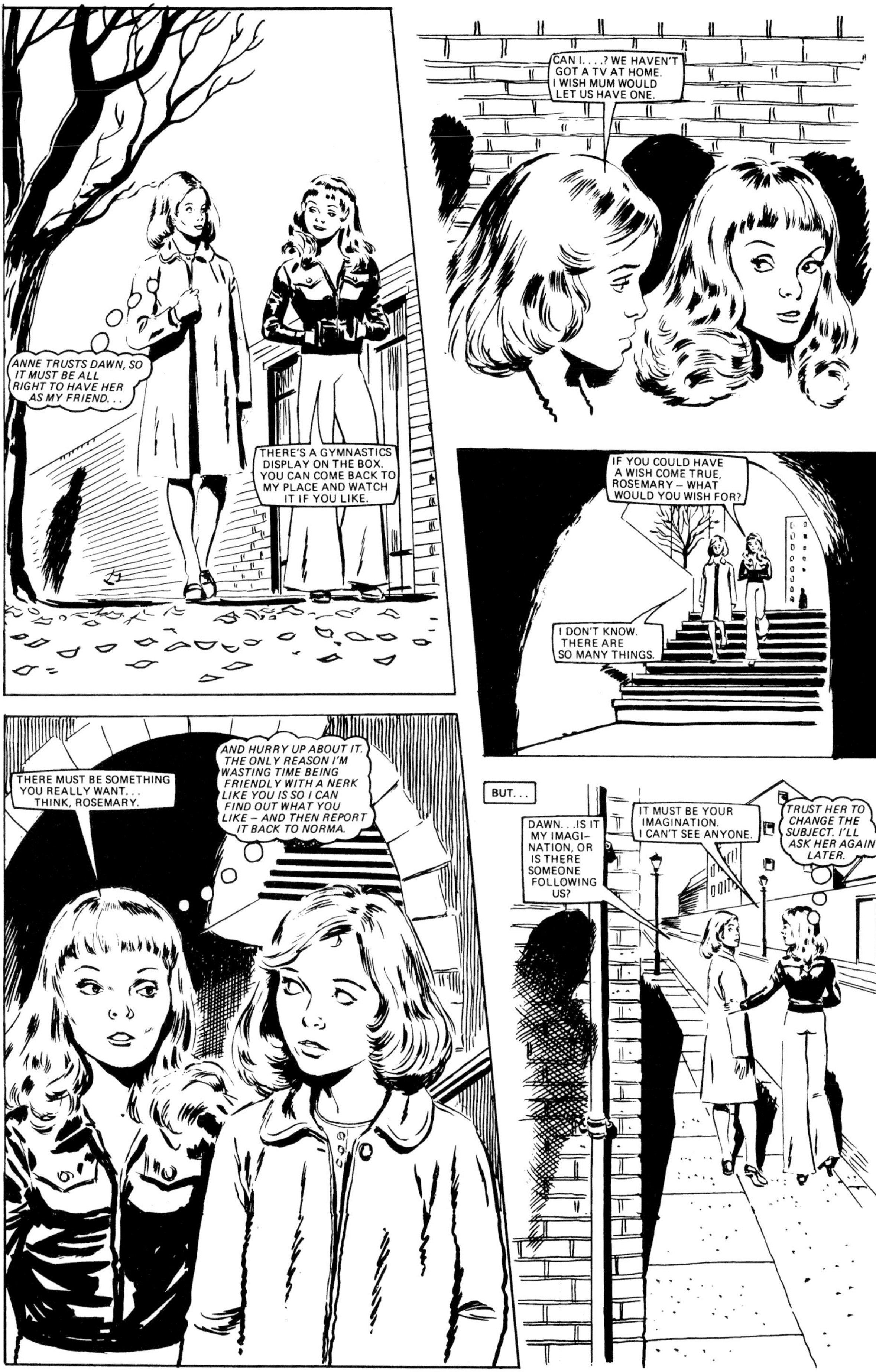

ANNE TRUSTS DAWN, SO IT MUST BE ALL RIGHT TO HAVE HER AS MY FRIEND. . .
THERE'S A GYMNASTICS DISPLAY ON THE BOX. YOU CAN COME BACK TO MY PLACE AND WATCH IT IF YOU LIKE.
CAN I. . . .? WE HAVEN'T GOT A TV AT HOME. I WISH MUM WOULD LET US HAVE ONE.
IF YOU COULD HAVE A WISH COME TRUE, ROSEMARY – WHAT WOULD YOU WISH FOR?
I DON'T KNOW. THERE ARE SO MANY THINGS.
THERE MUST BE SOMETHING YOU REALLY WANT. . . THINK, ROSEMARY.
AND HURRY UP ABOUT IT. THE ONLY REASON I'M WASTING TIME BEING FRIENDLY WITH A NERK LIKE YOU IS SO I CAN FIND OUT WHAT YOU LIKE – AND THEN REPORT IT BACK TO NORMA.
BUT. . .
DAWN. . .IS IT MY IMAGI-NATION, OR IS THERE SOMEONE FOLLOWING US?
IT MUST BE YOUR IMAGINATION. I CAN'T SEE ANYONE.
TRUST HER TO CHANGE THE SUBJECT. I'LL ASK HER AGAIN LATER.

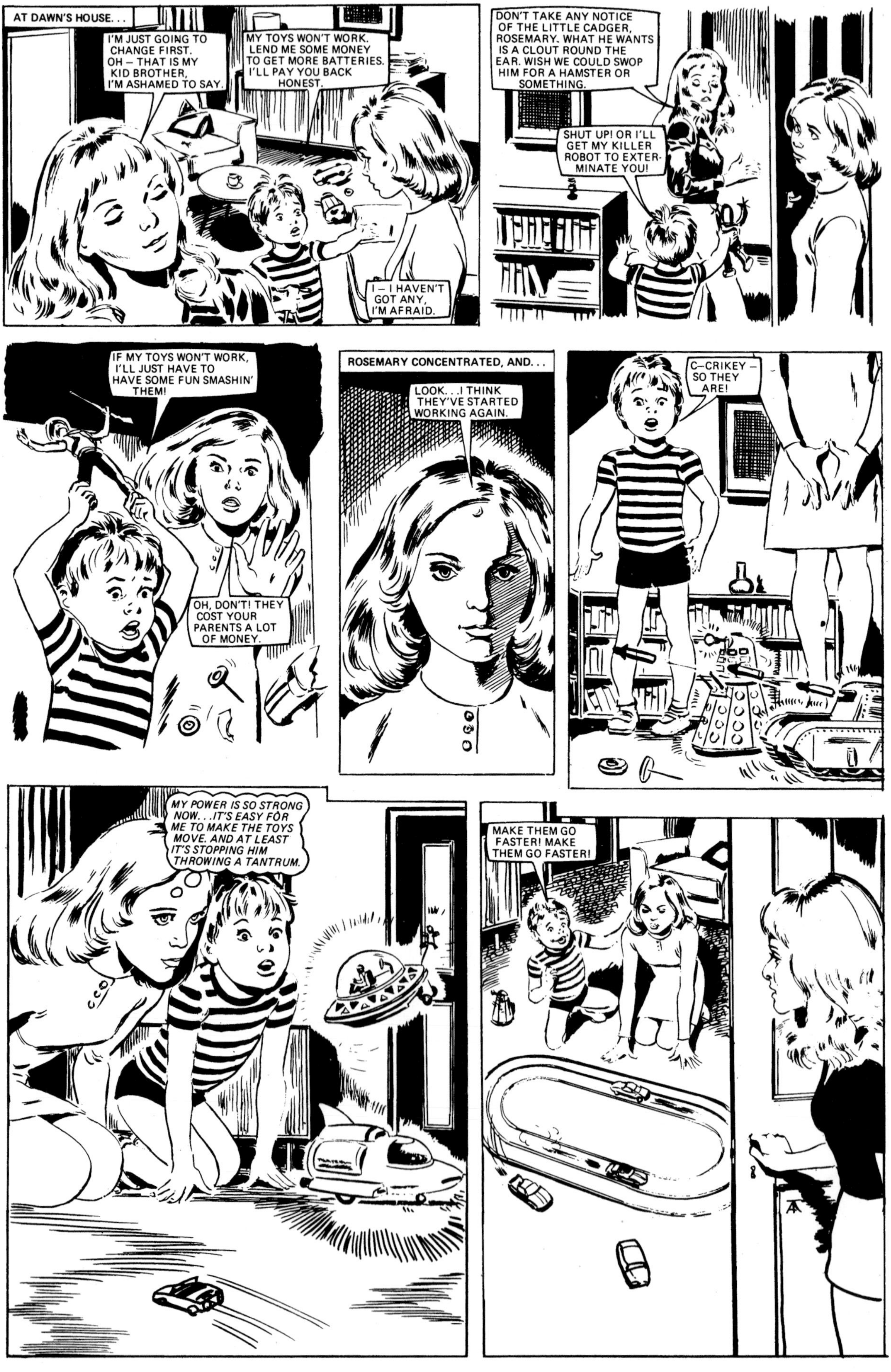
AT DAWN'S HOUSE. . .
I'M JUST GOING TO CHANGE FIRST. OH – THAT IS MY KID BROTHER, I'M ASHAMED TO SAY.
MY TOYS WON'T WORK. LEND ME SOME MONEY TO GET MORE BATTERIES. I'LL PAY YOU BACK HONEST.
I – I HAVEN'T GOT ANY, I'M AFRAID.
DON'T TAKE ANY NOTICE OF THE LITTLE CADGER, ROSEMARY. WHAT HE WANTS IS A CLOUT ROUND THE EAR. WISH WE COULD SWOP HIM FOR A HAMSTER OR SOMETHING.
SHUT UP! OR I'LL GET MY KILLER ROBOT TO EXTERMINATE YOU!
IF MY TOYS WON'T WORK, I'LL JUST HAVE TO HAVE SOME FUN SMASHIN' THEM!
OH, DON'T! THEY COST YOUR PARENTS A LOT OF MONEY.
ROSEMARY CONCENTRATED, AND. . .
LOOK. . .I THINK THEY'VE STARTED WORKING AGAIN.
C—CRIKEY – SO THEY ARE!
MY POWER IS SO STRONG NOW. . .IT'S EASY FOR ME TO MAKE THE TOYS MOVE. AND AT LEAST IT'S STOPPING HIM THROWING A TANTRUM.
MAKE THEM GO FASTER! MAKE THEM GO FASTER!

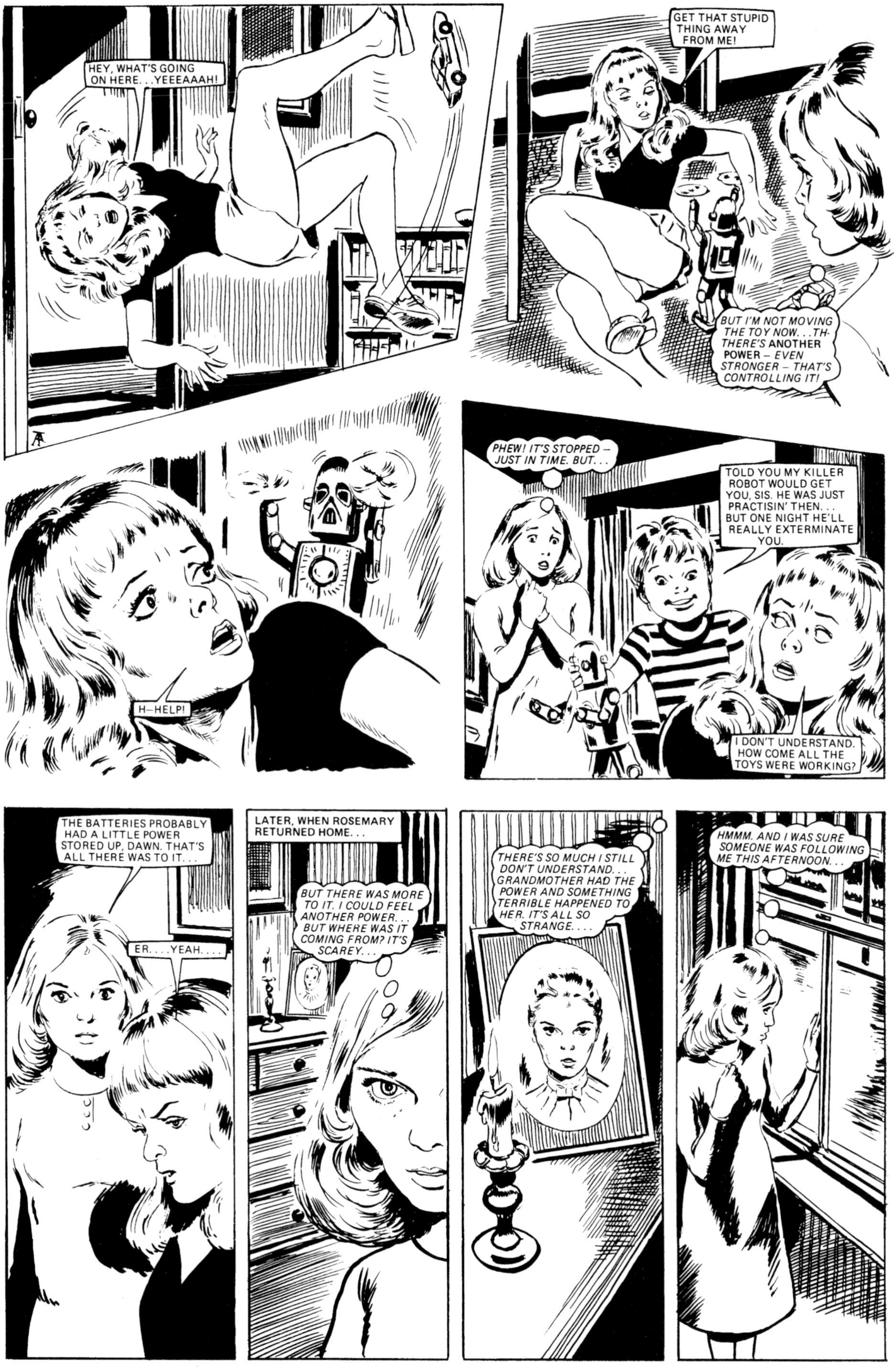

HEY, WHAT'S GOING ON HERE. . . YEEEAAAH!
GET THAT STUPID THING AWAY FROM ME!
BUT I'M NOT MOVING THE TOY NOW. . . TH-THERE'S ANOTHER POWER – EVEN STRONGER – THAT'S CONTROLLING IT!
H–HELP!
PHEW! IT'S STOPPED – JUST IN TIME. BUT. . .
TOLD YOU MY KILLER ROBOT WOULD GET YOU, SIS. HE WAS JUST PRACTISIN' THEN. . . BUT ONE NIGHT HE'LL REALLY EXTERMINATE YOU.
I DON'T UNDERSTAND. HOW COME ALL THE TOYS WERE WORKING?
THE BATTERIES PROBABLY HAD A LITTLE POWER STORED UP, DAWN. THAT'S ALL THERE WAS TO IT. . .
ER. . . . YEAH. . . .
LATER, WHEN ROSEMARY RETURNED HOME. . .
BUT THERE WAS MORE TO IT. I COULD FEEL ANOTHER POWER. . . BUT WHERE WAS IT COMING FROM? IT'S SCAREY. . .
THERE'S SO MUCH I STILL DON'T UNDERSTAND. . . GRANDMOTHER HAD THE POWER AND SOMETHING TERRIBLE HAPPENED TO HER. IT'S ALL SO STRANGE. . . .
HMMM. AND I WAS SURE SOMEONE WAS FOLLOWING ME THIS AFTERNOON. . .

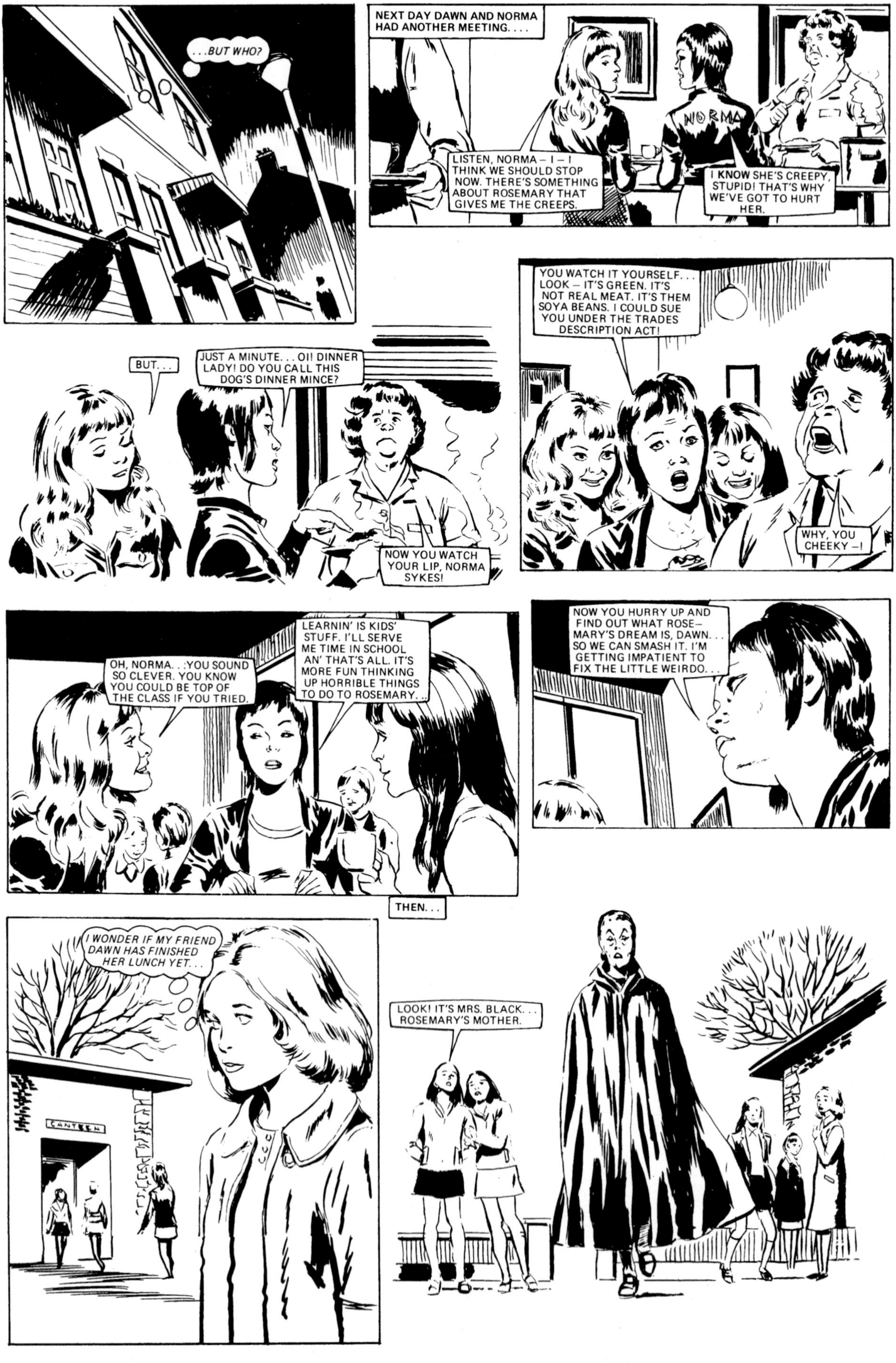
. . . BUT WHO?
NEXT DAY DAWN AND NORMA HAD ANOTHER MEETING. . . .
NORMA
LISTEN, NORMA – I – I THINK WE SHOULD STOP NOW. THERE'S SOMETHING ABOUT ROSEMARY THAT GIVES ME THE CREEPS.
I KNOW SHE'S CREEPY, STUPID! THAT'S WHY WE'VE GOT TO HURT HER.
BUT. . .
JUST A MINUTE. . . OI! DINNER LADY! DO YOU CALL THIS DOG'S DINNER MINCE?
NOW YOU WATCH YOUR LIP, NORMA SYKES!
YOU WATCH IT YOURSELF. . . LOOK – IT'S GREEN. IT'S NOT REAL MEAT. IT'S THEM SOYA BEANS. I COULD SUE YOU UNDER THE TRADES DESCRIPTION ACT!
WHY, YOU CHEEKY –!
OH, NORMA. . :YOU SOUND SO CLEVER. YOU KNOW YOU COULD BE TOP OF THE CLASS IF YOU TRIED.
LEARNIN' IS KIDS' STUFF. I'LL SERVE ME TIME IN SCHOOL AN' THAT'S ALL. IT'S MORE FUN THINKING UP HORRIBLE THINGS TO DO TO ROSEMARY. . .
NOW YOU HURRY UP AND FIND OUT WHAT ROSE-MARY'S DREAM IS, DAWN. . . SO WE CAN SMASH IT. I'M GETTING IMPATIENT TO FIX THE LITTLE WEIRDO. . .
THEN. . .
I WONDER IF MY FRIEND DAWN HAS FINISHED HER LUNCH YET. . .
CANTEEN
LOOK! IT'S MRS. BLACK. . . ROSEMARY'S MOTHER.

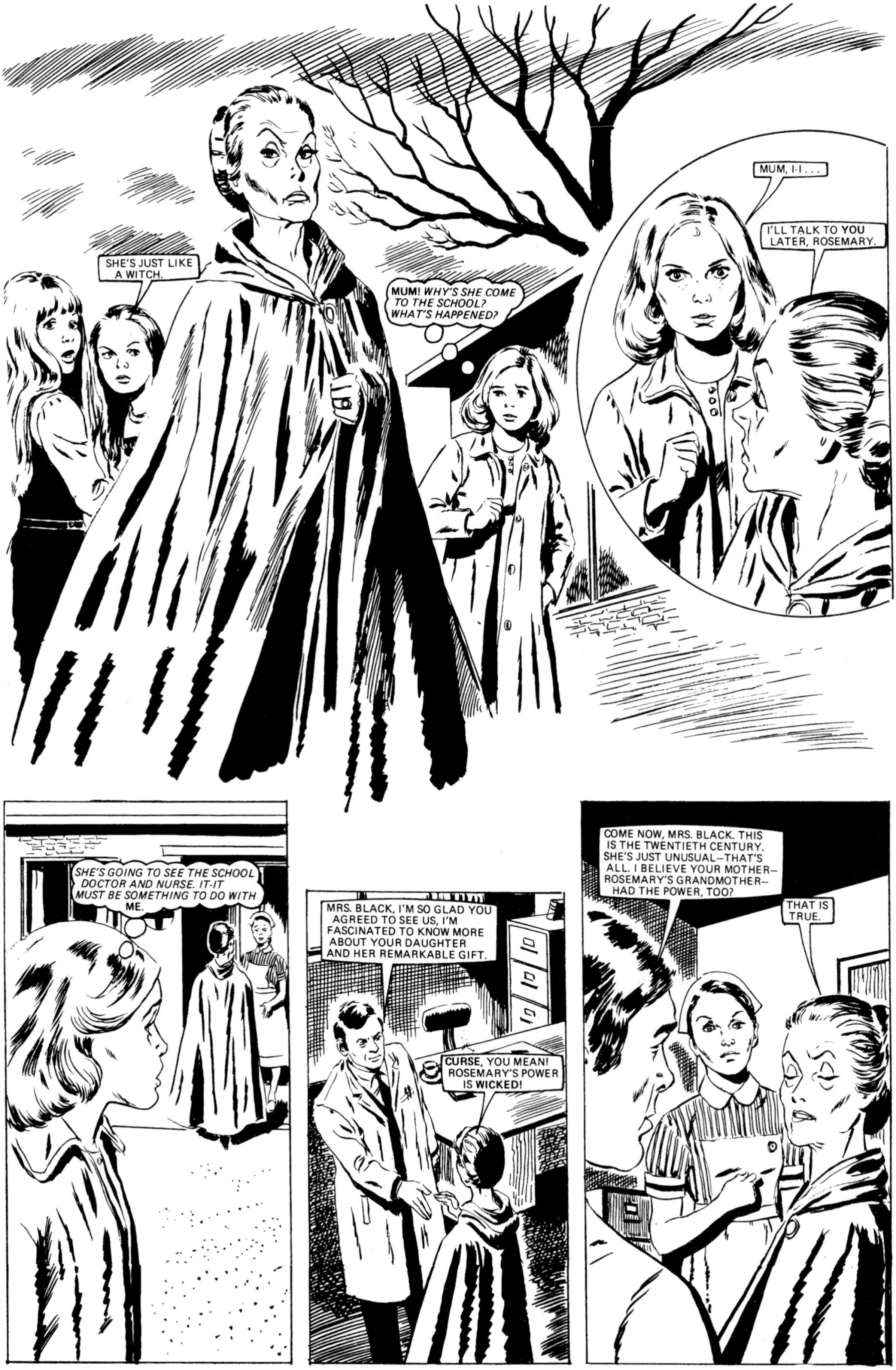
SHE'S JUST LIKE A WITCH.
MUM! WHY'S SHE COME TO THE SCHOOL? WHAT'S HAPPENED?
MUM, I-I . . .
I'LL TALK TO YOU LATER, ROSEMARY.
SHE'S GOING TO SEE THE SCHOOL DOCTOR AND NURSE. IT-IT MUST BE SOMETHING TO DO WITH ME.
MRS. BLACK, I'M SO GLAD YOU AGREED TO SEE US, I'M FASCINATED TO KNOW MORE ABOUT YOUR DAUGHTER AND HER REMARKABLE GIFT.
CURSE, YOU MEAN! ROSEMARY'S POWER IS WICKED!
COME NOW, MRS. BLACK. THIS IS THE TWENTIETH CENTURY. SHE'S JUST UNUSUAL—THAT'S ALL. I BELIEVE YOUR MOTHER—ROSEMARY'S GRANDMOTHER—HAD THE POWER, TOO?
THAT IS TRUE.

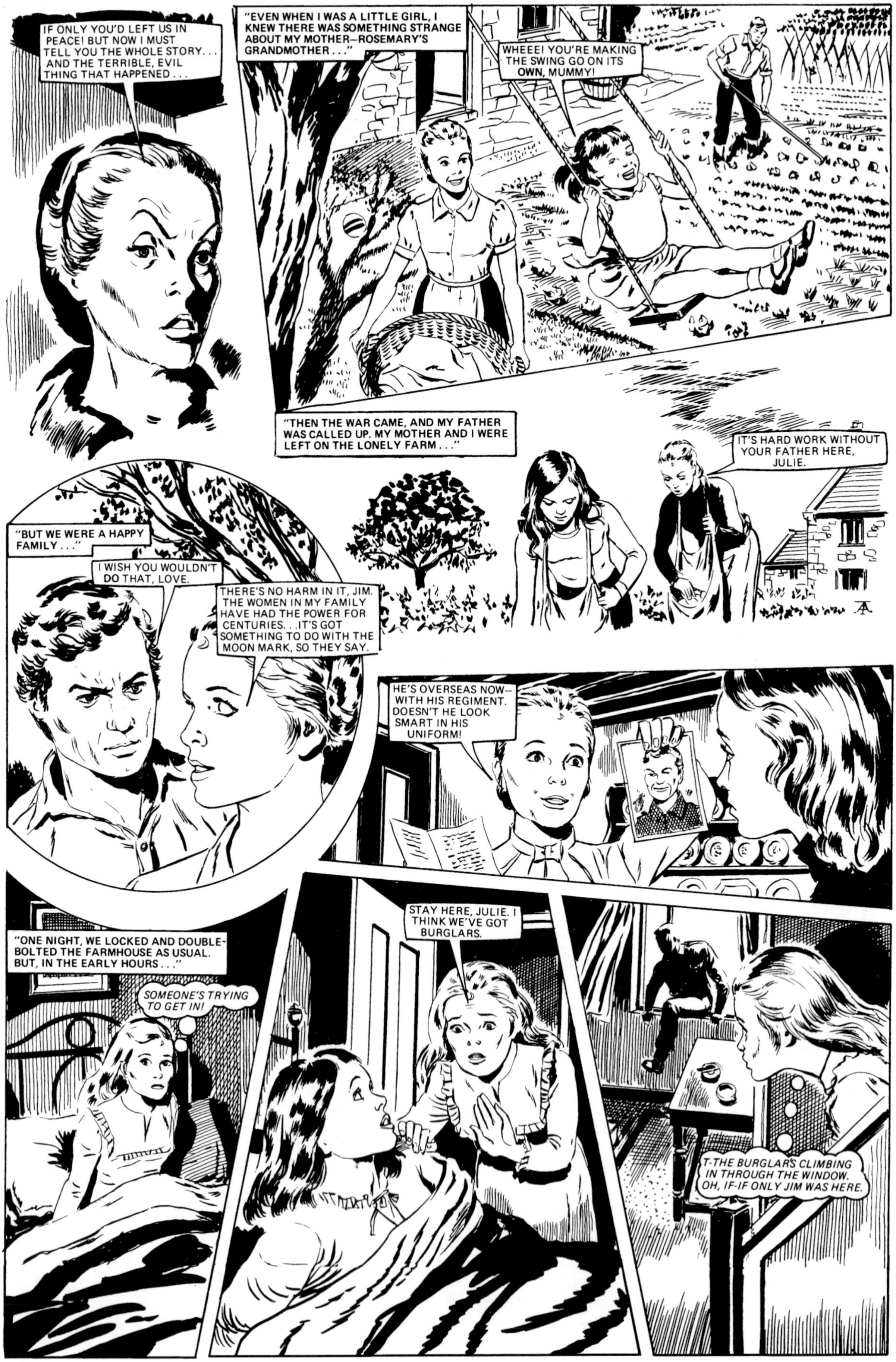

IF ONLY YOU'D LEFT US IN PEACE! BUT NOW I MUST TELL YOU THE WHOLE STORY... AND THE TERRIBLE, EVIL THING THAT HAPPENED...
"EVEN WHEN I WAS A LITTLE GIRL, I KNEW THERE WAS SOMETHING STRANGE ABOUT MY MOTHER—ROSEMARY'S GRANDMOTHER..."
WHEEE! YOU'RE MAKING THE SWING GO ON ITS OWN, MUMMY!
"THEN THE WAR CAME, AND MY FATHER WAS CALLED UP. MY MOTHER AND I WERE LEFT ON THE LONELY FARM..."
IT'S HARD WORK WITHOUT YOUR FATHER HERE, JULIE.
"BUT WE WERE A HAPPY FAMILY..."
I WISH YOU WOULDN'T DO THAT, LOVE.
THERE'S NO HARM IN IT, JIM. THE WOMEN IN MY FAMILY HAVE HAD THE POWER FOR CENTURIES...IT'S GOT SOMETHING TO DO WITH THE MOON MARK, SO THEY SAY.
HE'S OVERSEAS NOW—WITH HIS REGIMENT. DOESN'T HE LOOK SMART IN HIS UNIFORM!
"ONE NIGHT, WE LOCKED AND DOUBLE-BOLTED THE FARMHOUSE AS USUAL. BUT, IN THE EARLY HOURS..."
SOMEONE'S TRYING TO GET IN!
STAY HERE, JULIE. I THINK WE'VE GOT BURGLARS.
T-THE BURGLAR'S CLIMBING IN THROUGH THE WINDOW. OH, IF-IF ONLY JIM WAS HERE.

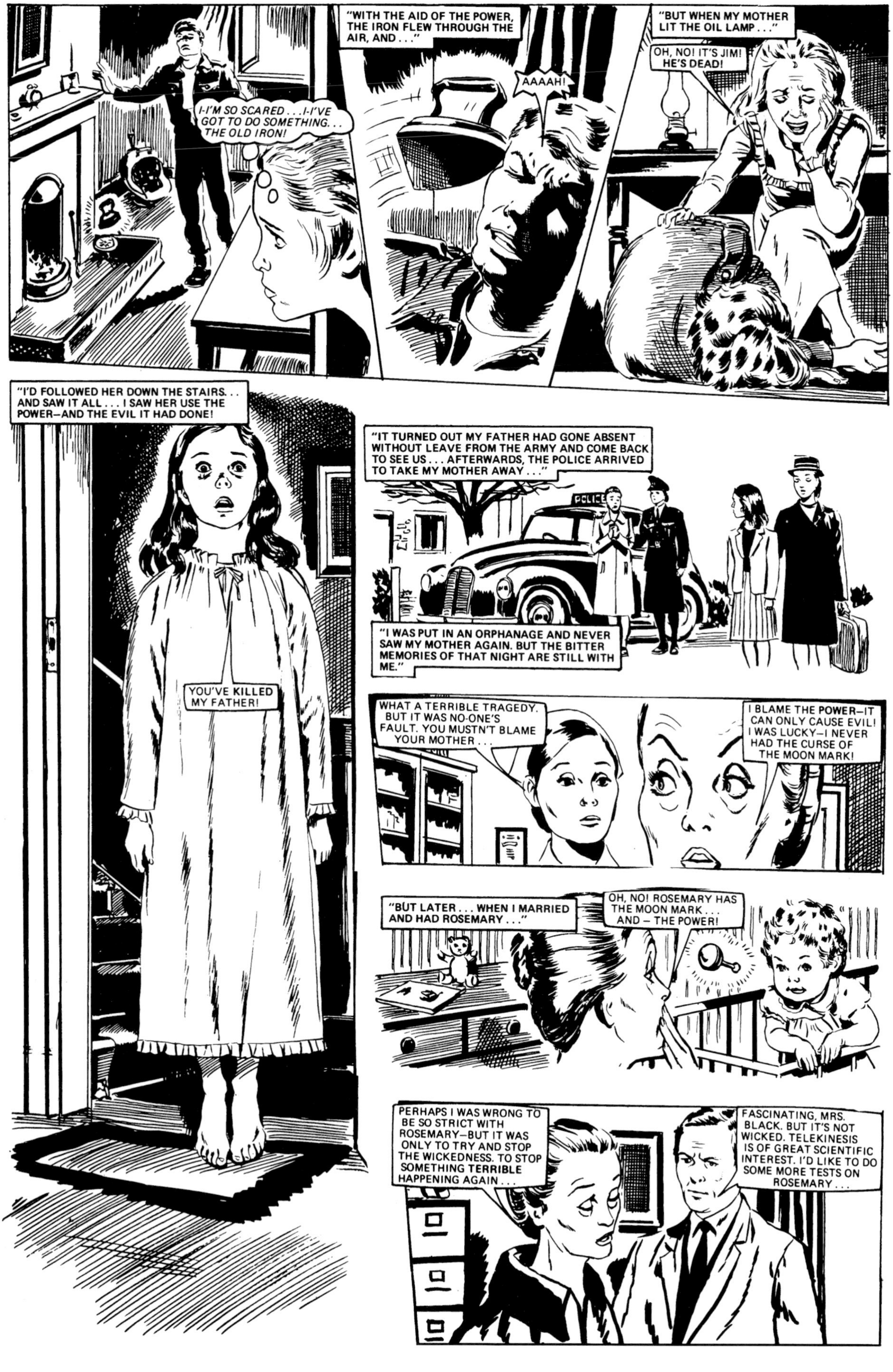

I-I'M SO SCARED . . . I-I'VE GOT TO DO SOMETHING. . . THE OLD IRON!
"WITH THE AID OF THE POWER, THE IRON FLEW THROUGH THE AIR, AND . . ."
AAAAH!
"BUT WHEN MY MOTHER LIT THE OIL LAMP . . ."
OH, NO! IT'S JIM! HE'S DEAD!
"I'D FOLLOWED HER DOWN THE STAIRS. . . AND SAW IT ALL . . . I SAW HER USE THE POWER—AND THE EVIL IT HAD DONE!
YOU'VE KILLED MY FATHER!
"IT TURNED OUT MY FATHER HAD GONE ABSENT WITHOUT LEAVE FROM THE ARMY AND COME BACK TO SEE US . . . AFTERWARDS, THE POLICE ARRIVED TO TAKE MY MOTHER AWAY . . ."
POLICE
"I WAS PUT IN AN ORPHANAGE AND NEVER SAW MY MOTHER AGAIN. BUT THE BITTER MEMORIES OF THAT NIGHT ARE STILL WITH ME."
WHAT A TERRIBLE TRAGEDY. BUT IT WAS NO-ONE'S FAULT. YOU MUSTN'T BLAME YOUR MOTHER . . .
I BLAME THE POWER—IT CAN ONLY CAUSE EVIL! I WAS LUCKY—I NEVER HAD THE CURSE OF THE MOON MARK!
"BUT LATER . . . WHEN I MARRIED AND HAD ROSEMARY . . ."
OH, NO! ROSEMARY HAS THE MOON MARK . . . AND – THE POWER!
PERHAPS I WAS WRONG TO BE SO STRICT WITH ROSEMARY—BUT IT WAS ONLY TO TRY AND STOP THE WICKEDNESS. TO STOP SOMETHING TERRIBLE HAPPENING AGAIN . . .
FASCINATING, MRS. BLACK. BUT IT'S NOT WICKED. TELEKINESIS IS OF GREAT SCIENTIFIC INTEREST. I'D LIKE TO DO SOME MORE TESTS ON ROSEMARY . . .

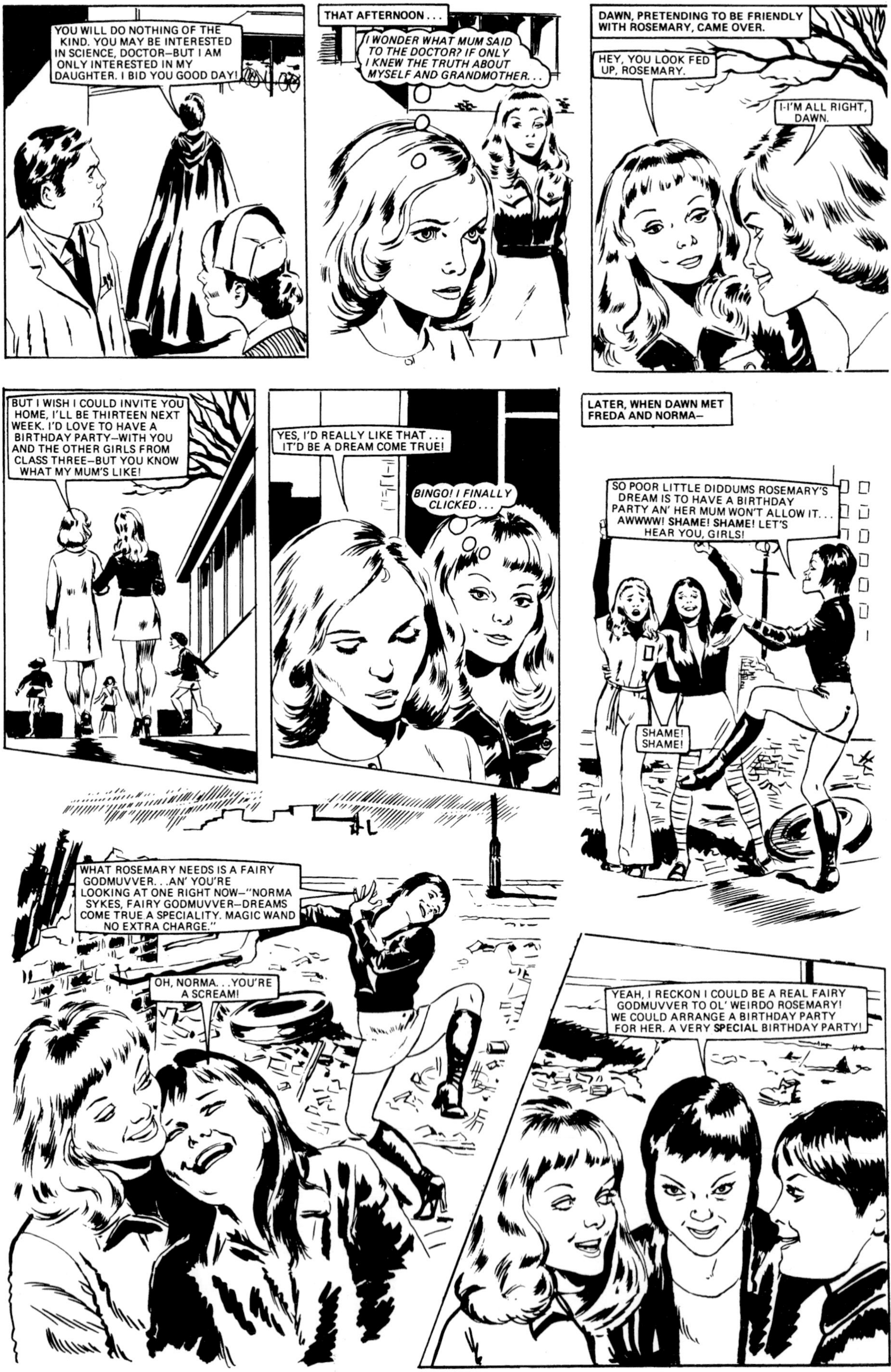
YOU WILL DO NOTHING OF THE KIND. YOU MAY BE INTERESTED IN SCIENCE, DOCTOR—BUT I AM ONLY INTERESTED IN MY DAUGHTER. I BID YOU GOOD DAY!
THAT AFTERNOON . . .
I WONDER WHAT MUM SAID TO THE DOCTOR? IF ONLY I KNEW THE TRUTH ABOUT MYSELF AND GRANDMOTHER . . .
DAWN, PRETENDING TO BE FRIENDLY WITH ROSEMARY, CAME OVER.
HEY, YOU LOOK FED UP, ROSEMARY.
I-I'M ALL RIGHT, DAWN.
BUT I WISH I COULD INVITE YOU HOME, I'LL BE THIRTEEN NEXT WEEK. I'D LOVE TO HAVE A BIRTHDAY PARTY—WITH YOU AND THE OTHER GIRLS FROM CLASS THREE—BUT YOU KNOW WHAT MY MUM'S LIKE!
YES, I'D REALLY LIKE THAT . . . IT'D BE A DREAM COME TRUE!
BINGO! I FINALLY CLICKED . . .
LATER, WHEN DAWN MET FREDA AND NORMA—
SO POOR LITTLE DIDDUMS ROSEMARY'S DREAM IS TO HAVE A BIRTHDAY PARTY AN' HER MUM WON'T ALLOW IT . . . AWWWW! SHAME! SHAME! LET'S HEAR YOU, GIRLS!
SHAME! SHAME!
WHAT ROSEMARY NEEDS IS A FAIRY GODMUVVER. . . AN' YOU'RE LOOKING AT ONE RIGHT NOW—"NORMA SYKES, FAIRY GODMUVVER—DREAMS COME TRUE A SPECIALITY. MAGIC WAND NO EXTRA CHARGE."
OH, NORMA. . . YOU'RE A SCREAM!
YEAH, I RECKON I COULD BE A REAL FAIRY GODMUVVER TO OL' WEIRDO ROSEMARY! WE COULD ARRANGE A BIRTHDAY PARTY FOR HER. A VERY SPECIAL BIRTHDAY PARTY!

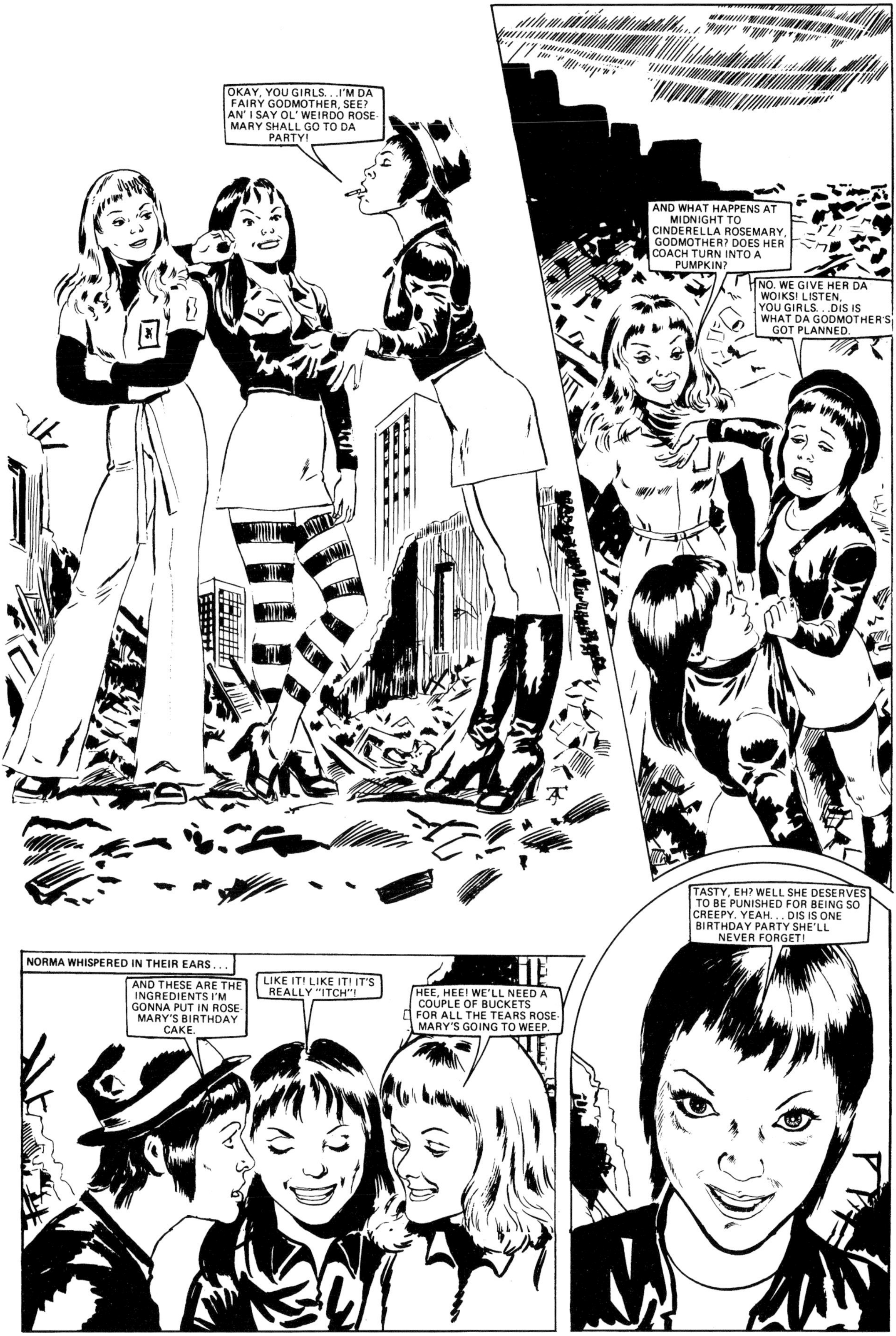
OKAY, YOU GIRLS. . . I'M DA FAIRY GODMOTHER, SEE? AN' I SAY OL' WEIRDO ROSE-MARY SHALL GO TO DA PARTY!
AND WHAT HAPPENS AT MIDNIGHT TO CINDERELLA ROSEMARY, GODMOTHER? DOES HER COACH TURN INTO A PUMPKIN?
NO. WE GIVE HER DA WOIKS! LISTEN, YOU GIRLS. . . DIS IS WHAT DA GODMOTHER'S GOT PLANNED.
NORMA WHISPERED IN THEIR EARS . . .
AND THESE ARE THE INGREDIENTS I'M GONNA PUT IN ROSE-MARY'S BIRTHDAY CAKE.
LIKE IT! LIKE IT! IT'S REALLY "ITCH"!
HEE, HEE! WE'LL NEED A COUPLE OF BUCKETS FOR ALL THE TEARS ROSE-MARY'S GOING TO WEEP.
TASTY, EH? WELL SHE DESERVES TO BE PUNISHED FOR BEING SO CREEPY. YEAH. . . DIS IS ONE BIRTHDAY PARTY SHE'LL NEVER FORGET!

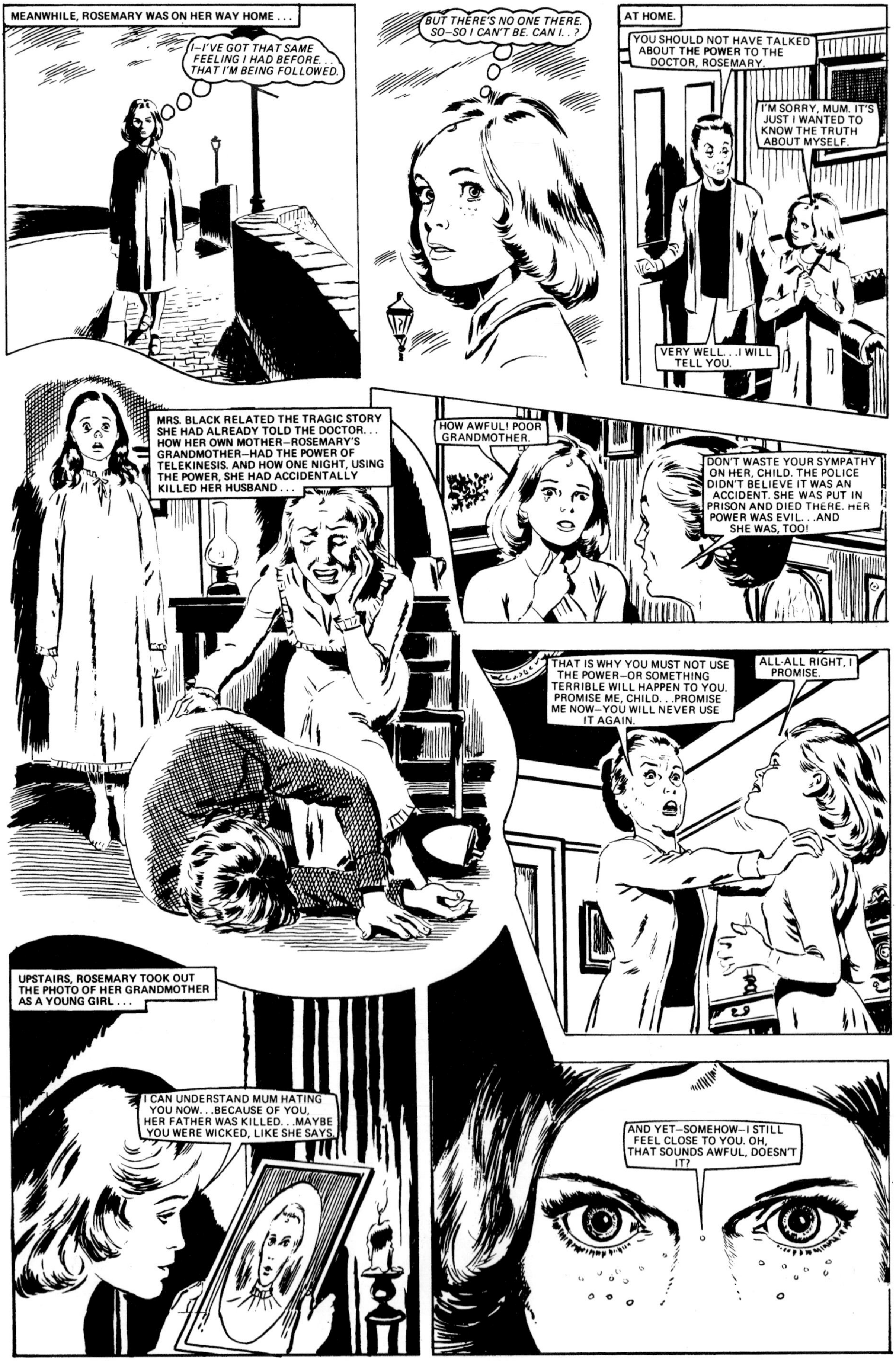
MEANWHILE, ROSEMARY WAS ON HER WAY HOME . . .
I–I'VE GOT THAT SAME FEELING I HAD BEFORE. . . THAT I'M BEING FOLLOWED.
BUT THERE'S NO ONE THERE. SO–SO I CAN'T BE. CAN I. . ?
AT HOME.
YOU SHOULD NOT HAVE TALKED ABOUT THE POWER TO THE DOCTOR, ROSEMARY.
I'M SORRY, MUM. IT'S JUST I WANTED TO KNOW THE TRUTH ABOUT MYSELF.
VERY WELL. . . I WILL TELL YOU.
MRS. BLACK RELATED THE TRAGIC STORY SHE HAD ALREADY TOLD THE DOCTOR. . . HOW HER OWN MOTHER–ROSEMARY'S GRANDMOTHER–HAD THE POWER OF TELEKINESIS. AND HOW ONE NIGHT, USING THE POWER, SHE HAD ACCIDENTALLY KILLED HER HUSBAND . . .
HOW AWFUL! POOR GRANDMOTHER.
DON'T WASTE YOUR SYMPATHY ON HER, CHILD. THE POLICE DIDN'T BELIEVE IT WAS AN ACCIDENT. SHE WAS PUT IN PRISON AND DIED THERE. HER POWER WAS EVIL. . . AND SHE WAS, TOO!
THAT IS WHY YOU MUST NOT USE THE POWER–OR SOMETHING TERRIBLE WILL HAPPEN TO YOU. PROMISE ME, CHILD. . . PROMISE ME NOW–YOU WILL NEVER USE IT AGAIN.
ALL-ALL RIGHT, I PROMISE.
UPSTAIRS, ROSEMARY TOOK OUT THE PHOTO OF HER GRANDMOTHER AS A YOUNG GIRL . . .
I CAN UNDERSTAND MUM HATING YOU NOW. . . BECAUSE OF YOU, HER FATHER WAS KILLED. . . MAYBE YOU WERE WICKED, LIKE SHE SAYS.
AND YET–SOMEHOW–I STILL FEEL CLOSE TO YOU. OH, THAT SOUNDS AWFUL, DOESN'T IT?

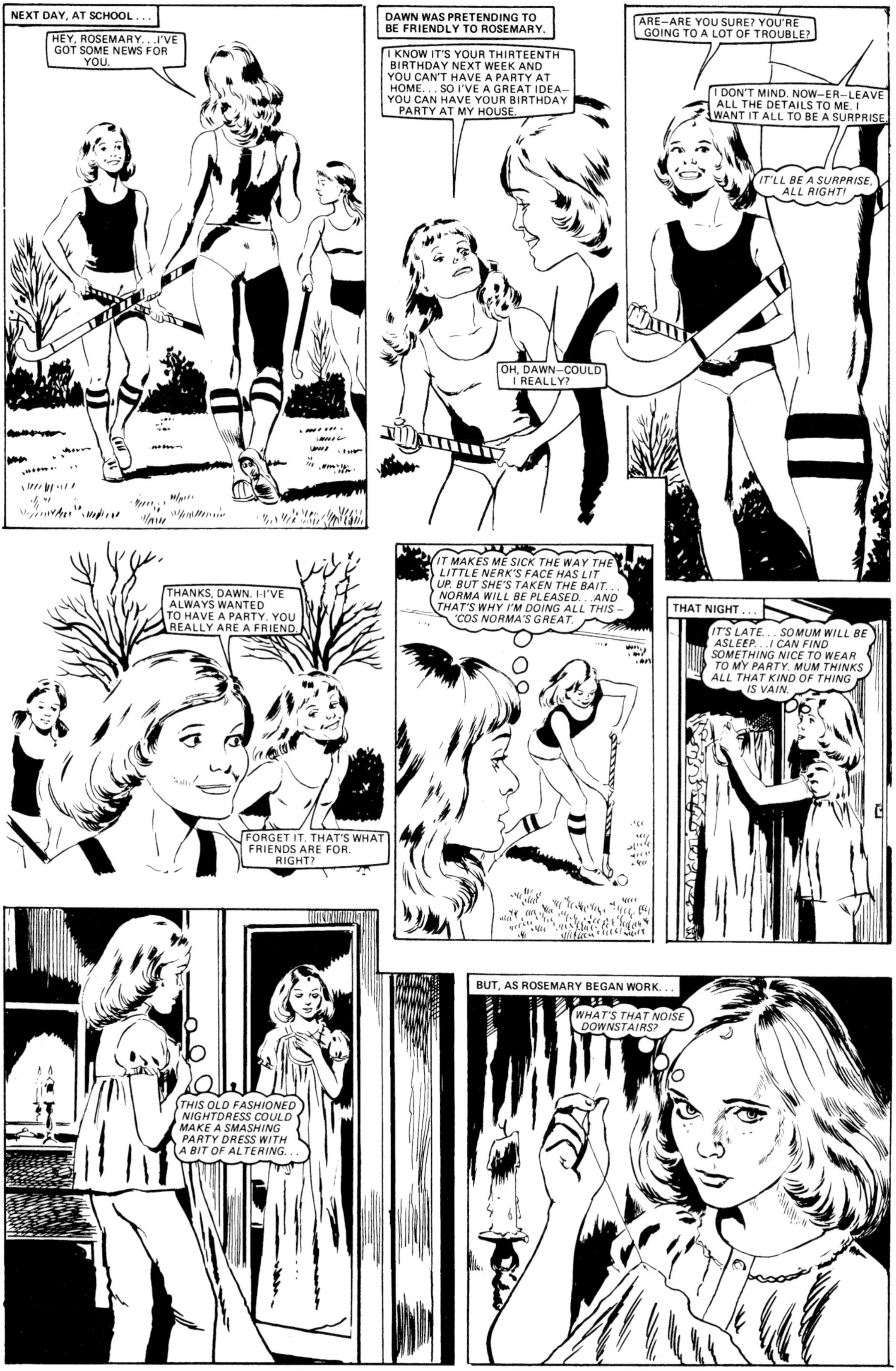
NEXT DAY, AT SCHOOL . . .
HEY, ROSEMARY. . .I'VE GOT SOME NEWS FOR YOU.
DAWN WAS PRETENDING TO BE FRIENDLY TO ROSEMARY.
I KNOW IT'S YOUR THIRTEENTH BIRTHDAY NEXT WEEK AND YOU CAN'T HAVE A PARTY AT HOME. . . SO I'VE A GREAT IDEA– YOU CAN HAVE YOUR BIRTHDAY PARTY AT MY HOUSE.
OH, DAWN–COULD I REALLY?
ARE–ARE YOU SURE? YOU'RE GOING TO A LOT OF TROUBLE?
I DON'T MIND. NOW–ER–LEAVE ALL THE DETAILS TO ME. I WANT IT ALL TO BE A SURPRISE.
IT'LL BE A SURPRISE, ALL RIGHT!
THANKS, DAWN. I-I'VE ALWAYS WANTED TO HAVE A PARTY. YOU REALLY ARE A FRIEND.
FORGET IT. THAT'S WHAT FRIENDS ARE FOR. RIGHT?
IT MAKES ME SICK THE WAY THE LITTLE NERK'S FACE HAS LIT UP. BUT SHE'S TAKEN THE BAIT. . . NORMA WILL BE PLEASED. . .AND THAT'S WHY I'M DOING ALL THIS – 'COS NORMA'S GREAT.
THAT NIGHT . . .
IT'S LATE. . . SO MUM WILL BE ASLEEP. . . I CAN FIND SOMETHING NICE TO WEAR TO MY PARTY. MUM THINKS ALL THAT KIND OF THING IS VAIN.
THIS OLD FASHIONED NIGHTDRESS COULD MAKE A SMASHING PARTY DRESS WITH A BIT OF ALTERING. . .
BUT, AS ROSEMARY BEGAN WORK. . .
WHAT'S THAT NOISE DOWNSTAIRS?

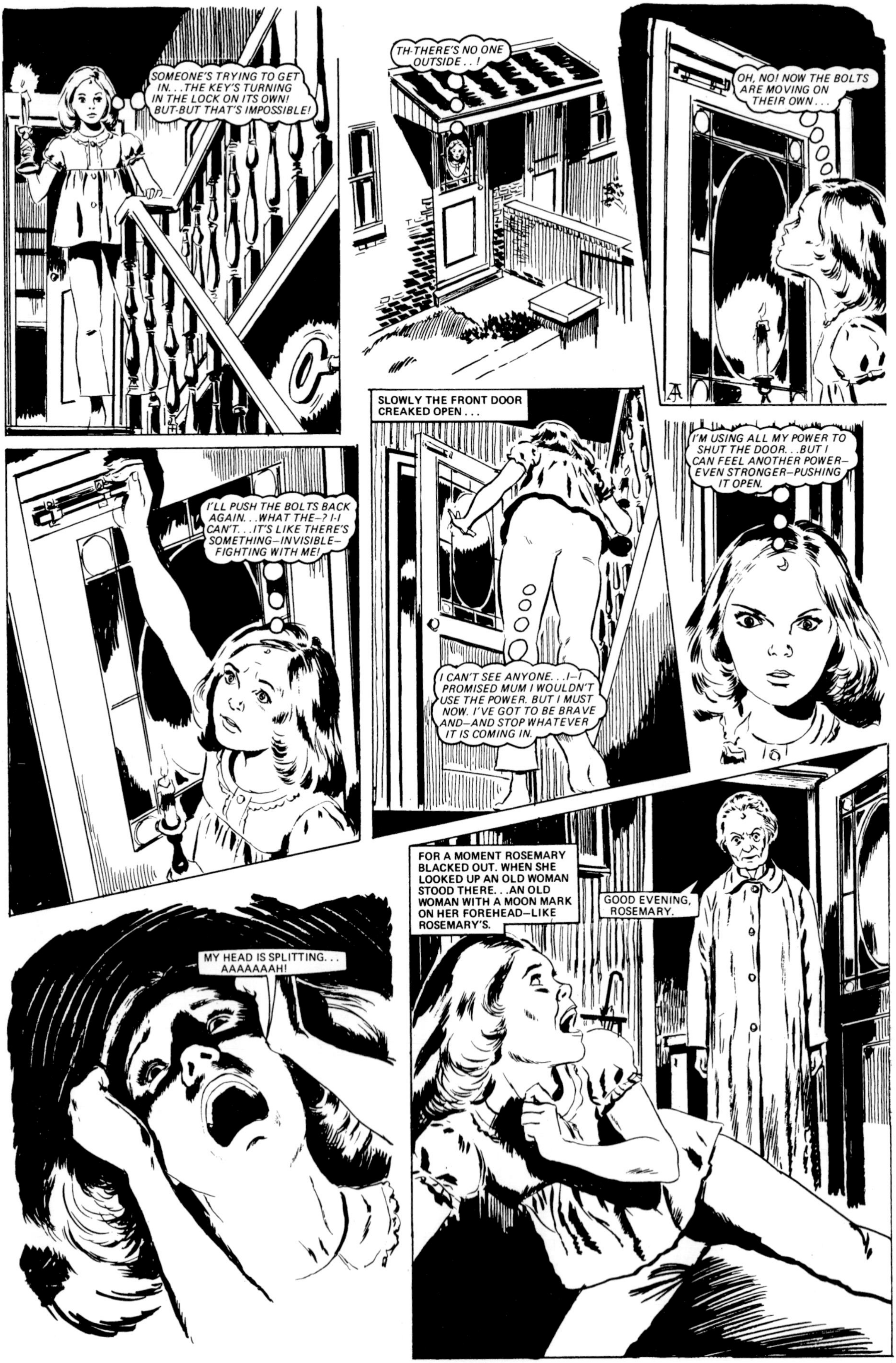

SOMEONE'S TRYING TO GET IN... THE KEY'S TURNING IN THE LOCK ON ITS OWN! BUT-BUT THAT'S IMPOSSIBLE!
TH-THERE'S NO ONE OUTSIDE..!
OH, NO! NOW THE BOLTS ARE MOVING ON THEIR OWN...
I'LL PUSH THE BOLTS BACK AGAIN...WHAT THE-? I-I CAN'T...IT'S LIKE THERE'S SOMETHING-INVISIBLE-FIGHTING WITH ME!
SLOWLY THE FRONT DOOR CREAKED OPEN...
I CAN'T SEE ANYONE...I-I PROMISED MUM I WOULDN'T USE THE POWER. BUT I MUST NOW. I'VE GOT TO BE BRAVE AND-AND STOP WHATEVER IT IS COMING IN.
I'M USING ALL MY POWER TO SHUT THE DOOR...BUT I CAN FEEL ANOTHER POWER-EVEN STRONGER-PUSHING IT OPEN.
MY HEAD IS SPLITTING... AAAAAAAH!
FOR A MOMENT ROSEMARY BLACKED OUT. WHEN SHE LOOKED UP AN OLD WOMAN STOOD THERE...AN OLD WOMAN WITH A MOON MARK ON HER FOREHEAD-LIKE ROSEMARY'S.
GOOD EVENING, ROSEMARY.

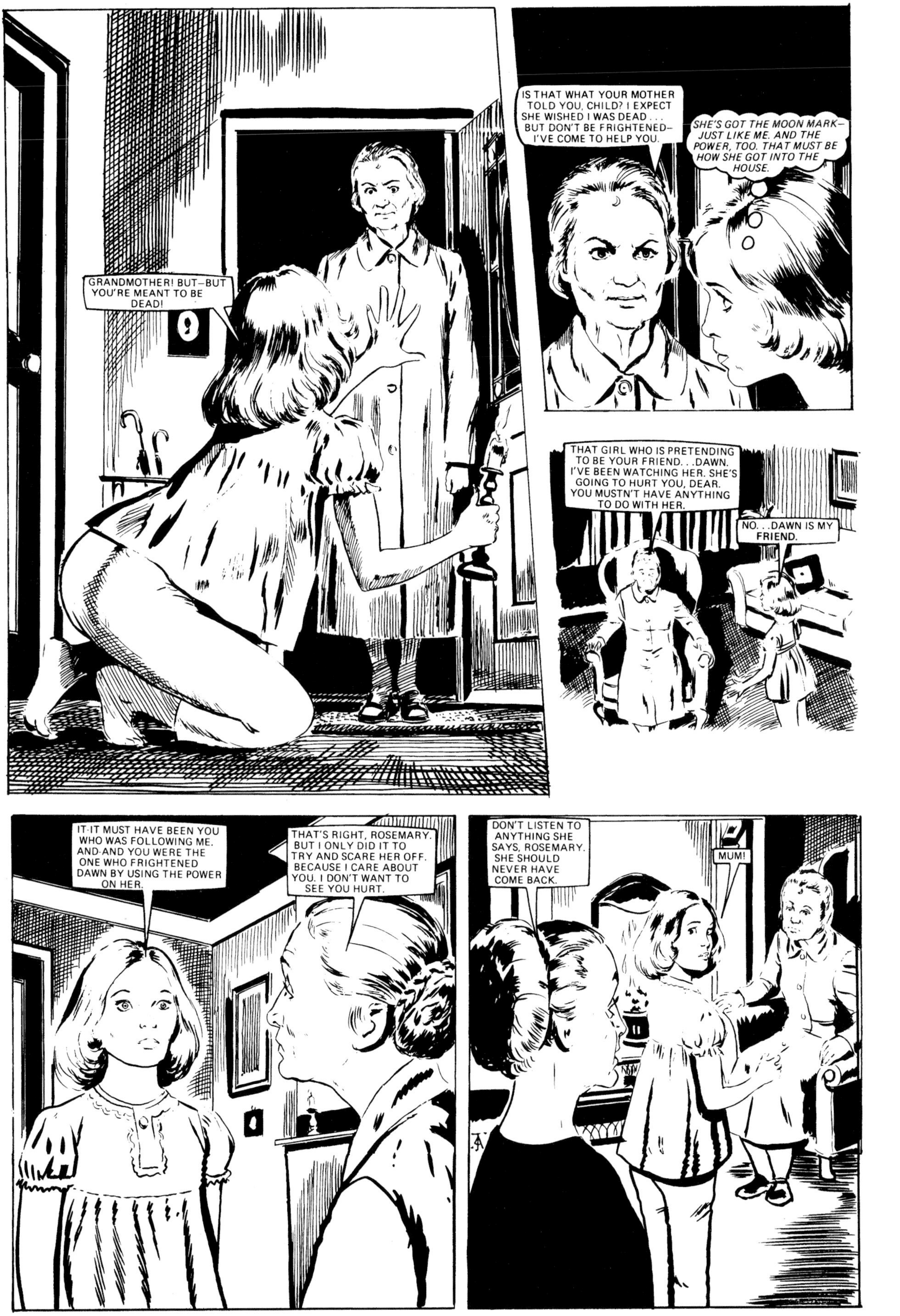

GRANDMOTHER! BUT—BUT YOU'RE MEANT TO BE DEAD!
IS THAT WHAT YOUR MOTHER TOLD YOU, CHILD? I EXPECT SHE WISHED I WAS DEAD . . . BUT DON'T BE FRIGHTENED—I'VE COME TO HELP YOU.
SHE'S GOT THE MOON MARK—JUST LIKE ME. AND THE POWER, TOO. THAT MUST BE HOW SHE GOT INTO THE HOUSE.
THAT GIRL WHO IS PRETENDING TO BE YOUR FRIEND. . .DAWN. I'VE BEEN WATCHING HER. SHE'S GOING TO HURT YOU, DEAR. YOU MUSTN'T HAVE ANYTHING TO DO WITH HER.
NO. . .DAWN IS MY FRIEND.
IT-IT MUST HAVE BEEN YOU WHO WAS FOLLOWING ME. AND-AND YOU WERE THE ONE WHO FRIGHTENED DAWN BY USING THE POWER ON HER.
THAT'S RIGHT, ROSEMARY. BUT I ONLY DID IT TO TRY AND SCARE HER OFF. BECAUSE I CARE ABOUT YOU. I DON'T WANT TO SEE YOU HURT.
DON'T LISTEN TO ANYTHING SHE SAYS, ROSEMARY. SHE SHOULD NEVER HAVE COME BACK.
MUM!

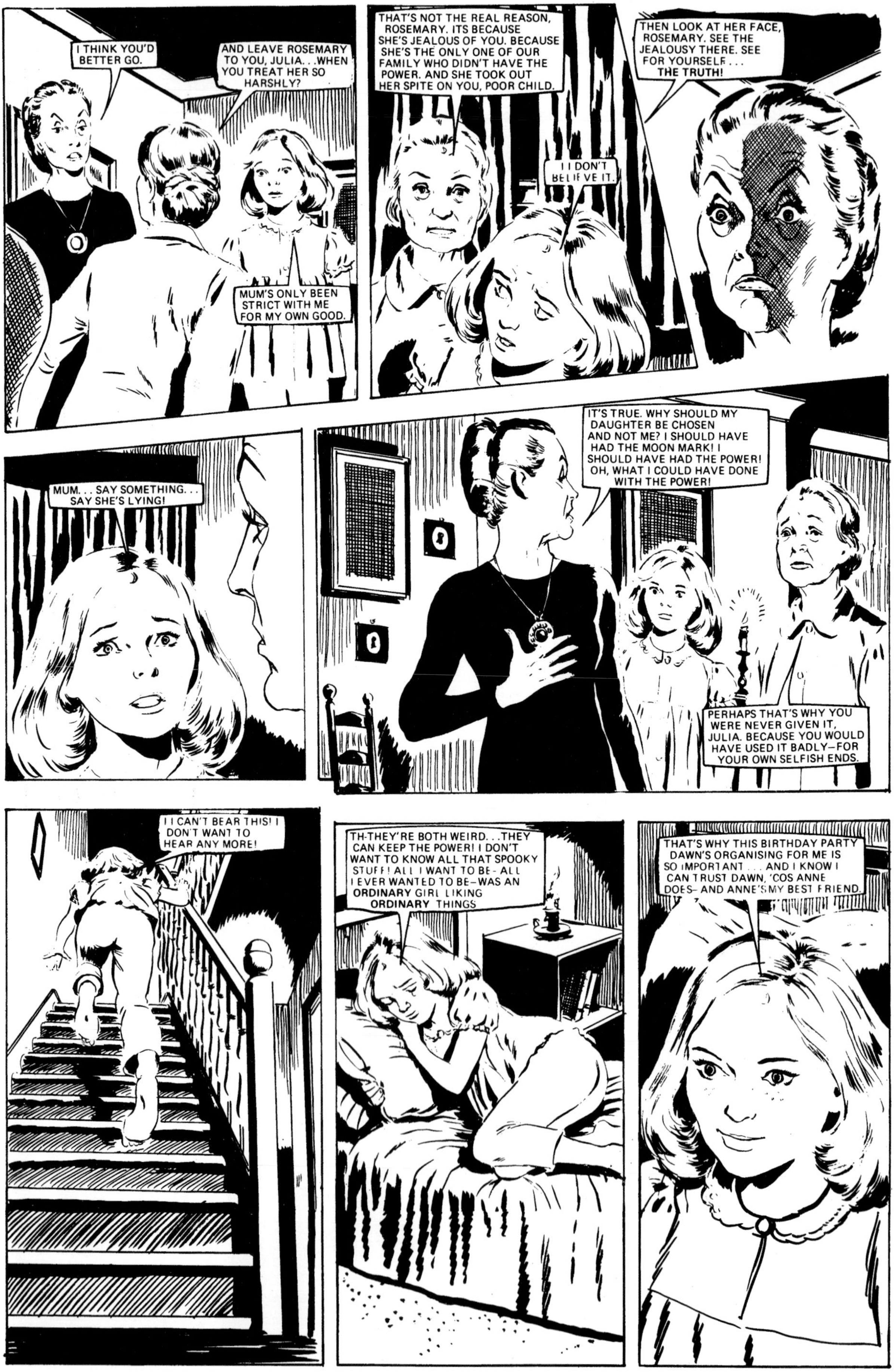
I THINK YOU'D BETTER GO.
AND LEAVE ROSEMARY TO YOU, JULIA. . . WHEN YOU TREAT HER SO HARSHLY?
MUM'S ONLY BEEN STRICT WITH ME FOR MY OWN GOOD.
THAT'S NOT THE REAL REASON, ROSEMARY. ITS BECAUSE SHE'S JEALOUS OF YOU. BECAUSE SHE'S THE ONLY ONE OF OUR FAMILY WHO DIDN'T HAVE THE POWER. AND SHE TOOK OUT HER SPITE ON YOU, POOR CHILD.
I-I DON'T BELIEVE IT.
THEN LOOK AT HER FACE, ROSEMARY. SEE THE JEALOUSY THERE. SEE FOR YOURSELF . . . THE TRUTH!
MUM. . . SAY SOMETHING. . . SAY SHE'S LYING!
IT'S TRUE. WHY SHOULD MY DAUGHTER BE CHOSEN AND NOT ME? I SHOULD HAVE HAD THE MOON MARK! I SHOULD HAVE HAD THE POWER! OH, WHAT I COULD HAVE DONE WITH THE POWER!
PERHAPS THAT'S WHY YOU WERE NEVER GIVEN IT, JULIA. BECAUSE YOU WOULD HAVE USED IT BADLY—FOR YOUR OWN SELFISH ENDS.
I-I CAN'T BEAR THIS! I DON'T WANT TO HEAR ANY MORE!
TH-THEY'RE BOTH WEIRD. . . THEY CAN KEEP THE POWER! I DON'T WANT TO KNOW ALL THAT SPOOKY STUFF! ALL I WANT TO BE- ALL I EVER WANTED TO BE- WAS AN ORDINARY GIRL LIKING ORDINARY THINGS
THAT'S WHY THIS BIRTHDAY PARTY DAWN'S ORGANISING FOR ME IS SO IMPORTANT . . . AND I KNOW I CAN TRUST DAWN, 'COS ANNE DOES- AND ANNE'S MY BEST FRIEND.

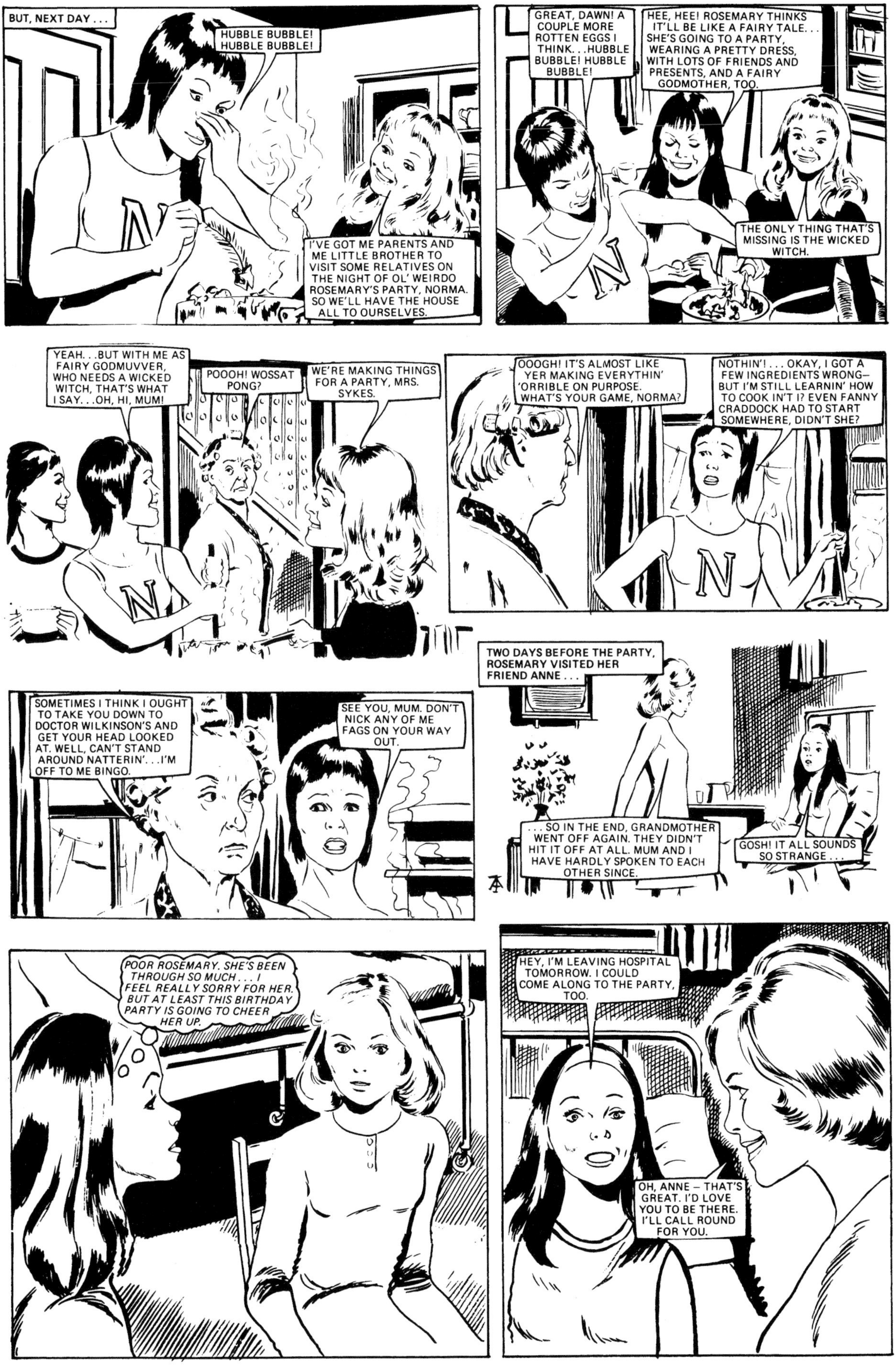
BUT, NEXT DAY . . .
HUBBLE BUBBLE! HUBBLE BUBBLE!
I'VE GOT ME PARENTS AND ME LITTLE BROTHER TO VISIT SOME RELATIVES ON THE NIGHT OF OL' WEIRDO ROSEMARY'S PARTY, NORMA. SO WE'LL HAVE THE HOUSE ALL TO OURSELVES.
GREAT, DAWN! A COUPLE MORE ROTTEN EGGS I THINK. . . HUBBLE BUBBLE! HUBBLE BUBBLE!
HEE, HEE! ROSEMARY THINKS IT'LL BE LIKE A FAIRY TALE. . . SHE'S GOING TO A PARTY, WEARING A PRETTY DRESS, WITH LOTS OF FRIENDS AND PRESENTS, AND A FAIRY GODMOTHER, TOO.
THE ONLY THING THAT'S MISSING IS THE WICKED WITCH.
YEAH. . . BUT WITH ME AS FAIRY GODMUVVER, WHO NEEDS A WICKED WITCH, THAT'S WHAT I SAY. . . OH, HI, MUM!
POOOH! WOSSAT PONG?
WE'RE MAKING THINGS FOR A PARTY, MRS. SYKES.
OOOGH! IT'S ALMOST LIKE YER MAKING EVERYTHIN' 'ORRIBLE ON PURPOSE. WHAT'S YOUR GAME, NORMA?
NOTHIN'! . . . OKAY, I GOT A FEW INGREDIENTS WRONG— BUT I'M STILL LEARNIN' HOW TO COOK IN'T I? EVEN FANNY CRADDOCK HAD TO START SOMEWHERE, DIDN'T SHE?
SOMETIMES I THINK I OUGHT TO TAKE YOU DOWN TO DOCTOR WILKINSON'S AND GET YOUR HEAD LOOKED AT. WELL, CAN'T STAND AROUND NATTERIN'. . . I'M OFF TO ME BINGO.
SEE YOU, MUM. DON'T NICK ANY OF ME FAGS ON YOUR WAY OUT.
TWO DAYS BEFORE THE PARTY, ROSEMARY VISITED HER FRIEND ANNE . . .
. . . SO IN THE END, GRANDMOTHER WENT OFF AGAIN. THEY DIDN'T HIT IT OFF AT ALL. MUM AND I HAVE HARDLY SPOKEN TO EACH OTHER SINCE.
GOSH! IT ALL SOUNDS SO STRANGE . . .
POOR ROSEMARY. SHE'S BEEN THROUGH SO MUCH . . . I FEEL REALLY SORRY FOR HER. BUT AT LEAST THIS BIRTHDAY PARTY IS GOING TO CHEER HER UP.
HEY, I'M LEAVING HOSPITAL TOMORROW. I COULD COME ALONG TO THE PARTY, TOO.
OH, ANNE – THAT'S GREAT. I'D LOVE YOU TO BE THERE. I'LL CALL ROUND FOR YOU.

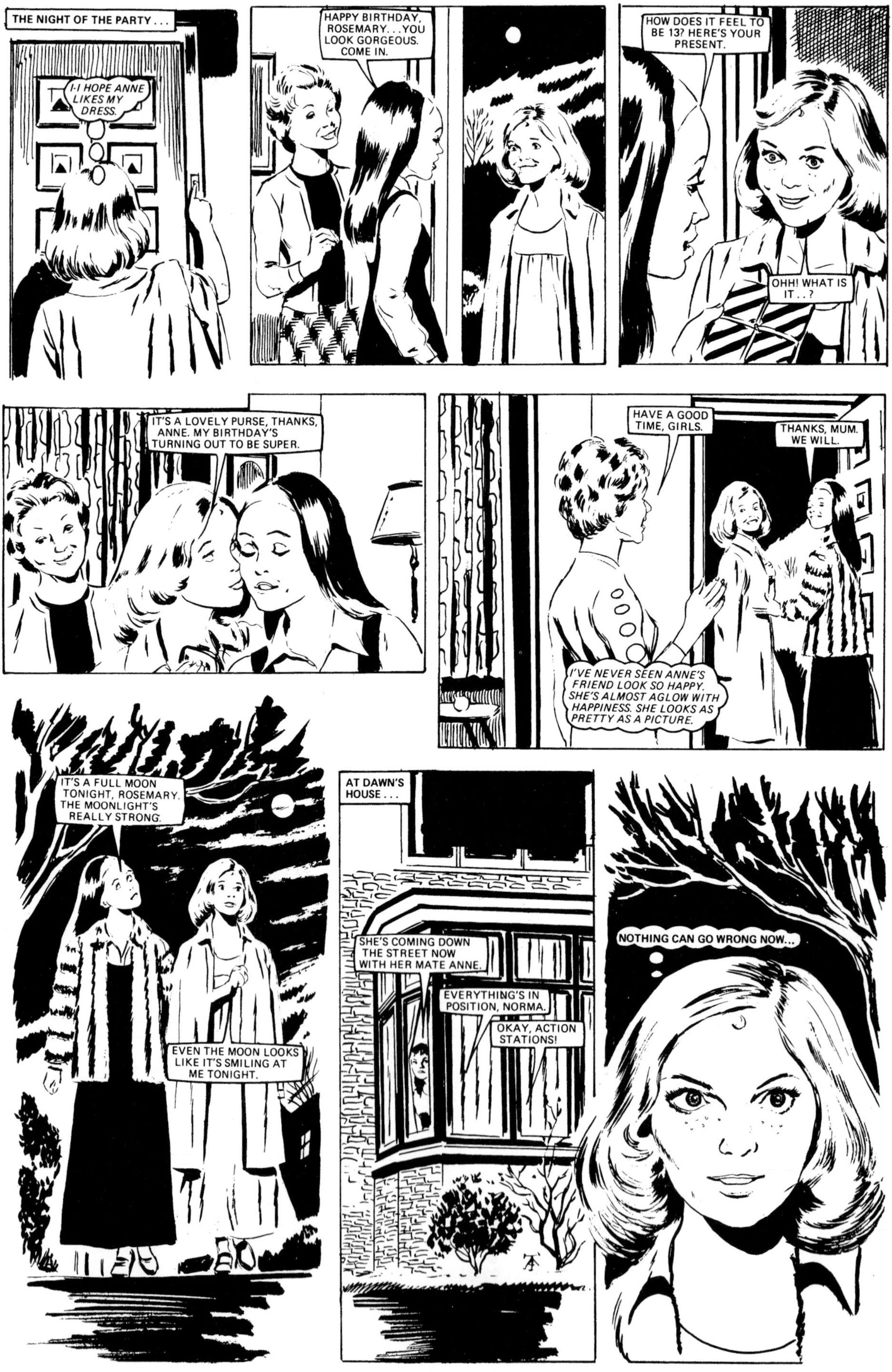

THE NIGHT OF THE PARTY . . .
I-I HOPE ANNE LIKES MY DRESS.
HAPPY BIRTHDAY, ROSEMARY . . . YOU LOOK GORGEOUS. COME IN.
HOW DOES IT FEEL TO BE 13? HERE'S YOUR PRESENT.
OHH! WHAT IS IT . . ?
IT'S A LOVELY PURSE, THANKS, ANNE. MY BIRTHDAY'S TURNING OUT TO BE SUPER.
HAVE A GOOD TIME, GIRLS.
THANKS, MUM. WE WILL.
I'VE NEVER SEEN ANNE'S FRIEND LOOK SO HAPPY. SHE'S ALMOST AGLOW WITH HAPPINESS. SHE LOOKS AS PRETTY AS A PICTURE.
IT'S A FULL MOON TONIGHT, ROSEMARY. THE MOONLIGHT'S REALLY STRONG.
EVEN THE MOON LOOKS LIKE IT'S SMILING AT ME TONIGHT.
AT DAWN'S HOUSE . . .
SHE'S COMING DOWN THE STREET NOW WITH HER MATE ANNE.
EVERYTHING'S IN POSITION, NORMA.
OKAY, ACTION STATIONS!
NOTHING CAN GO WRONG NOW . . .

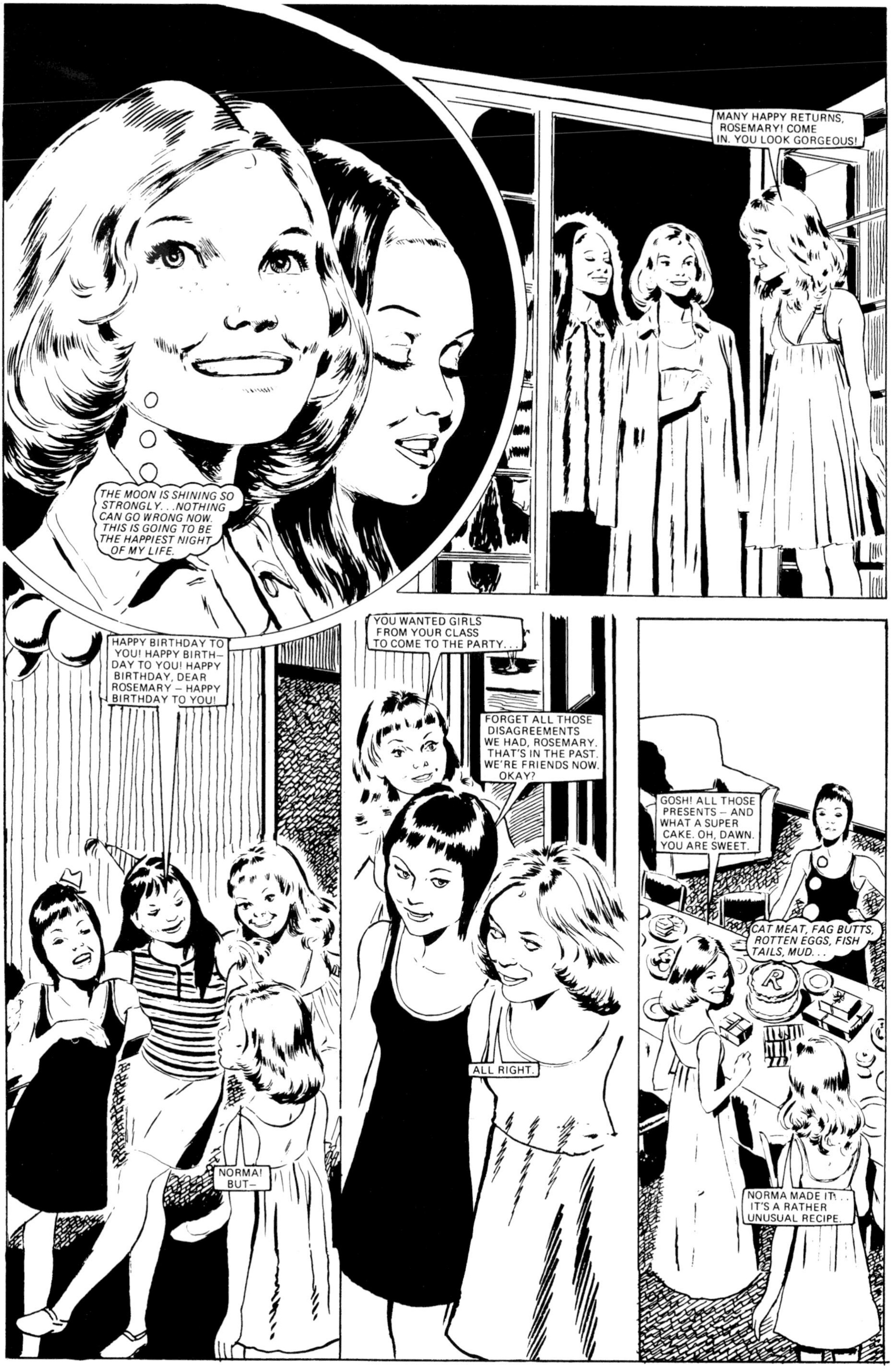
THE MOON IS SHINING SO STRONGLY. . .NOTHING CAN GO WRONG NOW. THIS IS GOING TO BE THE HAPPIEST NIGHT OF MY LIFE.
MANY HAPPY RETURNS, ROSEMARY! COME IN. YOU LOOK GORGEOUS!
HAPPY BIRTHDAY TO YOU! HAPPY BIRTH-DAY TO YOU! HAPPY BIRTHDAY, DEAR ROSEMARY – HAPPY BIRTHDAY TO YOU!
NORMA! BUT–
YOU WANTED GIRLS FROM YOUR CLASS TO COME TO THE PARTY. . .
FORGET ALL THOSE DISAGREEMENTS WE HAD, ROSEMARY. THAT'S IN THE PAST. WE'RE FRIENDS NOW. OKAY?
ALL RIGHT.
GOSH! ALL THOSE PRESENTS – AND WHAT A SUPER CAKE. OH, DAWN. YOU ARE SWEET.
CAT MEAT, FAG BUTTS, ROTTEN EGGS, FISH TAILS, MUD. . .
NORMA MADE IT. . . IT'S A RATHER UNUSUAL RECIPE.

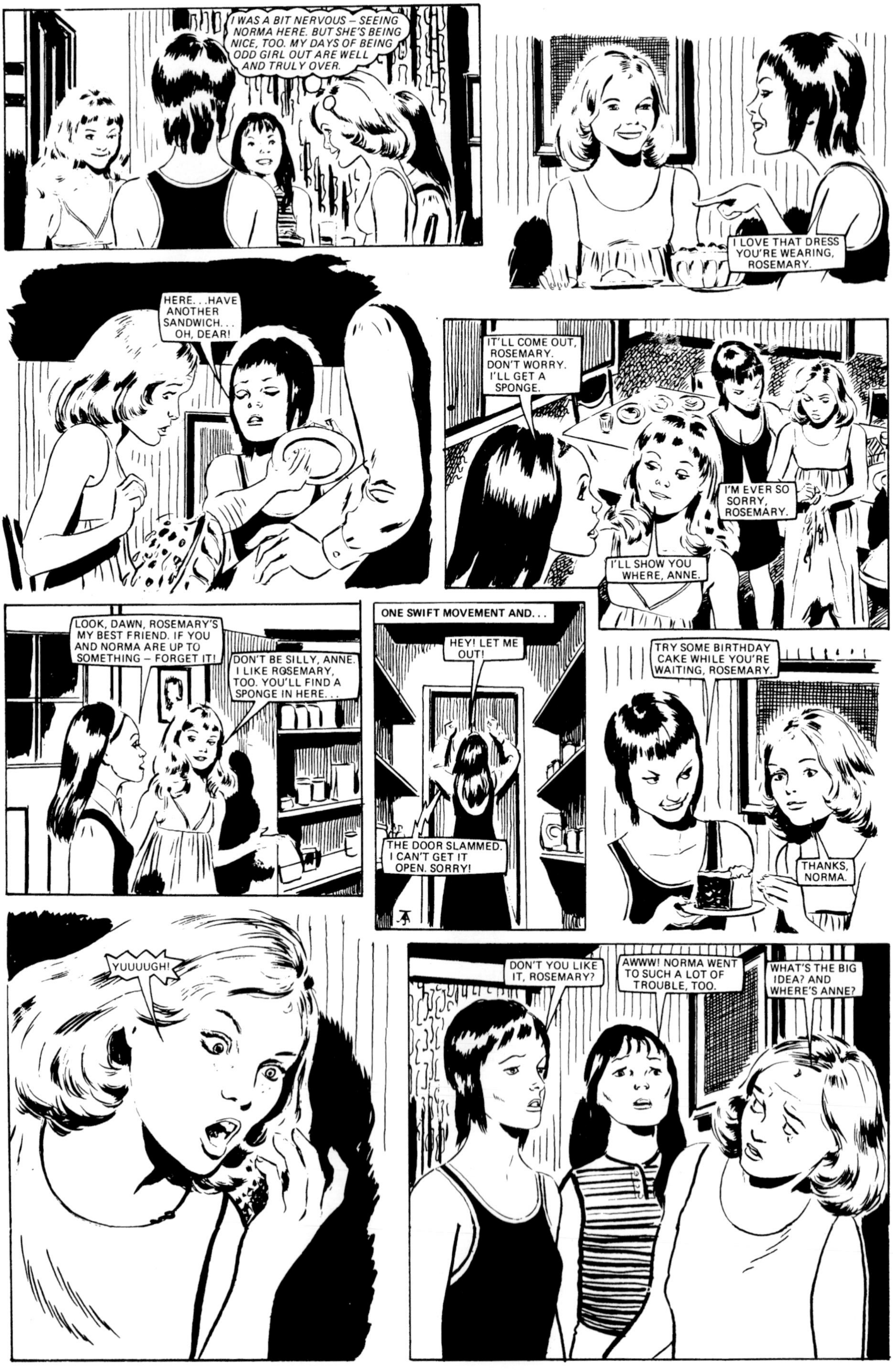
I WAS A BIT NERVOUS – SEEING NORMA HERE. BUT SHE'S BEING NICE, TOO. MY DAYS OF BEING ODD GIRL OUT ARE WELL AND TRULY OVER.
I LOVE THAT DRESS YOU'RE WEARING, ROSEMARY.
HERE. . .HAVE ANOTHER SANDWICH. . . OH, DEAR!
IT'LL COME OUT, ROSEMARY. DON'T WORRY. I'LL GET A SPONGE.
I'M EVER SO SORRY, ROSEMARY.
I'LL SHOW YOU WHERE, ANNE.
LOOK, DAWN, ROSEMARY'S MY BEST FRIEND. IF YOU AND NORMA ARE UP TO SOMETHING – FORGET IT!
DON'T BE SILLY, ANNE. I LIKE ROSEMARY, TOO. YOU'LL FIND A SPONGE IN HERE. . .
ONE SWIFT MOVEMENT AND. . .
HEY! LET ME OUT!
THE DOOR SLAMMED. I CAN'T GET IT OPEN. SORRY!
TRY SOME BIRTHDAY CAKE WHILE YOU'RE WAITING, ROSEMARY.
THANKS, NORMA.
YUUUUGH!
DON'T YOU LIKE IT, ROSEMARY?
AWWW! NORMA WENT TO SUCH A LOT OF TROUBLE, TOO.
WHAT'S THE BIG IDEA? AND WHERE'S ANNE?

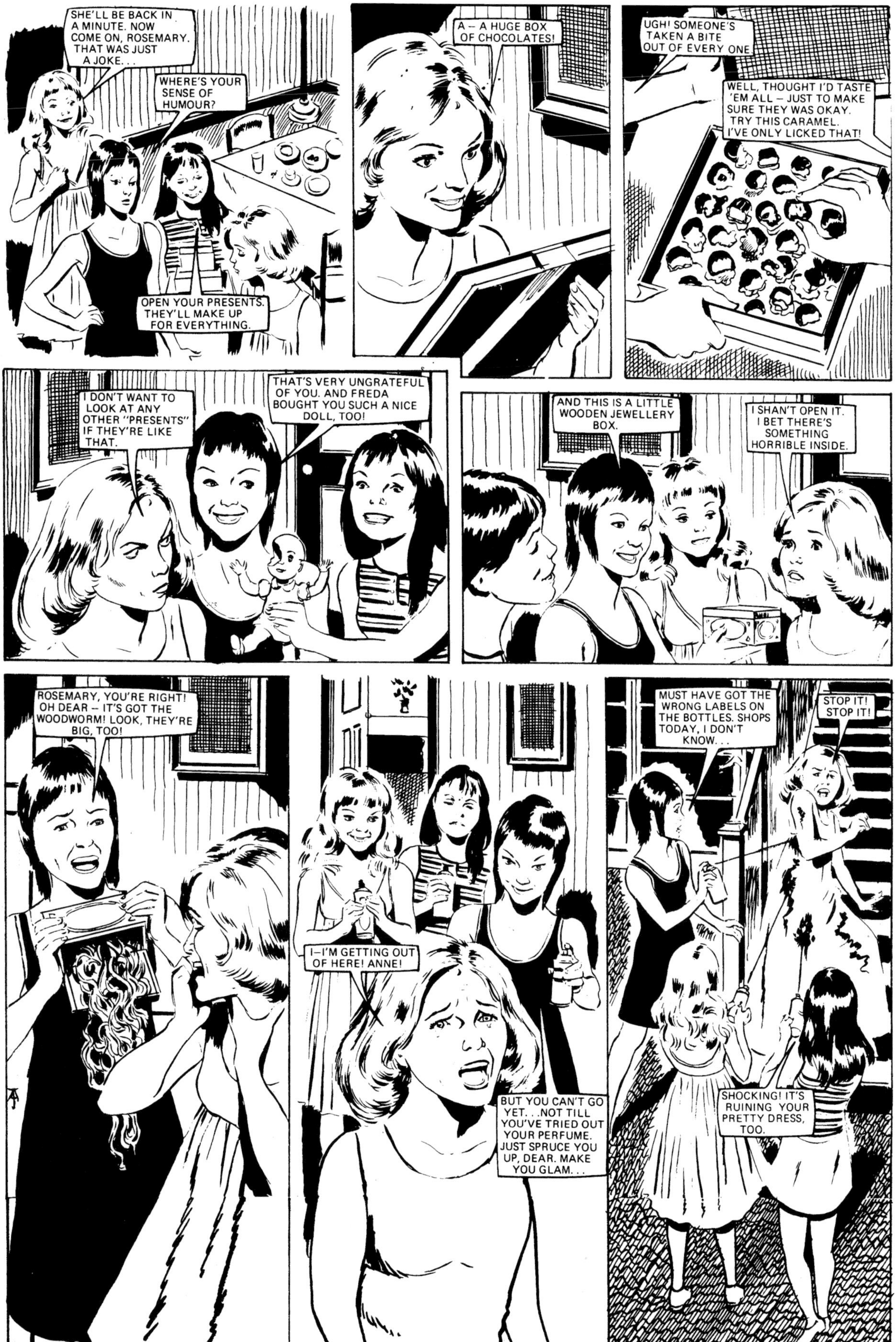
SHE'LL BE BACK IN A MINUTE. NOW COME ON, ROSEMARY. THAT WAS JUST A JOKE...
WHERE'S YOUR SENSE OF HUMOUR?
OPEN YOUR PRESENTS. THEY'LL MAKE UP FOR EVERYTHING.
A – A HUGE BOX OF CHOCOLATES!
UGH! SOMEONE'S TAKEN A BITE OUT OF EVERY ONE.
WELL, THOUGHT I'D TASTE 'EM ALL – JUST TO MAKE SURE THEY WAS OKAY. TRY THIS CARAMEL. I'VE ONLY LICKED THAT!
I DON'T WANT TO LOOK AT ANY OTHER "PRESENTS" IF THEY'RE LIKE THAT.
THAT'S VERY UNGRATEFUL OF YOU. AND FREDA BOUGHT YOU SUCH A NICE DOLL, TOO!
AND THIS IS A LITTLE WOODEN JEWELLERY BOX.
I SHAN'T OPEN IT. I BET THERE'S SOMETHING HORRIBLE INSIDE.
ROSEMARY, YOU'RE RIGHT! OH DEAR – IT'S GOT THE WOODWORM! LOOK, THEY'RE BIG, TOO!
I–I'M GETTING OUT OF HERE! ANNE!
BUT YOU CAN'T GO YET. . .NOT TILL YOU'VE TRIED OUT YOUR PERFUME. JUST SPRUCE YOU UP, DEAR. MAKE YOU GLAM. . .
MUST HAVE GOT THE WRONG LABELS ON THE BOTTLES. SHOPS TODAY, I DON'T KNOW. . .
STOP IT! STOP IT!
SHOCKING! IT'S RUINING YOUR PRETTY DRESS, TOO.

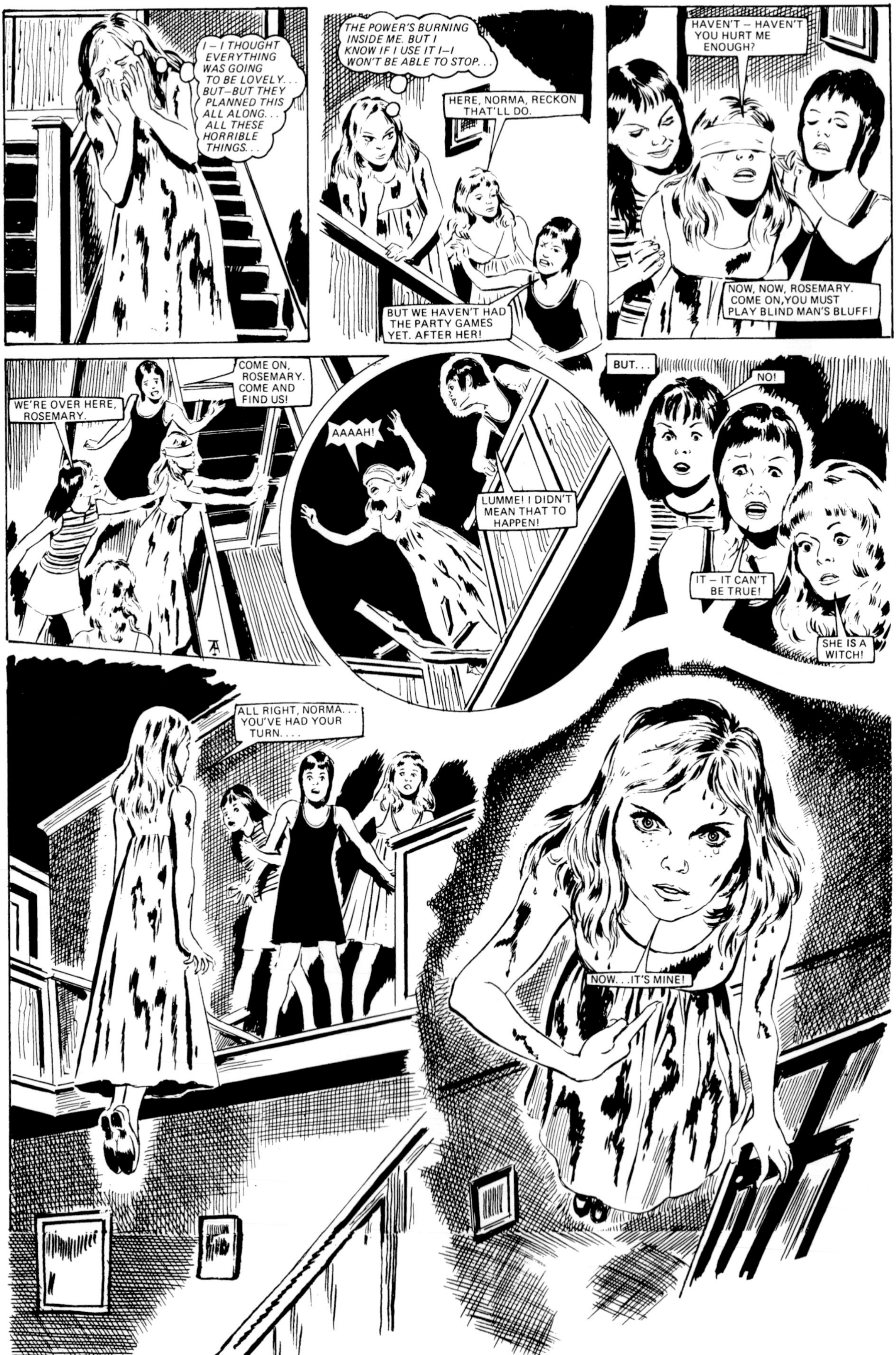
I – I THOUGHT EVERYTHING WAS GOING TO BE LOVELY... BUT–BUT THEY PLANNED THIS ALL ALONG... ALL THESE HORRIBLE THINGS...
THE POWER'S BURNING INSIDE ME. BUT I KNOW IF I USE IT I–I WON'T BE ABLE TO STOP...
HERE, NORMA, RECKON THAT'LL DO.
BUT WE HAVEN'T HAD THE PARTY GAMES YET. AFTER HER!
HAVEN'T – HAVEN'T YOU HURT ME ENOUGH?
NOW, NOW, ROSEMARY. COME ON, YOU MUST PLAY BLIND MAN'S BLUFF!
WE'RE OVER HERE, ROSEMARY.
COME ON, ROSEMARY. COME AND FIND US!
AAAAH!
LUMME! I DIDN'T MEAN THAT TO HAPPEN!
BUT...
NO!
IT – IT CAN'T BE TRUE!
SHE IS A WITCH!
ALL RIGHT, NORMA... YOU'VE HAD YOUR TURN....
NOW...IT'S MINE!

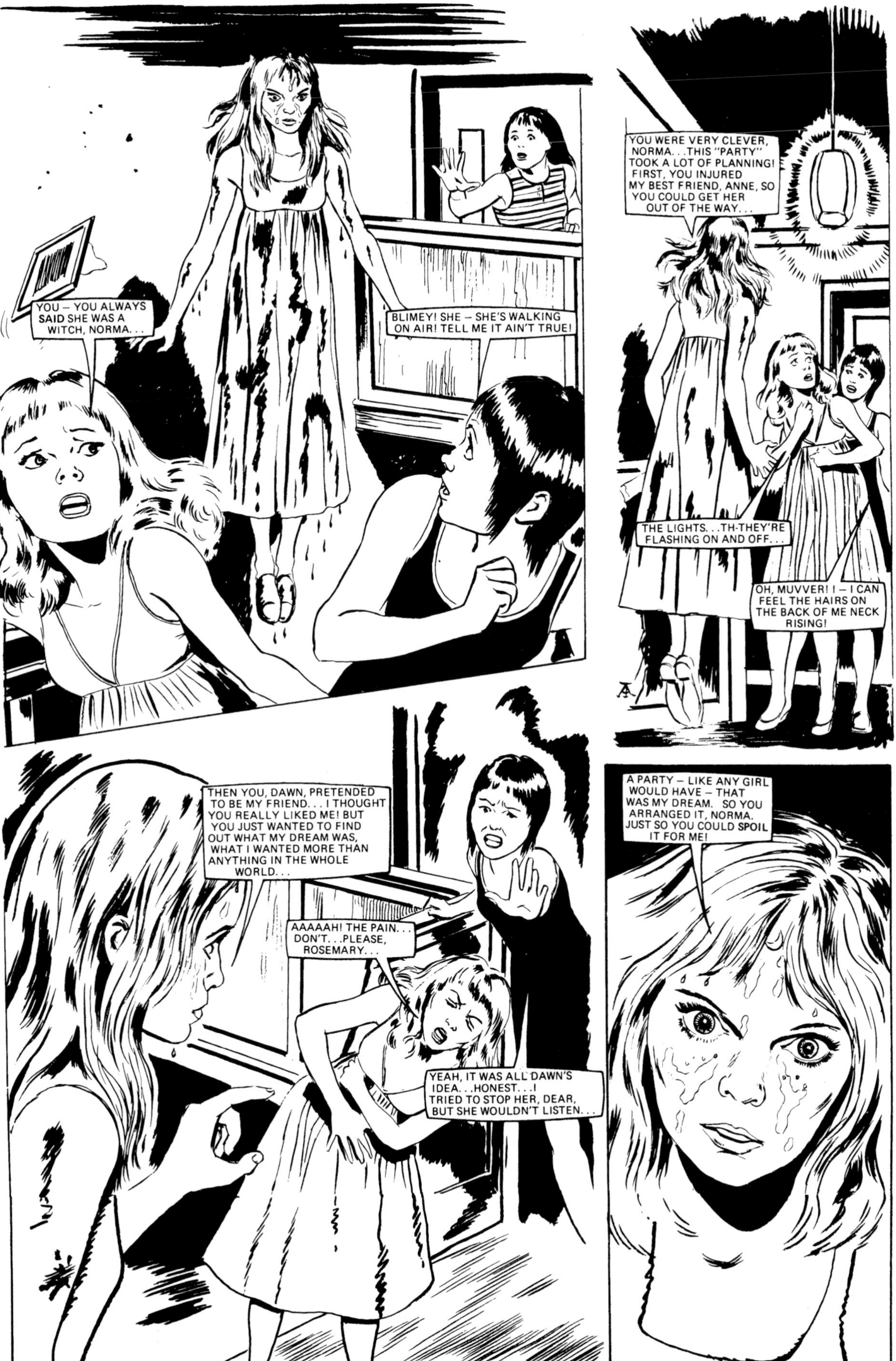

YOU – YOU ALWAYS SAID SHE WAS A WITCH, NORMA...
BLIMEY! SHE – SHE'S WALKING ON AIR! TELL ME IT AIN'T TRUE!
YOU WERE VERY CLEVER, NORMA... THIS "PARTY" TOOK A LOT OF PLANNING! FIRST, YOU INJURED MY BEST FRIEND, ANNE, SO YOU COULD GET HER OUT OF THE WAY...
THE LIGHTS... TH-THEY'RE FLASHING ON AND OFF...
OH, MUVVER! I – I CAN FEEL THE HAIRS ON THE BACK OF ME NECK RISING!
THEN YOU, DAWN, PRETENDED TO BE MY FRIEND... I THOUGHT YOU REALLY LIKED ME! BUT YOU JUST WANTED TO FIND OUT WHAT MY DREAM WAS, WHAT I WANTED MORE THAN ANYTHING IN THE WHOLE WORLD...
AAAAAH! THE PAIN... DON'T... PLEASE, ROSEMARY...
YEAH, IT WAS ALL DAWN'S IDEA... HONEST... I TRIED TO STOP HER, DEAR, BUT SHE WOULDN'T LISTEN...
A PARTY – LIKE ANY GIRL WOULD HAVE – THAT WAS MY DREAM. SO YOU ARRANGED IT, NORMA. JUST SO YOU COULD SPOIL IT FOR ME!

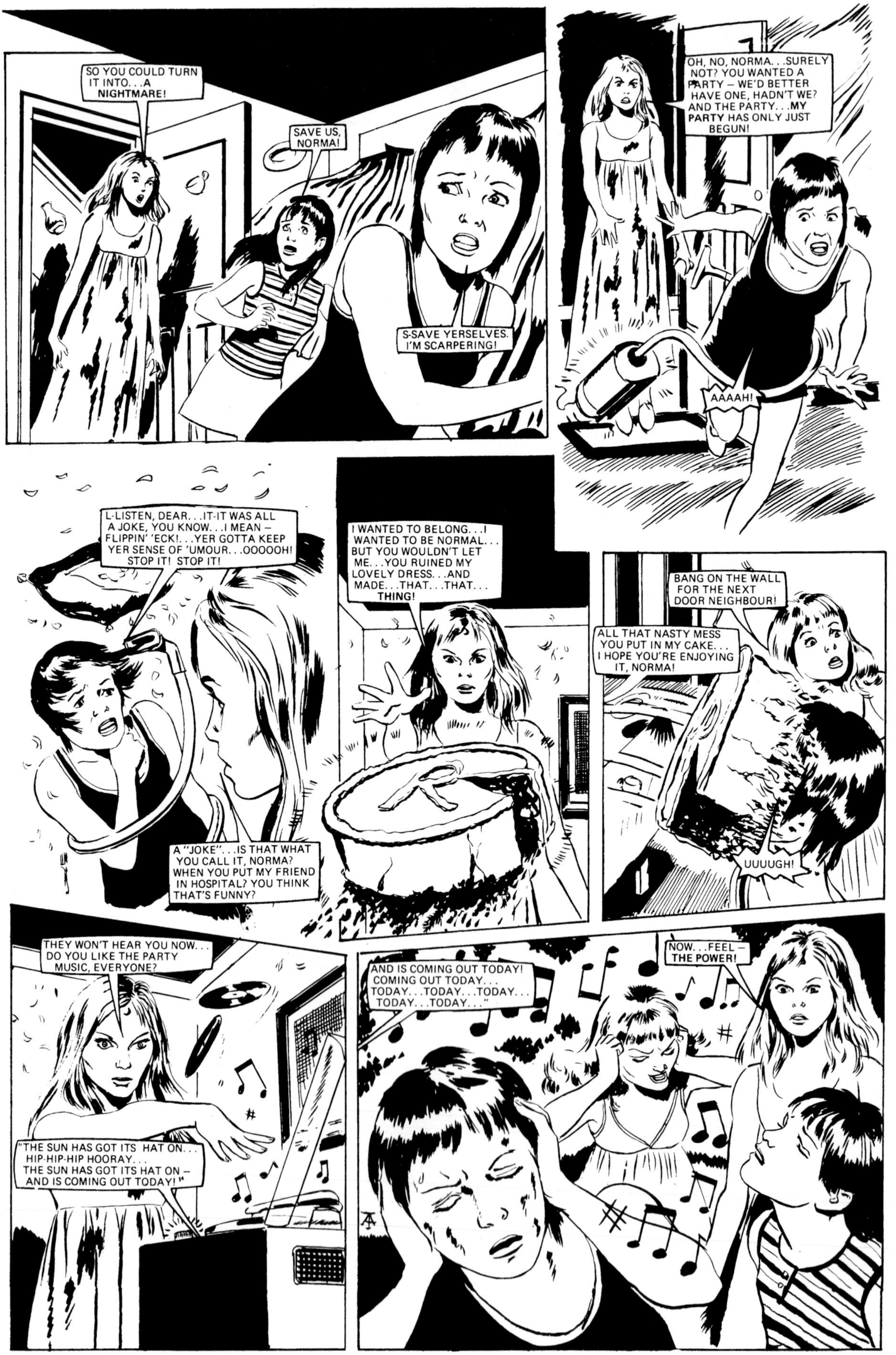

SO YOU COULD TURN IT INTO. . . A NIGHTMARE!
SAVE US, NORMA!
S-SAVE YERSELVES. I'M SCARPERING!
OH, NO, NORMA. . . SURELY NOT? YOU WANTED A PARTY – WE'D BETTER HAVE ONE, HADN'T WE? AND THE PARTY. . . MY PARTY HAS ONLY JUST BEGUN!
AAAAH!
L-LISTEN, DEAR. . . IT-IT WAS ALL A JOKE, YOU KNOW. . . I MEAN – FLIPPIN' 'ECK!. . . YER GOTTA KEEP YER SENSE OF 'UMOUR. . . OOOOOH! STOP IT! STOP IT!
A "JOKE". . . IS THAT WHAT YOU CALL IT, NORMA? WHEN YOU PUT MY FRIEND IN HOSPITAL? YOU THINK THAT'S FUNNY?
I WANTED TO BELONG. . . I WANTED TO BE NORMAL. . . BUT YOU WOULDN'T LET ME. . . YOU RUINED MY LOVELY DRESS. . . AND MADE. . . THAT. . . THAT. . . THING!
BANG ON THE WALL FOR THE NEXT DOOR NEIGHBOUR!
ALL THAT NASTY MESS YOU PUT IN MY CAKE. . . I HOPE YOU'RE ENJOYING IT, NORMA!
UUUUGH!
THEY WON'T HEAR YOU NOW. . . DO YOU LIKE THE PARTY MUSIC, EVERYONE?
"THE SUN HAS GOT ITS HAT ON. . . HIP-HIP-HIP HOORAY. . . THE SUN HAS GOT ITS HAT ON – AND IS COMING OUT TODAY!"
AND IS COMING OUT TODAY! COMING OUT TODAY. . . TODAY. . . TODAY. . . TODAY. . . TODAY. . . TODAY. . ."
NOW. . . FEEL – THE POWER!

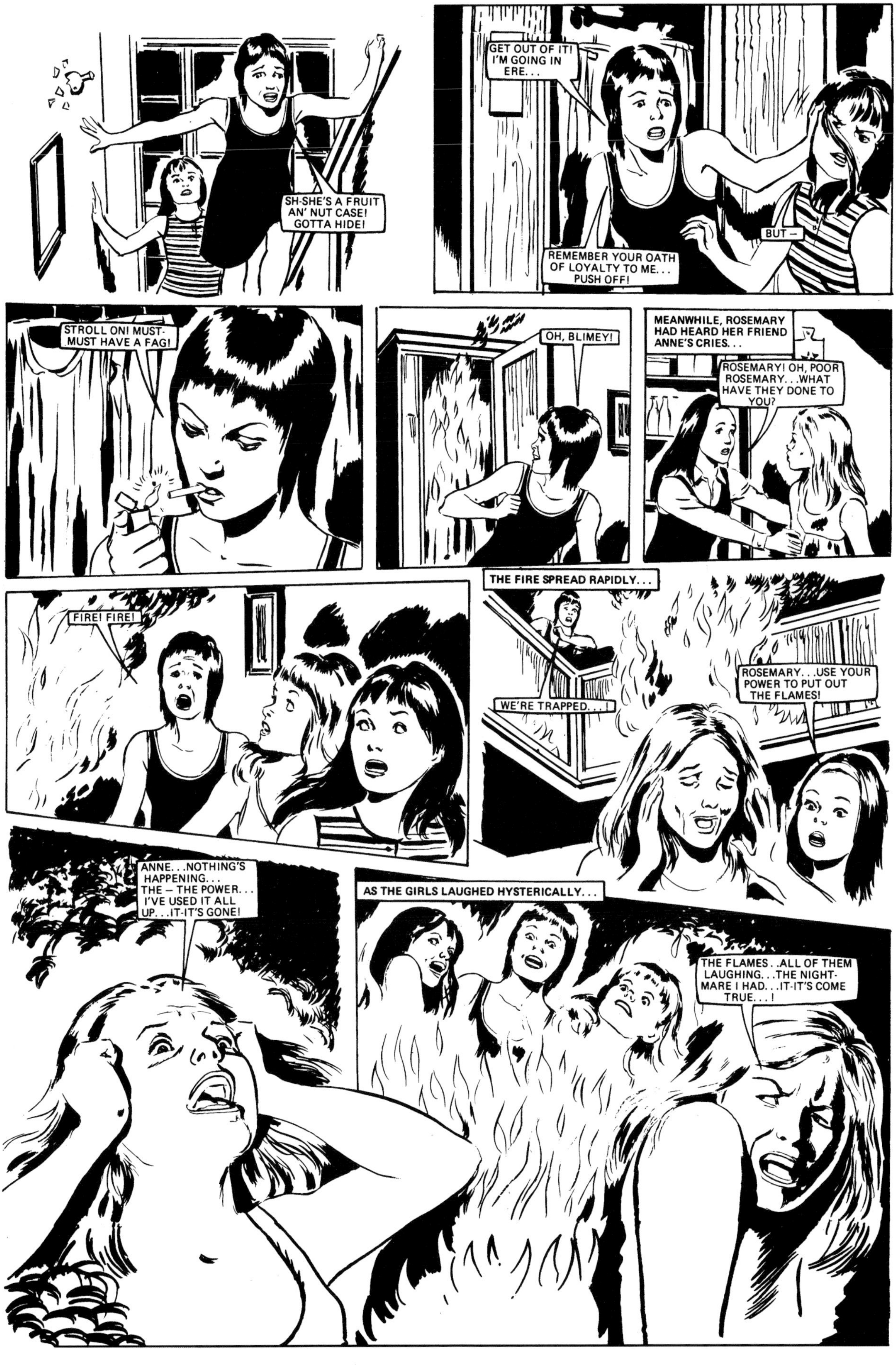
SH-SHE'S A FRUIT AN' NUT CASE! GOTTA HIDE!
GET OUT OF IT! I'M GOING IN ERE...
BUT —
REMEMBER YOUR OATH OF LOYALTY TO ME... PUSH OFF!
STROLL ON! MUST-MUST HAVE A FAG!
OH, BLIMEY!
MEANWHILE, ROSEMARY HAD HEARD HER FRIEND ANNE'S CRIES...
ROSEMARY! OH, POOR ROSEMARY...WHAT HAVE THEY DONE TO YOU?
FIRE! FIRE!
THE FIRE SPREAD RAPIDLY...
WE'RE TRAPPED...
ROSEMARY...USE YOUR POWER TO PUT OUT THE FLAMES!
ANNE...NOTHING'S HAPPENING... THE — THE POWER... I'VE USED IT ALL UP...IT-IT'S GONE!
AS THE GIRLS LAUGHED HYSTERICALLY...
THE FLAMES..ALL OF THEM LAUGHING...THE NIGHT-MARE I HAD...IT-IT'S COME TRUE...!

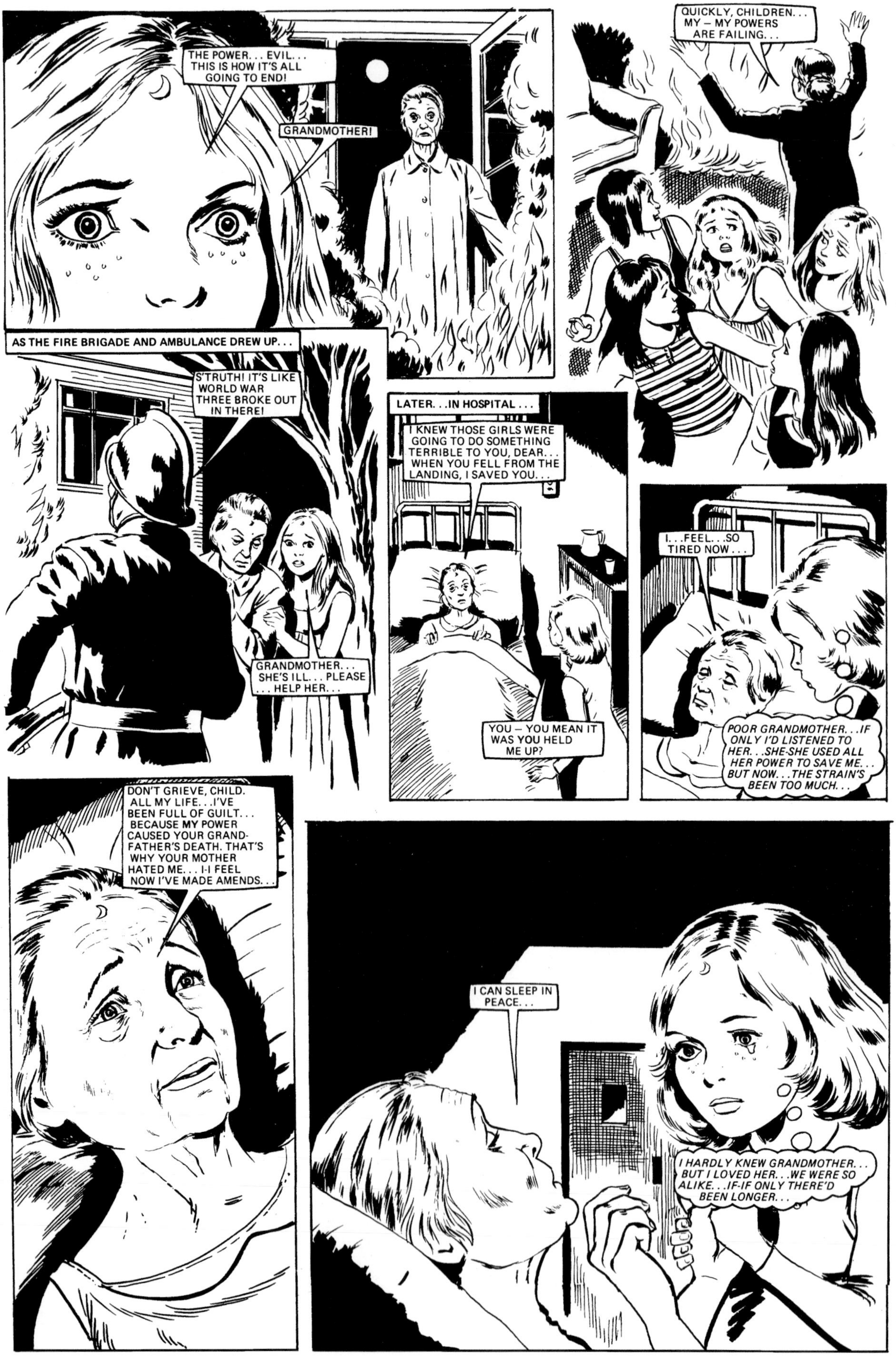
THE POWER. . . EVIL. . . THIS IS HOW IT'S ALL GOING TO END!
GRANDMOTHER!
QUICKLY, CHILDREN. . . MY — MY POWERS ARE FAILING. . .
AS THE FIRE BRIGADE AND AMBULANCE DREW UP. . .
S'TRUTH! IT'S LIKE WORLD WAR THREE BROKE OUT IN THERE!
GRANDMOTHER. . . SHE'S ILL. . . PLEASE . . . HELP HER. . .
LATER. . . IN HOSPITAL . . .
I KNEW THOSE GIRLS WERE GOING TO DO SOMETHING TERRIBLE TO YOU, DEAR. . . WHEN YOU FELL FROM THE LANDING, I SAVED YOU. . .
YOU — YOU MEAN IT WAS YOU HELD ME UP?
I. . . FEEL. . . SO TIRED NOW . . .
POOR GRANDMOTHER. . . IF ONLY I'D LISTENED TO HER. . . SHE-SHE USED ALL HER POWER TO SAVE ME. . . BUT NOW. . . THE STRAIN'S BEEN TOO MUCH. . .
DON'T GRIEVE, CHILD. ALL MY LIFE. . . I'VE BEEN FULL OF GUILT. . . BECAUSE MY POWER CAUSED YOUR GRAND-FATHER'S DEATH. THAT'S WHY YOUR MOTHER HATED ME. . . I-I FEEL NOW I'VE MADE AMENDS. . .
I CAN SLEEP IN PEACE. . .
I HARDLY KNEW GRANDMOTHER. . . BUT I LOVED HER. . . WE WERE SO ALIKE. . . IF-IF ONLY THERE'D BEEN LONGER. . .

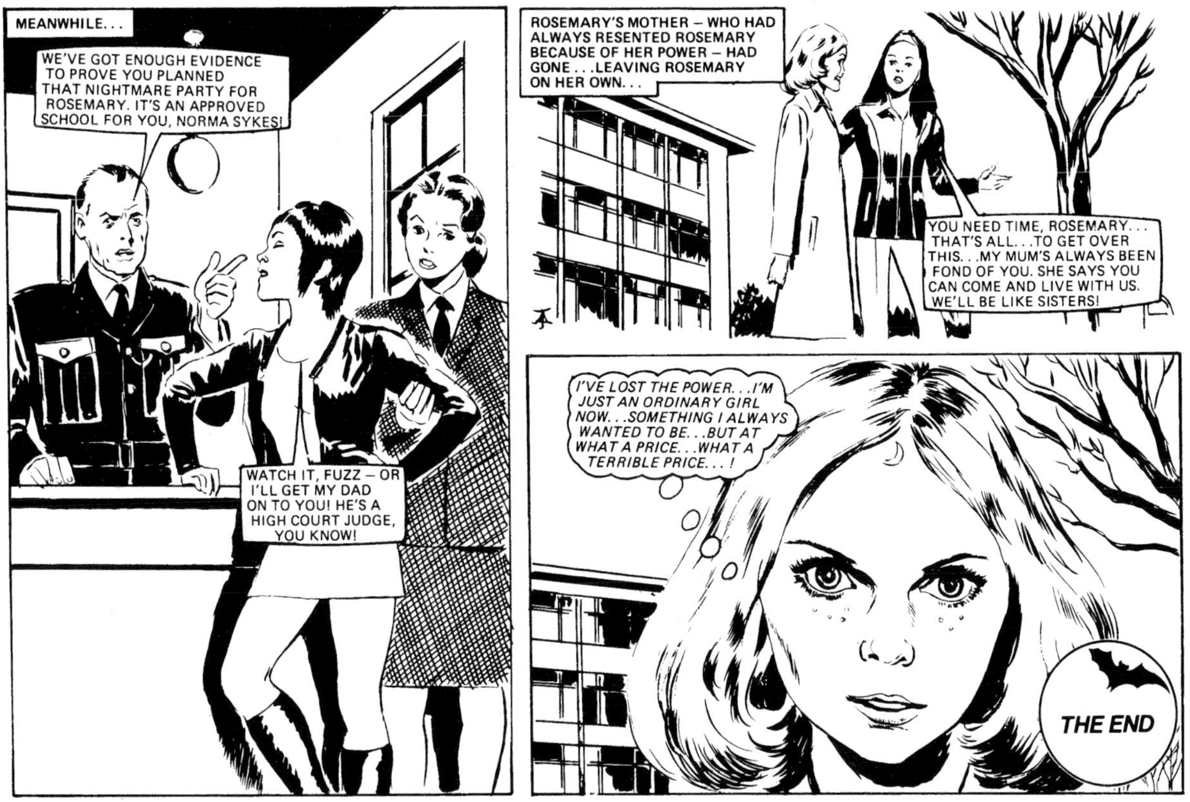
MEANWHILE...
WE'VE GOT ENOUGH EVIDENCE TO PROVE YOU PLANNED THAT NIGHTMARE PARTY FOR ROSEMARY. IT'S AN APPROVED SCHOOL FOR YOU, NORMA SYKES!
WATCH IT, FUZZ – OR I'LL GET MY DAD ON TO YOU! HE'S A HIGH COURT JUDGE, YOU KNOW!
ROSEMARY'S MOTHER – WHO HAD ALWAYS RESENTED ROSEMARY BECAUSE OF HER POWER – HAD GONE . . . LEAVING ROSEMARY ON HER OWN. . .
YOU NEED TIME, ROSEMARY... THAT'S ALL...TO GET OVER THIS...MY MUM'S ALWAYS BEEN FOND OF YOU. SHE SAYS YOU CAN COME AND LIVE WITH US. WE'LL BE LIKE SISTERS!
I'VE LOST THE POWER...I'M JUST AN ORDINARY GIRL NOW...SOMETHING I ALWAYS WANTED TO BE...BUT AT WHAT A PRICE...WHAT A TERRIBLE PRICE... !
THE END

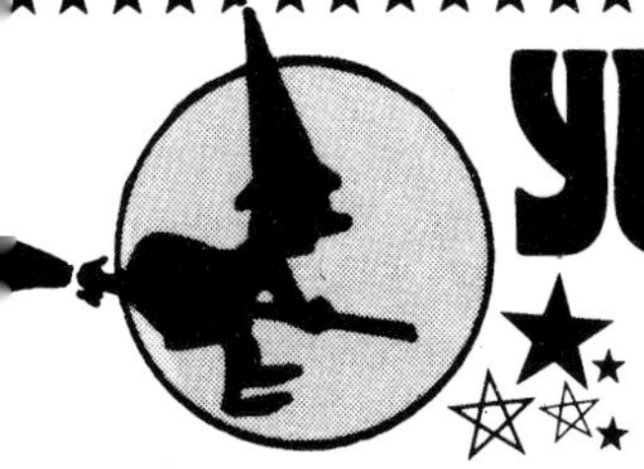

# YOUR WITCH'S HAT

**A witch's hat is easy to make – once you know how. Just follow our simple, step-by-step guide.**

You will need:

*1. One large sheet of black stiff paper approx 63 centimetres by 85 centimetres.*
*2. Glue and sellotape.*
*3. Scissors.*
*4. Patience.*
*5. Gold spray (optional).*

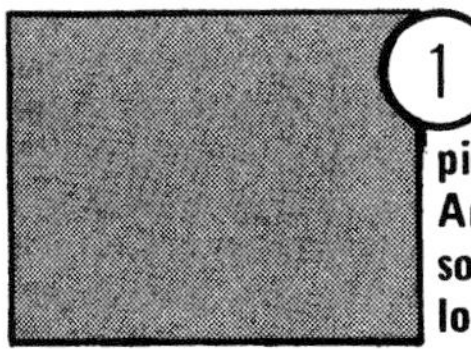

**1** Use a fairly stiff piece of black paper. An art shop will sell you some, which should be long enough and wide enough to fit your head.

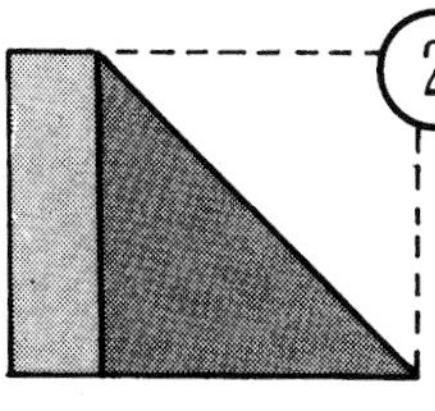

**2** Fold it down to form a square.

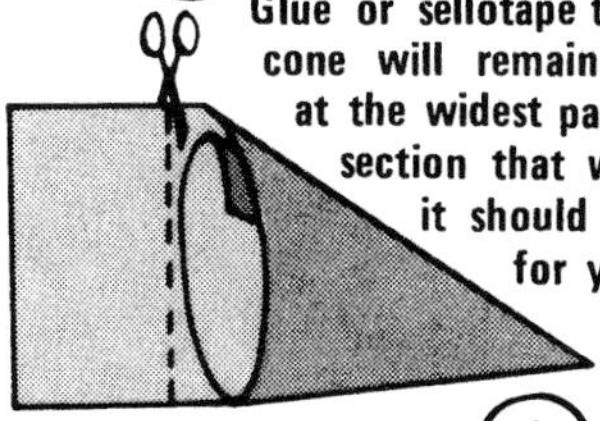

**3** Twist it round until it becomes a cone shape. Glue or sellotape the insides together so that the cone will remain as illustrated. Trim off the piece at the widest part of the cone – this is the section that will go round your head. Now it should be all neat and tidy – all ready for you to put on the brim.

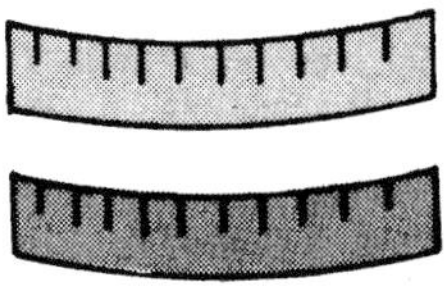

**4** With the paper that's left over, cut out two rounded sections, to be used as the brim. Cut 10mm inserts every 10mms – so that they look rather like the end of a Christmas cracker.

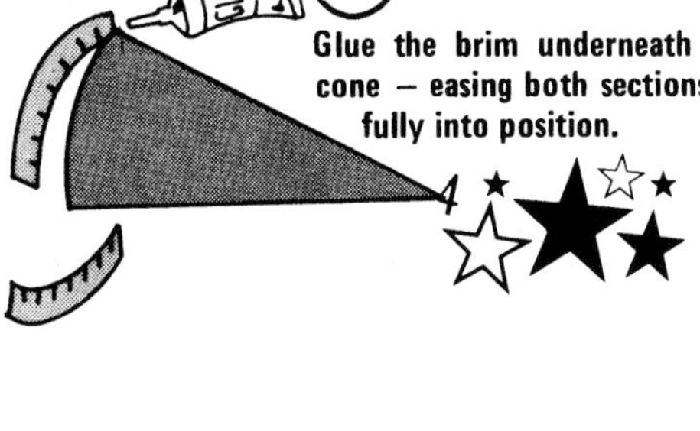
GLUE

**5** Glue the brim underneath the cone – easing both sections carefully into position.

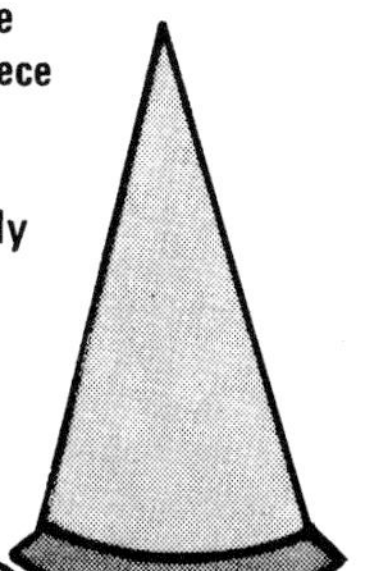

**6** You now have your witch's hat. Have fun wearing it – and for a final effect, why not spray some gold glitter over it?

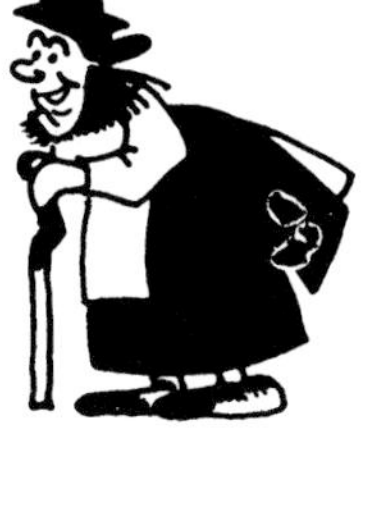

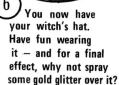

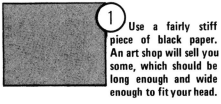

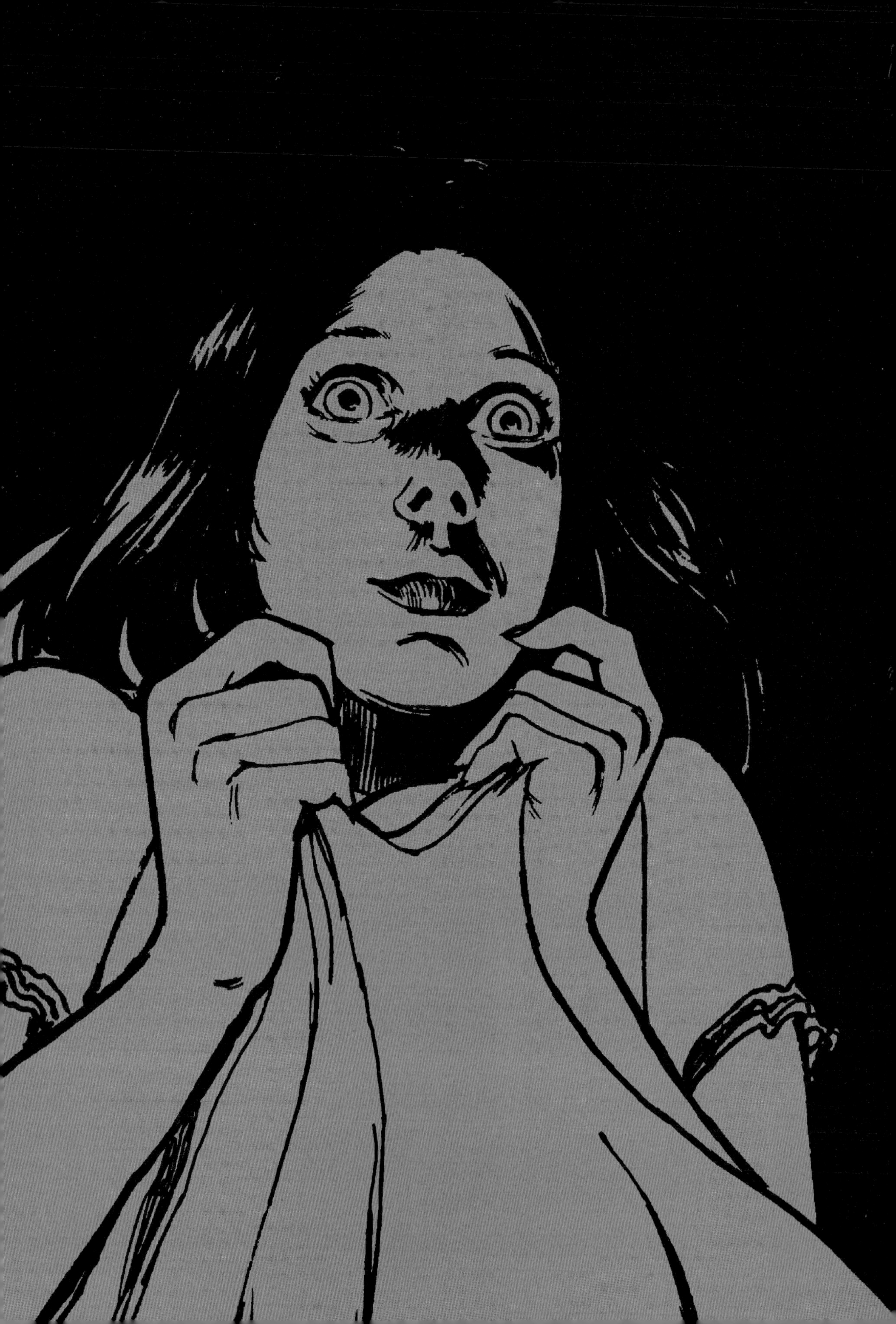

# THE FOUR FACES OF EVE

Script: Malcolm Shaw
Art: Brian Delaney

Originally published in *Misty* issues 20-31

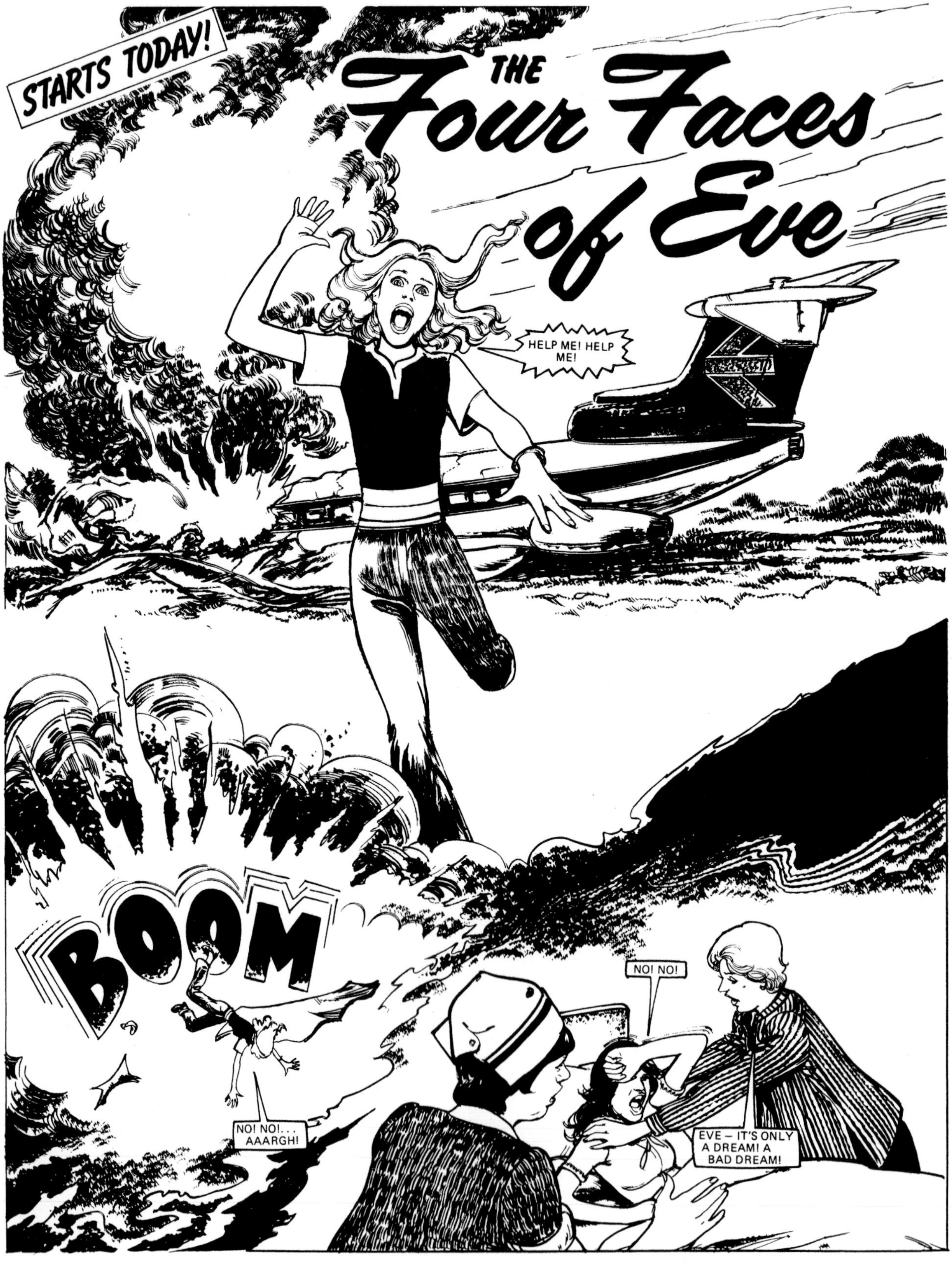
STARTS TODAY!
THE Four Faces of Eve
HELP ME! HELP ME!
BOOM
NO! NO!... AAARGH!
NO! NO!
EVE – IT'S ONLY A DREAM! A BAD DREAM!

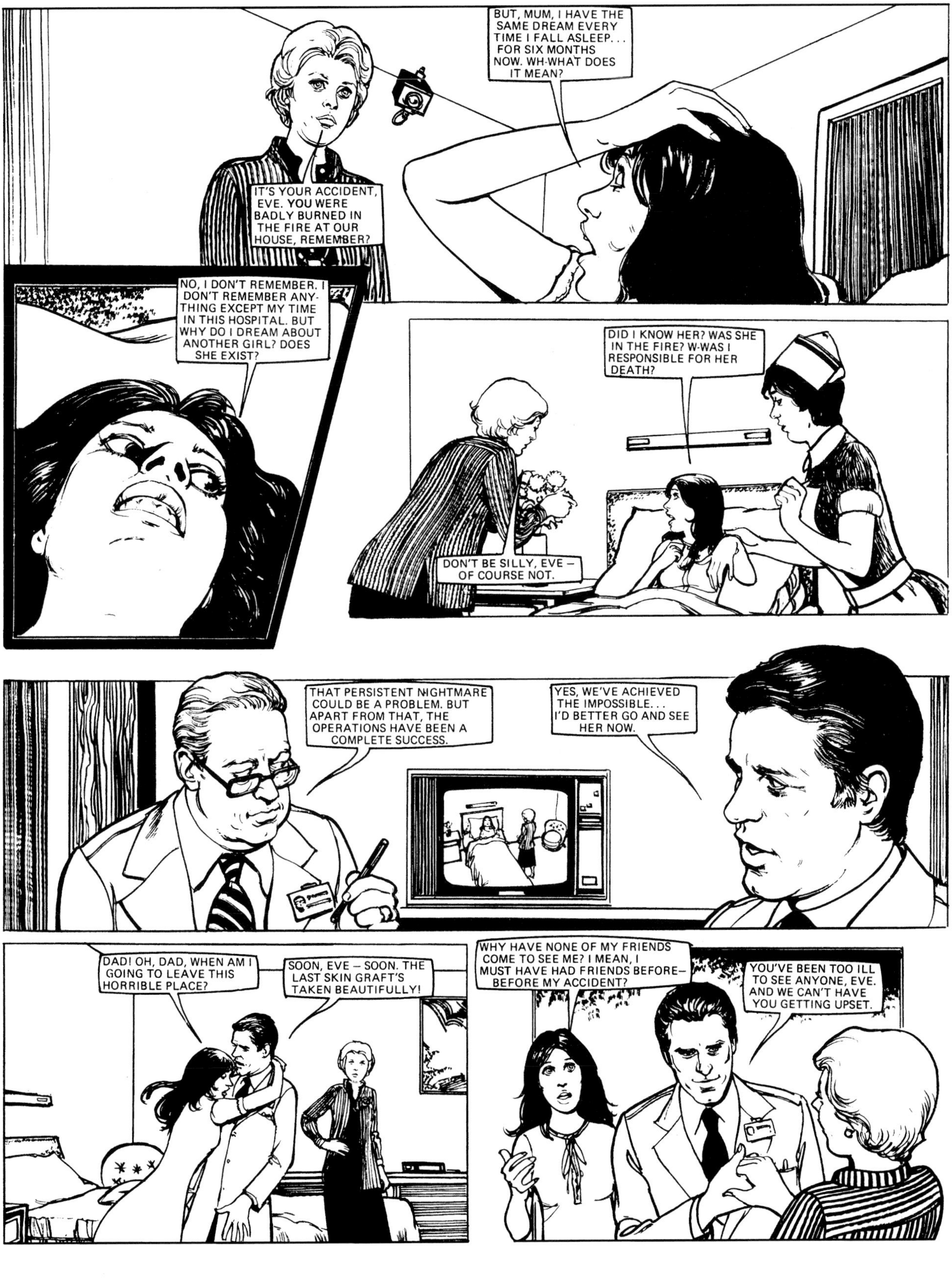
BUT, MUM, I HAVE THE SAME DREAM EVERY TIME I FALL ASLEEP. . . FOR SIX MONTHS NOW. WH-WHAT DOES IT MEAN?
IT'S YOUR ACCIDENT, EVE. YOU WERE BADLY BURNED IN THE FIRE AT OUR HOUSE, REMEMBER?
NO, I DON'T REMEMBER. I DON'T REMEMBER ANYTHING EXCEPT MY TIME IN THIS HOSPITAL. BUT WHY DO I DREAM ABOUT ANOTHER GIRL? DOES SHE EXIST?
DID I KNOW HER? WAS SHE IN THE FIRE? W-WAS I RESPONSIBLE FOR HER DEATH?
DON'T BE SILLY, EVE — OF COURSE NOT.
THAT PERSISTENT NIGHTMARE COULD BE A PROBLEM. BUT APART FROM THAT, THE OPERATIONS HAVE BEEN A COMPLETE SUCCESS.
YES, WE'VE ACHIEVED THE IMPOSSIBLE. . . I'D BETTER GO AND SEE HER NOW.
DAD! OH, DAD, WHEN AM I GOING TO LEAVE THIS HORRIBLE PLACE?
SOON, EVE — SOON. THE LAST SKIN GRAFT'S TAKEN BEAUTIFULLY!
WHY HAVE NONE OF MY FRIENDS COME TO SEE ME? I MEAN, I MUST HAVE HAD FRIENDS BEFORE— BEFORE MY ACCIDENT?
YOU'VE BEEN TOO ILL TO SEE ANYONE, EVE. AND WE CAN'T HAVE YOU GETTING UPSET.

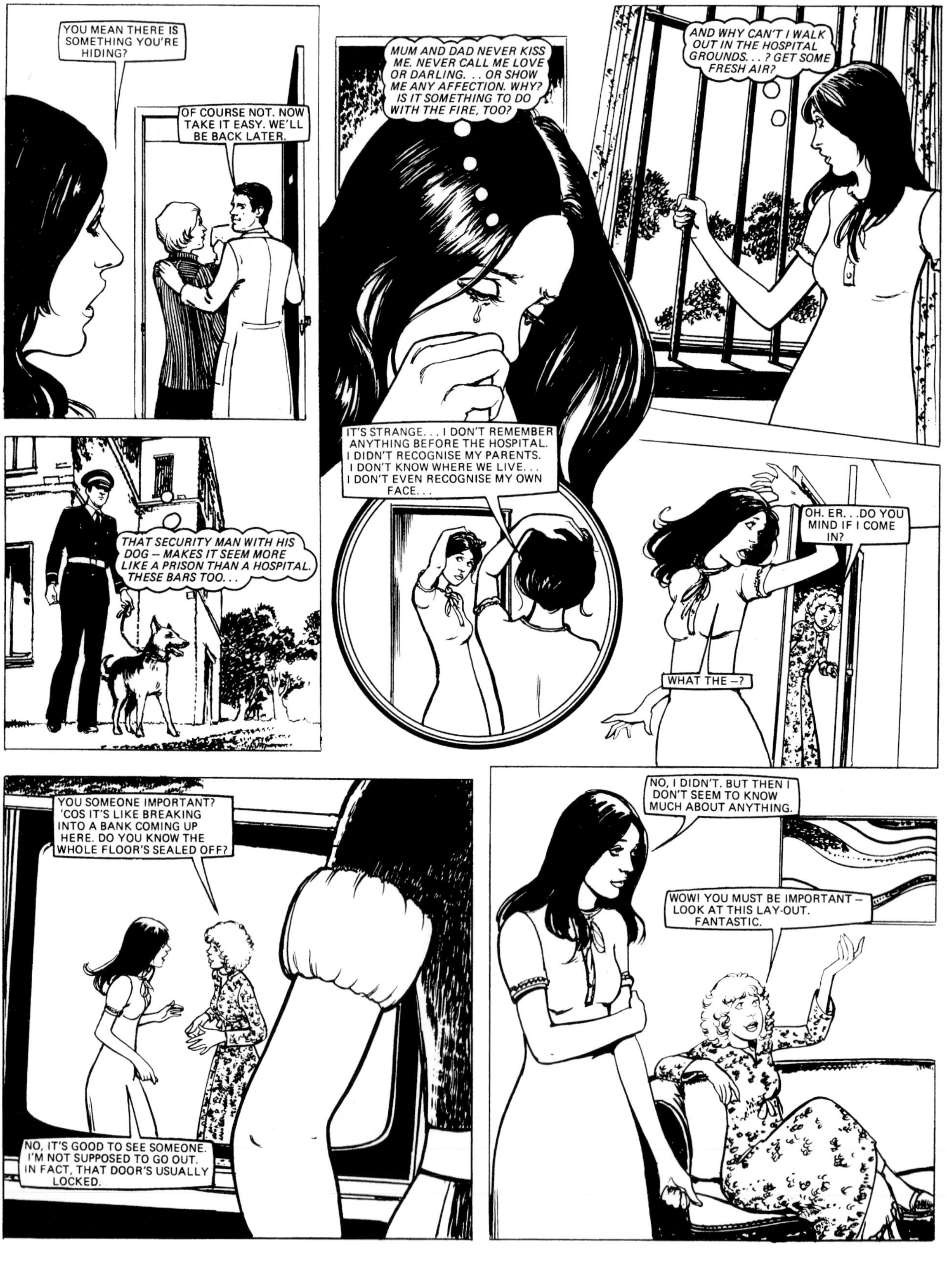
YOU MEAN THERE IS SOMETHING YOU'RE HIDING?
OF COURSE NOT. NOW TAKE IT EASY. WE'LL BE BACK LATER.
MUM AND DAD NEVER KISS ME. NEVER CALL ME LOVE OR DARLING. . . OR SHOW ME ANY AFFECTION. WHY? IS IT SOMETHING TO DO WITH THE FIRE, TOO?
AND WHY CAN'T I WALK OUT IN THE HOSPITAL GROUNDS. . . ? GET SOME FRESH AIR?
THAT SECURITY MAN WITH HIS DOG – MAKES IT SEEM MORE LIKE A PRISON THAN A HOSPITAL. THESE BARS TOO. . .
IT'S STRANGE. . . I DON'T REMEMBER ANYTHING BEFORE THE HOSPITAL. I DIDN'T RECOGNISE MY PARENTS. I DON'T KNOW WHERE WE LIVE. . . I DON'T EVEN RECOGNISE MY OWN FACE. . .
OH. ER. . .DO YOU MIND IF I COME IN?
WHAT THE –?
YOU SOMEONE IMPORTANT? 'COS IT'S LIKE BREAKING INTO A BANK COMING UP HERE. DO YOU KNOW THE WHOLE FLOOR'S SEALED OFF?
NO, IT'S GOOD TO SEE SOMEONE. I'M NOT SUPPOSED TO GO OUT. IN FACT, THAT DOOR'S USUALLY LOCKED.
NO, I DIDN'T. BUT THEN I DON'T SEEM TO KNOW MUCH ABOUT ANYTHING.
WOW! YOU MUST BE IMPORTANT – LOOK AT THIS LAY-OUT. FANTASTIC.

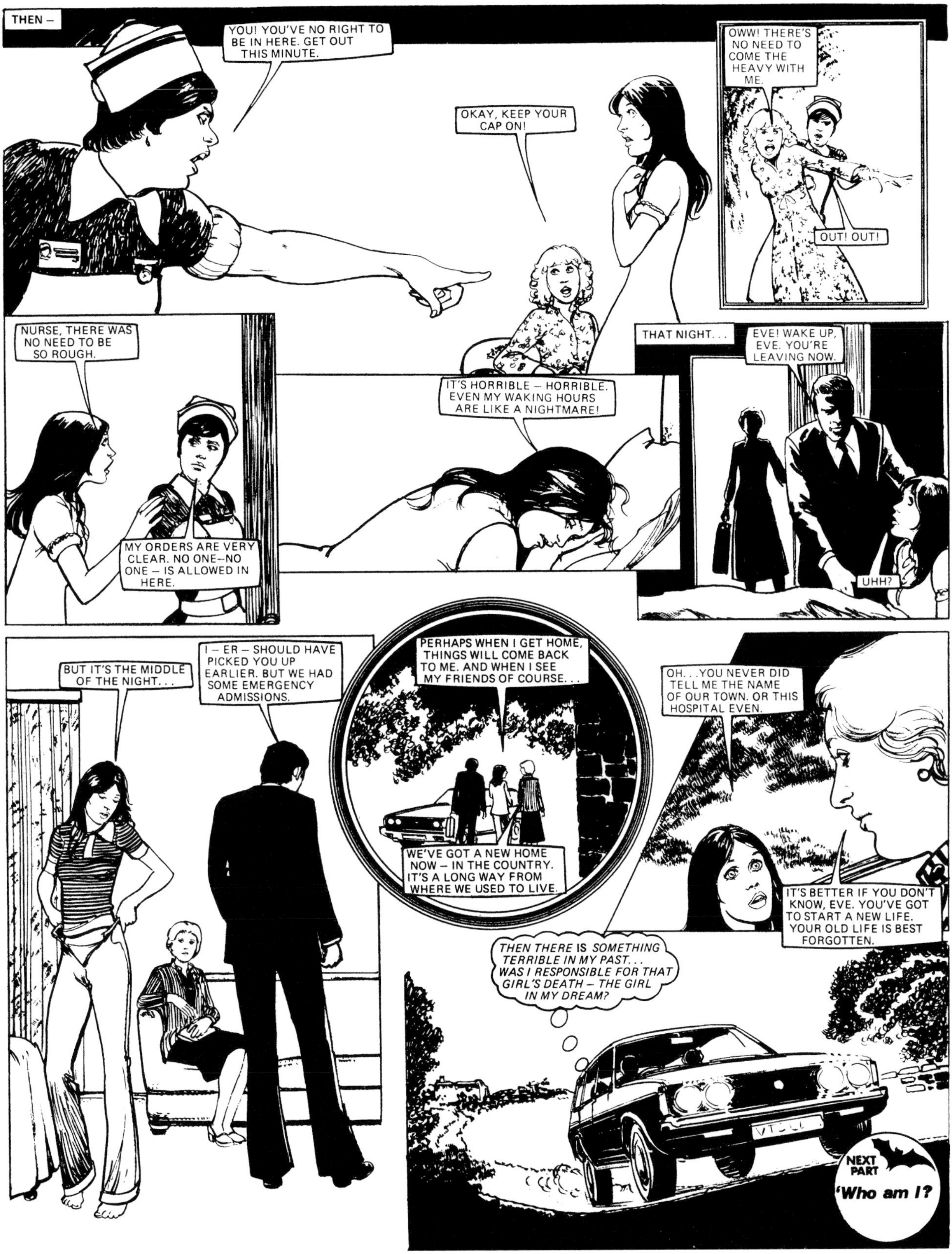
THEN –
YOU! YOU'VE NO RIGHT TO BE IN HERE. GET OUT THIS MINUTE.
OKAY, KEEP YOUR CAP ON!
OWW! THERE'S NO NEED TO COME THE HEAVY WITH ME.
OUT! OUT!
NURSE, THERE WAS NO NEED TO BE SO ROUGH.
MY ORDERS ARE VERY CLEAR. NO ONE–NO ONE – IS ALLOWED IN HERE.
IT'S HORRIBLE – HORRIBLE. EVEN MY WAKING HOURS ARE LIKE A NIGHTMARE!
THAT NIGHT...
EVE! WAKE UP, EVE. YOU'RE LEAVING NOW.
UHH?
BUT IT'S THE MIDDLE OF THE NIGHT...
I – ER – SHOULD HAVE PICKED YOU UP EARLIER. BUT WE HAD SOME EMERGENCY ADMISSIONS.
PERHAPS WHEN I GET HOME, THINGS WILL COME BACK TO ME. AND WHEN I SEE MY FRIENDS OF COURSE...
WE'VE GOT A NEW HOME NOW – IN THE COUNTRY. IT'S A LONG WAY FROM WHERE WE USED TO LIVE.
OH... YOU NEVER DID TELL ME THE NAME OF OUR TOWN. OR THIS HOSPITAL EVEN.
IT'S BETTER IF YOU DON'T KNOW, EVE. YOU'VE GOT TO START A NEW LIFE. YOUR OLD LIFE IS BEST FORGOTTEN.
THEN THERE IS SOMETHING TERRIBLE IN MY PAST... WAS I RESPONSIBLE FOR THAT GIRL'S DEATH – THE GIRL IN MY DREAM?
NEXT PART
'Who am I?

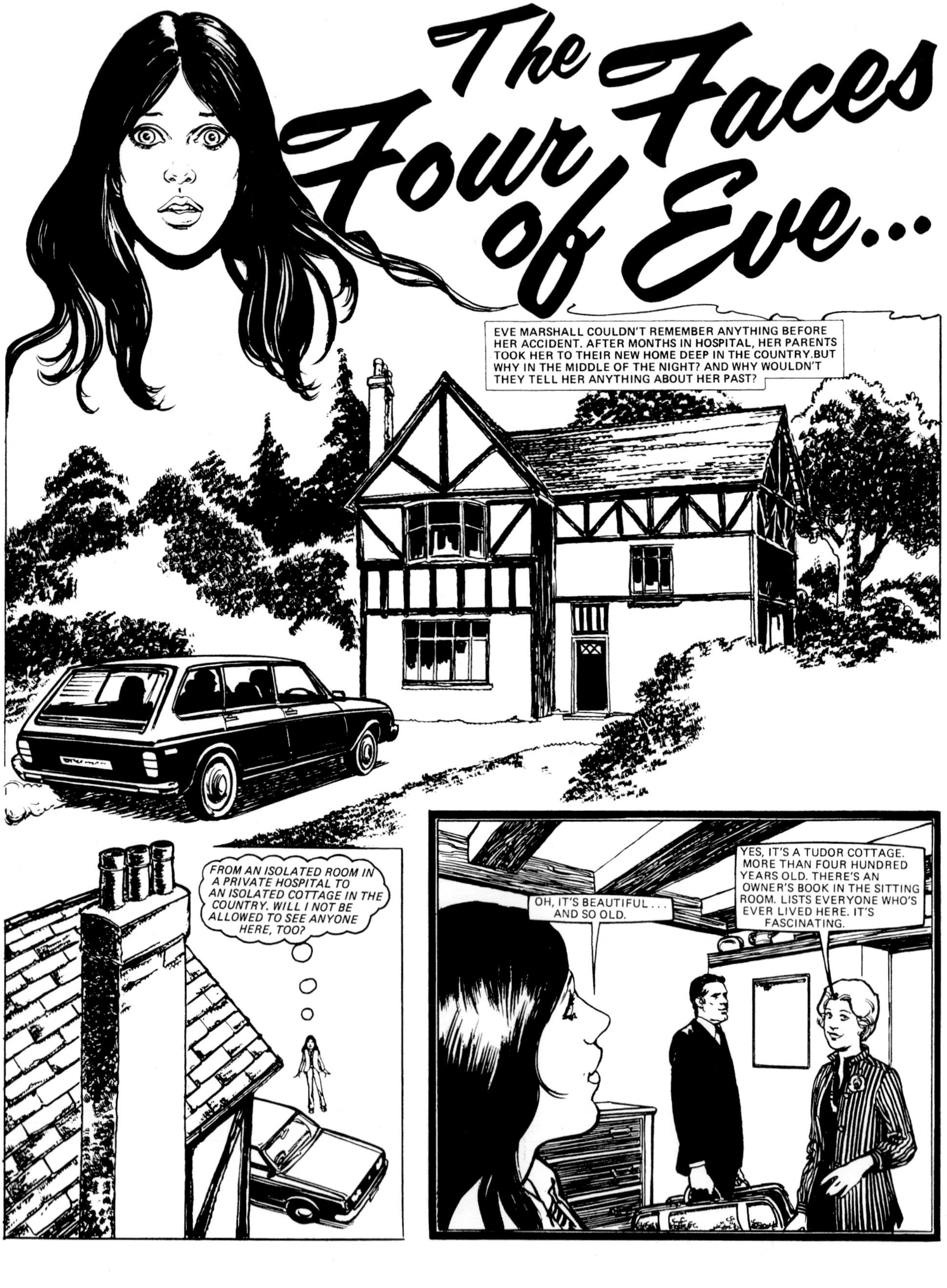
The Four Faces of Eve...
EVE MARSHALL COULDN'T REMEMBER ANYTHING BEFORE HER ACCIDENT. AFTER MONTHS IN HOSPITAL, HER PARENTS TOOK HER TO THEIR NEW HOME DEEP IN THE COUNTRY.BUT WHY IN THE MIDDLE OF THE NIGHT? AND WHY WOULDN'T THEY TELL HER ANYTHING ABOUT HER PAST?
FROM AN ISOLATED ROOM IN A PRIVATE HOSPITAL TO AN ISOLATED COTTAGE IN THE COUNTRY. WILL I NOT BE ALLOWED TO SEE ANYONE HERE, TOO?
OH, IT'S BEAUTIFUL . . . AND SO OLD.
YES, IT'S A TUDOR COTTAGE. MORE THAN FOUR HUNDRED YEARS OLD. THERE'S AN OWNER'S BOOK IN THE SITTING ROOM. LISTS EVERYONE WHO'S EVER LIVED HERE. IT'S FASCINATING.

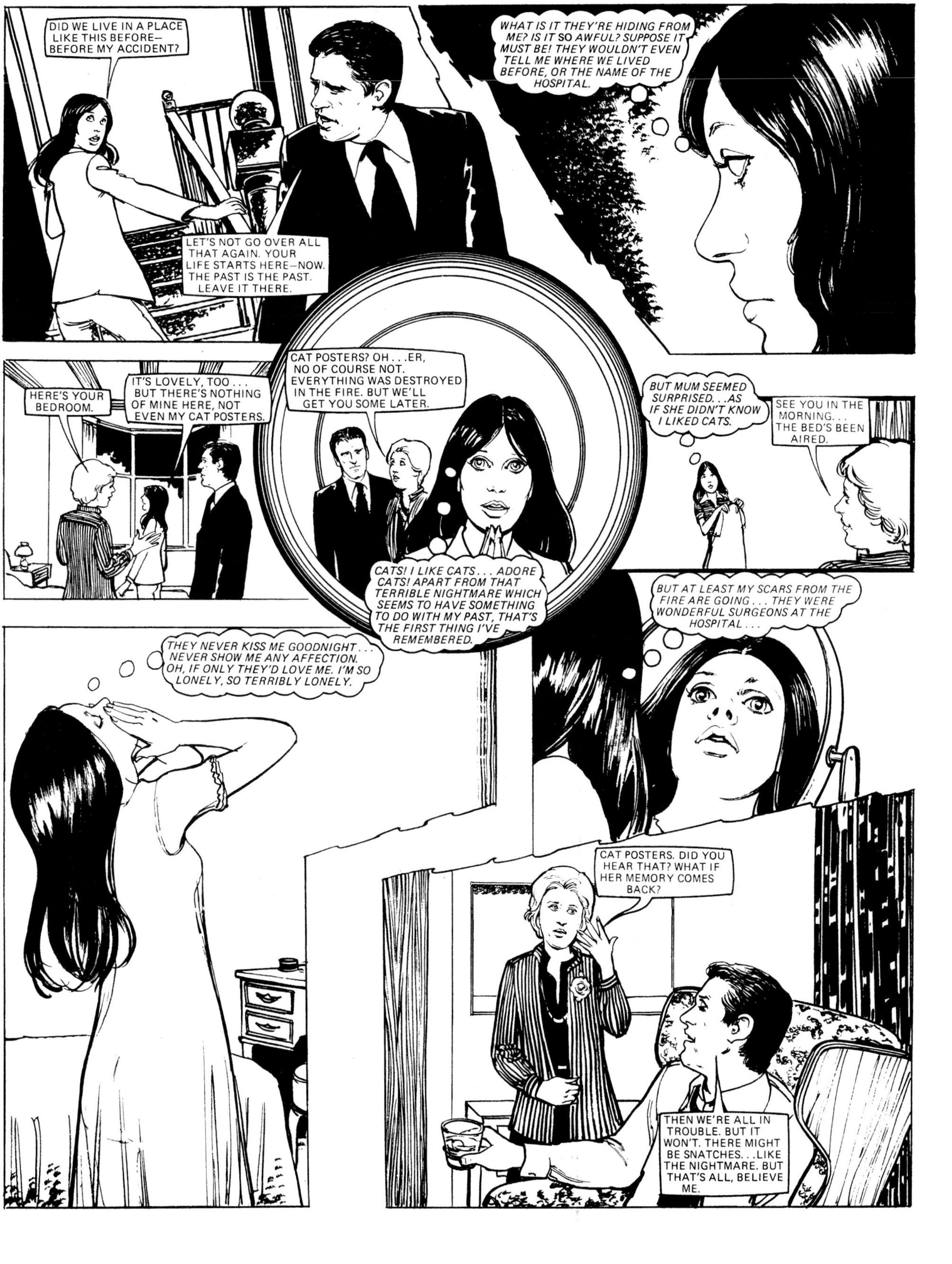
DID WE LIVE IN A PLACE LIKE THIS BEFORE— BEFORE MY ACCIDENT?
LET'S NOT GO OVER ALL THAT AGAIN. YOUR LIFE STARTS HERE—NOW. THE PAST IS THE PAST. LEAVE IT THERE.
WHAT IS IT THEY'RE HIDING FROM ME? IS IT SO AWFUL? SUPPOSE IT MUST BE! THEY WOULDN'T EVEN TELL ME WHERE WE LIVED BEFORE, OR THE NAME OF THE HOSPITAL.
HERE'S YOUR BEDROOM.
IT'S LOVELY, TOO . . . BUT THERE'S NOTHING OF MINE HERE, NOT EVEN MY CAT POSTERS.
CAT POSTERS? OH . . .ER, NO OF COURSE NOT. EVERYTHING WAS DESTROYED IN THE FIRE. BUT WE'LL GET YOU SOME LATER.
CATS! I LIKE CATS . . . ADORE CATS! APART FROM THAT TERRIBLE NIGHTMARE WHICH SEEMS TO HAVE SOMETHING TO DO WITH MY PAST, THAT'S THE FIRST THING I'VE REMEMBERED.
BUT MUM SEEMED SURPRISED. . .AS IF SHE DIDN'T KNOW I LIKED CATS.
SEE YOU IN THE MORNING. . . THE BED'S BEEN AIRED.
THEY NEVER KISS ME GOODNIGHT . . . NEVER SHOW ME ANY AFFECTION. OH, IF ONLY THEY'D LOVE ME. I'M SO LONELY, SO TERRIBLY LONELY.
BUT AT LEAST MY SCARS FROM THE FIRE ARE GOING . . . THEY WERE WONDERFUL SURGEONS AT THE HOSPITAL . . .
CAT POSTERS. DID YOU HEAR THAT? WHAT IF HER MEMORY COMES BACK?
THEN WE'RE ALL IN TROUBLE. BUT IT WON'T. THERE MIGHT BE SNATCHES. . .LIKE THE NIGHTMARE. BUT THAT'S ALL, BELIEVE ME.

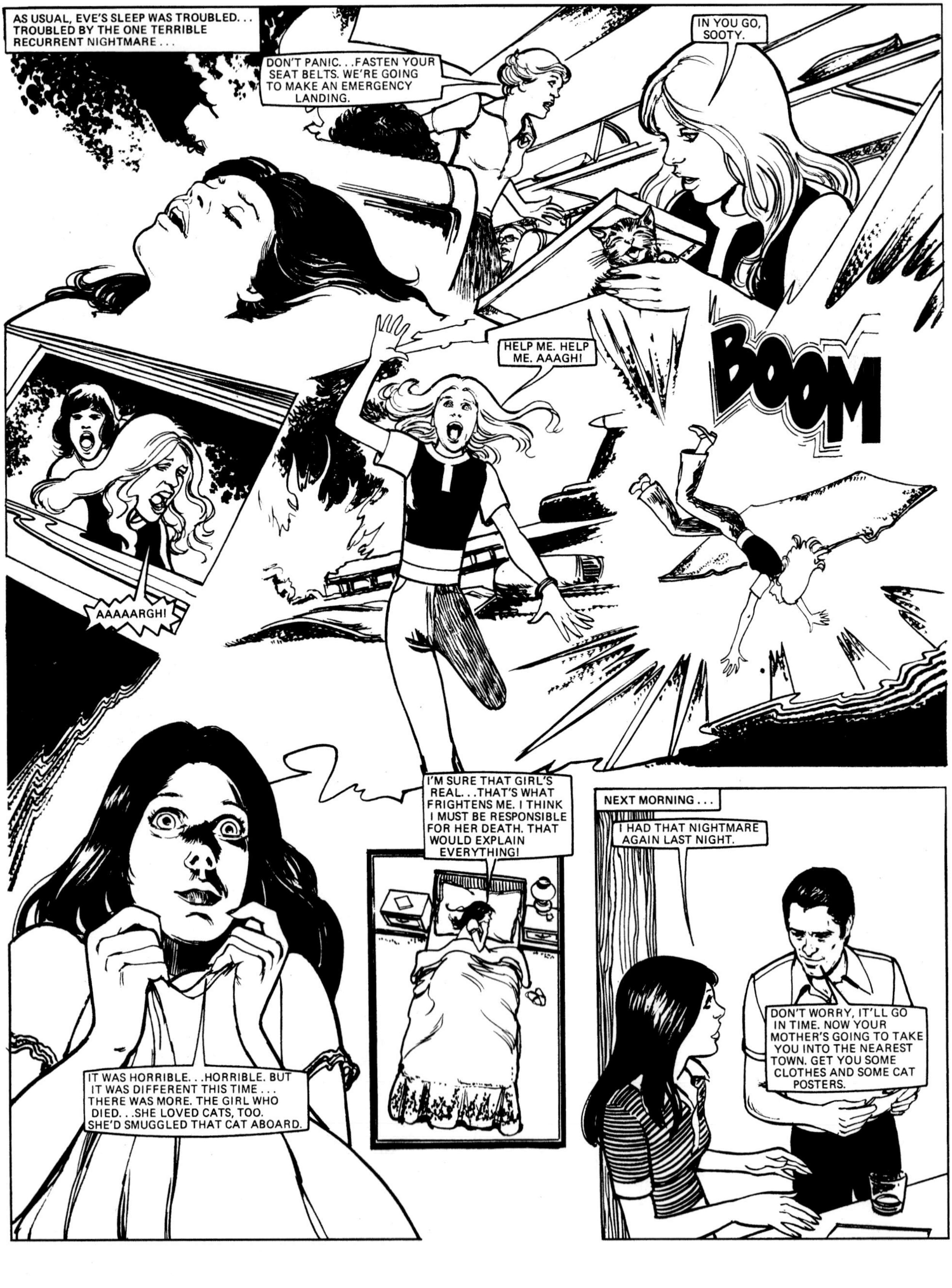
AS USUAL, EVE'S SLEEP WAS TROUBLED... TROUBLED BY THE ONE TERRIBLE RECURRENT NIGHTMARE...
DON'T PANIC...FASTEN YOUR SEAT BELTS. WE'RE GOING TO MAKE AN EMERGENCY LANDING.
IN YOU GO, SOOTY.
HELP ME. HELP ME. AAAGH!
BOOM
AAAAARGH!
I'M SURE THAT GIRL'S REAL...THAT'S WHAT FRIGHTENS ME. I THINK I MUST BE RESPONSIBLE FOR HER DEATH. THAT WOULD EXPLAIN EVERYTHING!
IT WAS HORRIBLE...HORRIBLE. BUT IT WAS DIFFERENT THIS TIME... THERE WAS MORE. THE GIRL WHO DIED...SHE LOVED CATS, TOO. SHE'D SMUGGLED THAT CAT ABOARD.
NEXT MORNING...
I HAD THAT NIGHTMARE AGAIN LAST NIGHT.
DON'T WORRY, IT'LL GO IN TIME. NOW YOUR MOTHER'S GOING TO TAKE YOU INTO THE NEAREST TOWN. GET YOU SOME CLOTHES AND SOME CAT POSTERS.

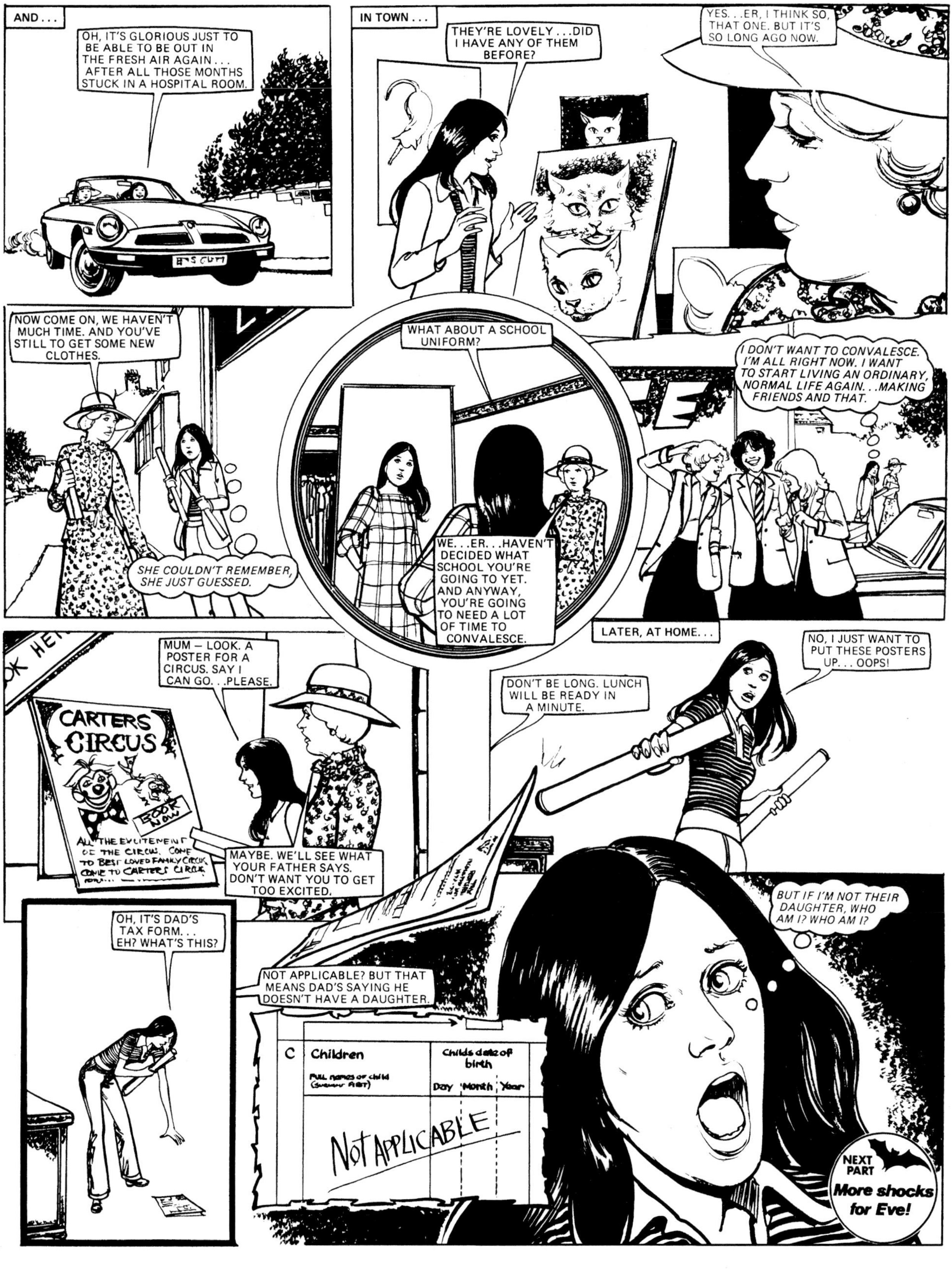

AND . . .
OH, IT'S GLORIOUS JUST TO BE ABLE TO BE OUT IN THE FRESH AIR AGAIN . . . AFTER ALL THOSE MONTHS STUCK IN A HOSPITAL ROOM.
IN TOWN . . .
THEY'RE LOVELY . . . DID I HAVE ANY OF THEM BEFORE?
YES. . . ER, I THINK SO, THAT ONE. BUT IT'S SO LONG AGO NOW.
NOW COME ON, WE HAVEN'T MUCH TIME. AND YOU'VE STILL TO GET SOME NEW CLOTHES.
SHE COULDN'T REMEMBER, SHE JUST GUESSED.
WHAT ABOUT A SCHOOL UNIFORM?
WE. . . ER. . . HAVEN'T DECIDED WHAT SCHOOL YOU'RE GOING TO YET. AND ANYWAY, YOU'RE GOING TO NEED A LOT OF TIME TO CONVALESCE.
I DON'T WANT TO CONVALESCE. I'M ALL RIGHT NOW. I WANT TO START LIVING AN ORDINARY, NORMAL LIFE AGAIN. . . MAKING FRIENDS AND THAT.
MUM — LOOK. A POSTER FOR A CIRCUS. SAY I CAN GO. . . PLEASE.
CARTERS CIRCUS
BOOK NOW
ALL THE EXCITEMENT OF THE CIRCUS. COME TO BEST LOVED FAMILY CIRCUS COME TO CARTERS CIRCUS
MAYBE. WE'LL SEE WHAT YOUR FATHER SAYS. DON'T WANT YOU TO GET TOO EXCITED.
LATER, AT HOME. . .
DON'T BE LONG. LUNCH WILL BE READY IN A MINUTE.
NO, I JUST WANT TO PUT THESE POSTERS UP. . . OOPS!
OH, IT'S DAD'S TAX FORM. . . EH? WHAT'S THIS?
NOT APPLICABLE? BUT THAT MEANS DAD'S SAYING HE DOESN'T HAVE A DAUGHTER.
C Children
Full names of child (Surname first)
Childs date of birth
Day Month Year
NOT APPLICABLE
BUT IF I'M NOT THEIR DAUGHTER, WHO AM I? WHO AM I?
NEXT PART
More shocks for Eve!

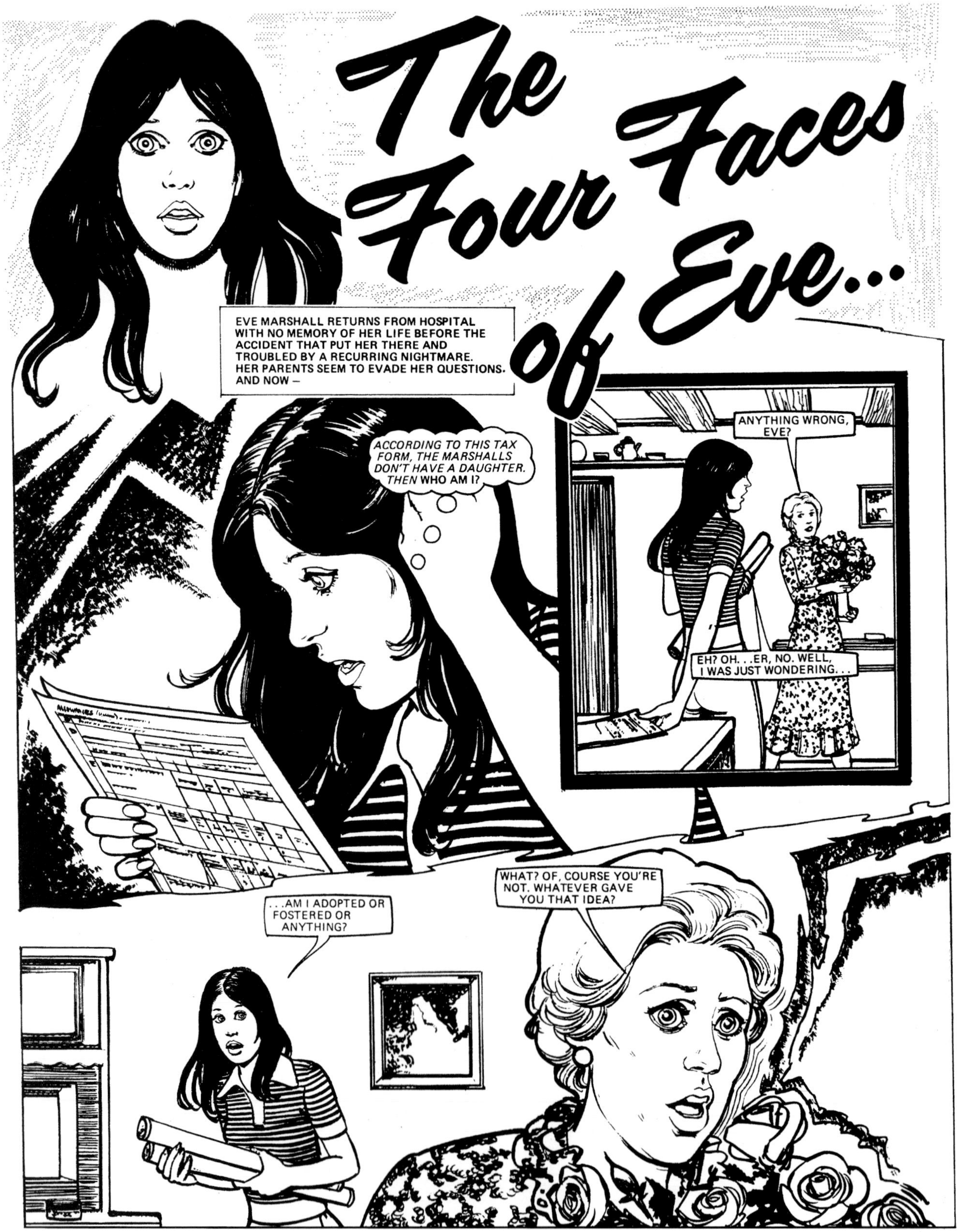
The Four Faces of Eve...
EVE MARSHALL RETURNS FROM HOSPITAL WITH NO MEMORY OF HER LIFE BEFORE THE ACCIDENT THAT PUT HER THERE AND TROUBLED BY A RECURRING NIGHTMARE. HER PARENTS SEEM TO EVADE HER QUESTIONS. AND NOW –
ACCORDING TO THIS TAX FORM, THE MARSHALLS DON'T HAVE A DAUGHTER. THEN WHO AM I?
ANYTHING WRONG, EVE?
EH? OH. . .ER, NO. WELL, I WAS JUST WONDERING. . .
. . .AM I ADOPTED OR FOSTERED OR ANYTHING?
WHAT? OF, COURSE YOU'RE NOT. WHATEVER GAVE YOU THAT IDEA?

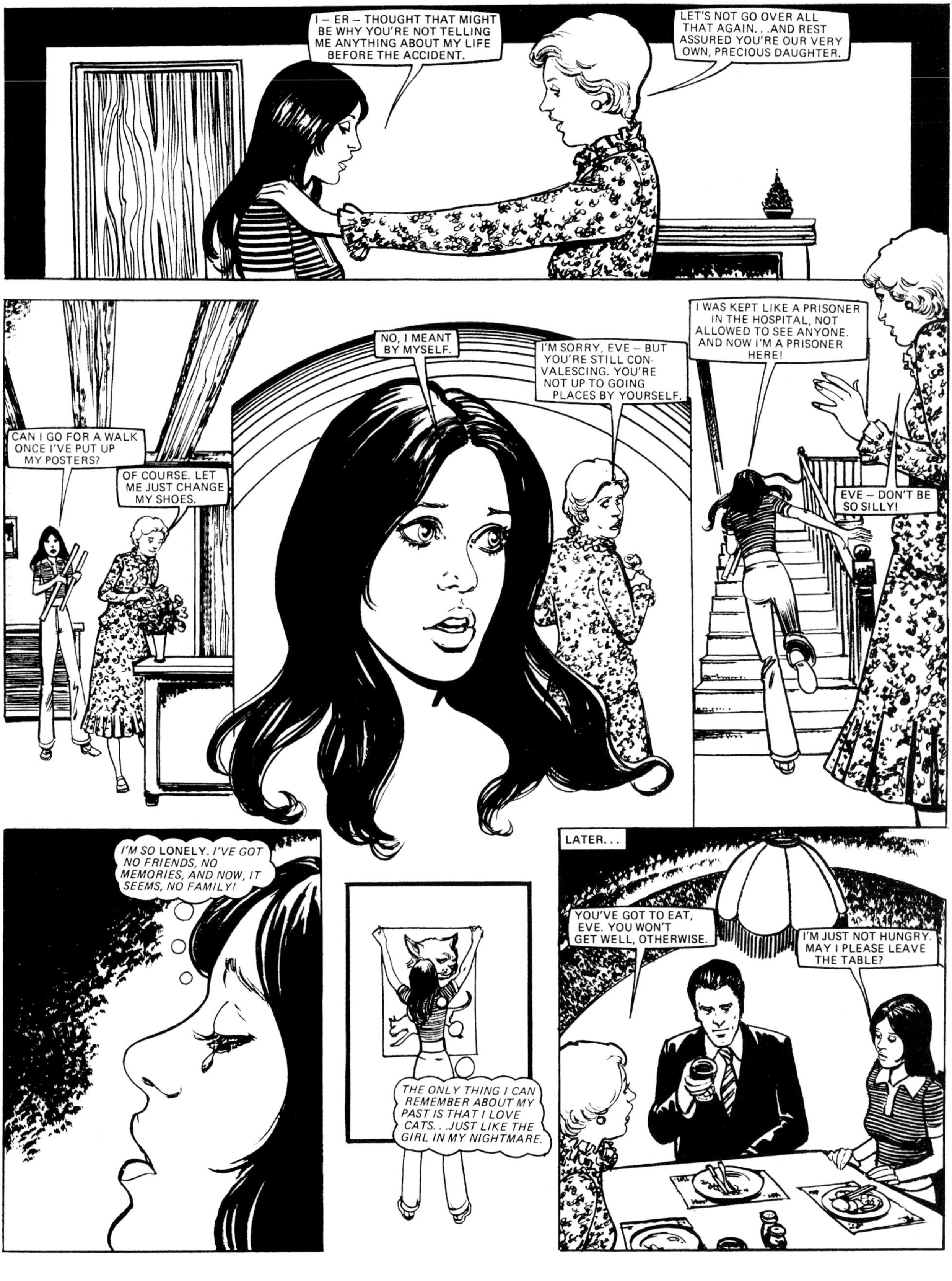

I – ER – THOUGHT THAT MIGHT BE WHY YOU'RE NOT TELLING ME ANYTHING ABOUT MY LIFE BEFORE THE ACCIDENT.
LET'S NOT GO OVER ALL THAT AGAIN. . .AND REST ASSURED YOU'RE OUR VERY OWN, PRECIOUS DAUGHTER.
CAN I GO FOR A WALK ONCE I'VE PUT UP MY POSTERS?
OF COURSE. LET ME JUST CHANGE MY SHOES.
NO, I MEANT BY MYSELF.
I'M SORRY, EVE – BUT YOU'RE STILL CONVALESCING. YOU'RE NOT UP TO GOING PLACES BY YOURSELF.
I WAS KEPT LIKE A PRISONER IN THE HOSPITAL, NOT ALLOWED TO SEE ANYONE. AND NOW I'M A PRISONER HERE!
EVE – DON'T BE SO SILLY!
I'M SO LONELY. I'VE GOT NO FRIENDS, NO MEMORIES, AND NOW, IT SEEMS, NO FAMILY!
THE ONLY THING I CAN REMEMBER ABOUT MY PAST IS THAT I LOVE CATS. . .JUST LIKE THE GIRL IN MY NIGHTMARE.
LATER. . .
YOU'VE GOT TO EAT, EVE. YOU WON'T GET WELL, OTHERWISE.
I'M JUST NOT HUNGRY. MAY I PLEASE LEAVE THE TABLE?

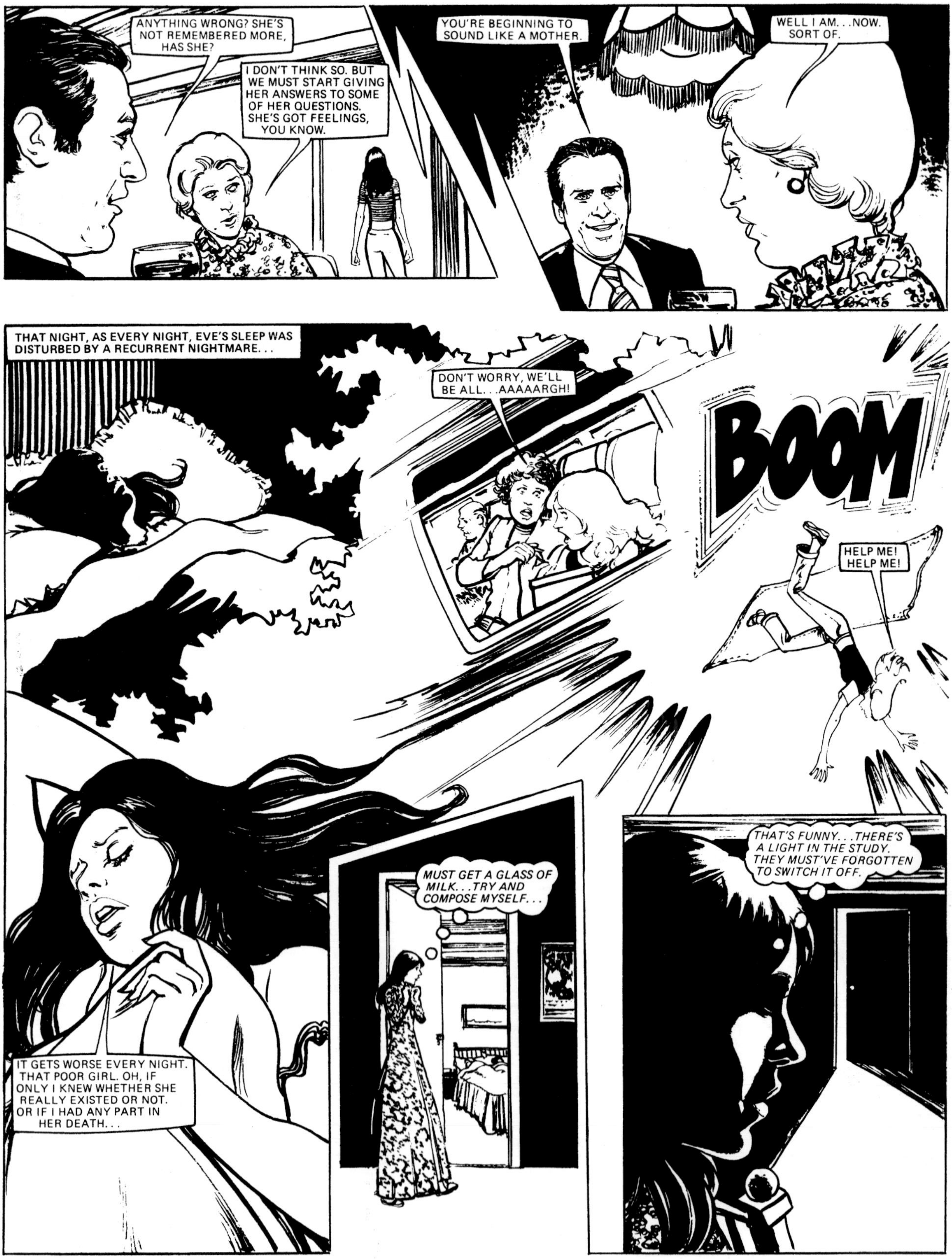

ANYTHING WRONG? SHE'S NOT REMEMBERED MORE, HAS SHE?
I DON'T THINK SO. BUT WE MUST START GIVING HER ANSWERS TO SOME OF HER QUESTIONS. SHE'S GOT FEELINGS, YOU KNOW.
YOU'RE BEGINNING TO SOUND LIKE A MOTHER.
WELL I AM. . .NOW. SORT OF.
THAT NIGHT, AS EVERY NIGHT, EVE'S SLEEP WAS DISTURBED BY A RECURRENT NIGHTMARE. . .
DON'T WORRY, WE'LL BE ALL. . .AAAAARGH!
BOOM
HELP ME! HELP ME!
IT GETS WORSE EVERY NIGHT. THAT POOR GIRL. OH, IF ONLY I KNEW WHETHER SHE REALLY EXISTED OR NOT. OR IF I HAD ANY PART IN HER DEATH. . .
MUST GET A GLASS OF MILK. . .TRY AND COMPOSE MYSELF. . .
THAT'S FUNNY. . .THERE'S A LIGHT IN THE STUDY. THEY MUST'VE FORGOTTEN TO SWITCH IT OFF.

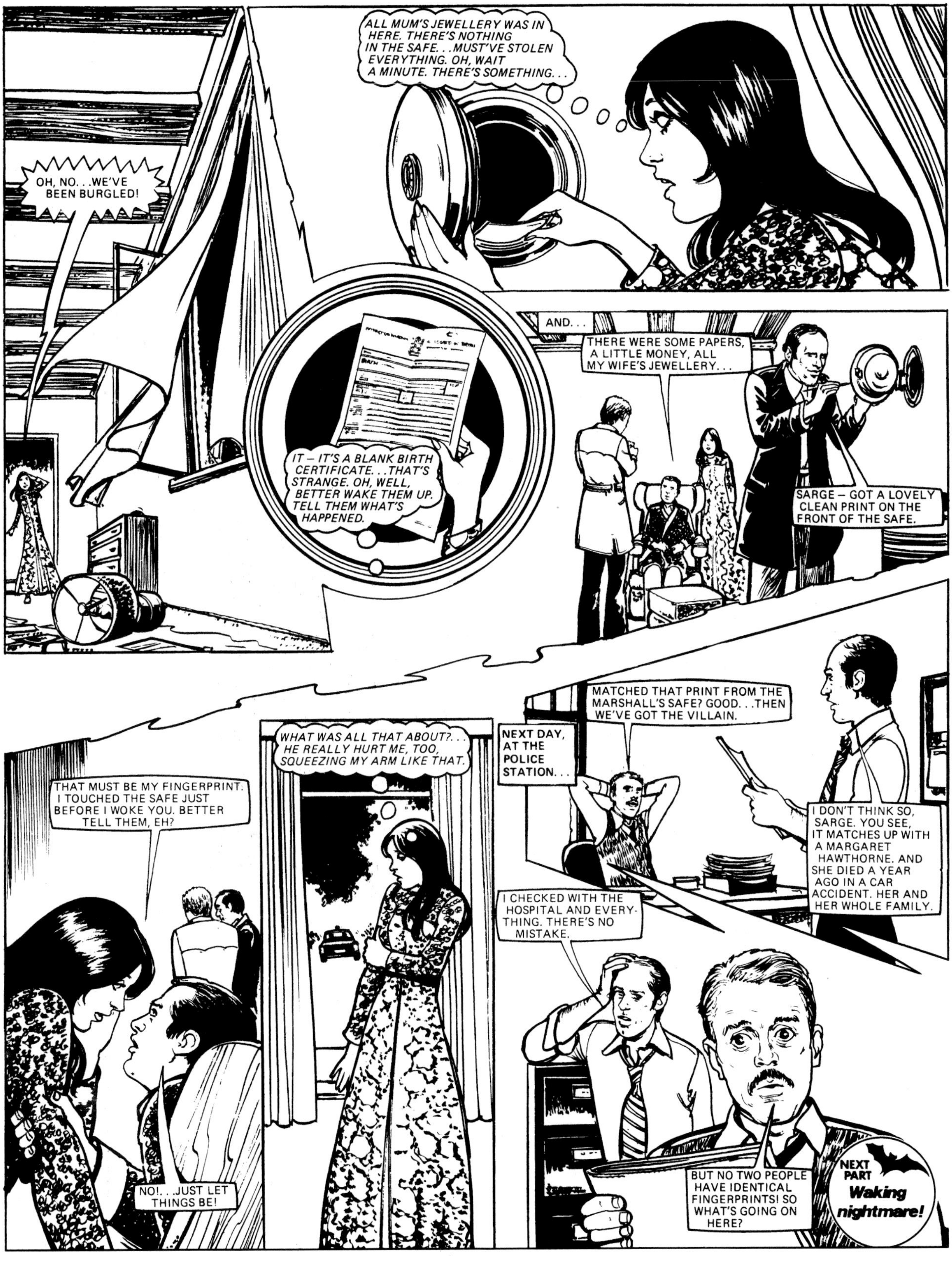

ALL MUM'S JEWELLERY WAS IN HERE. THERE'S NOTHING IN THE SAFE. . .MUST'VE STOLEN EVERYTHING. OH, WAIT A MINUTE. THERE'S SOMETHING. . .
OH, NO. . .WE'VE BEEN BURGLED!
IT – IT'S A BLANK BIRTH CERTIFICATE. . .THAT'S STRANGE. OH, WELL, BETTER WAKE THEM UP. TELL THEM WHAT'S HAPPENED.
AND. . .
THERE WERE SOME PAPERS, A LITTLE MONEY, ALL MY WIFE'S JEWELLERY. . .
SARGE – GOT A LOVELY CLEAN PRINT ON THE FRONT OF THE SAFE.
THAT MUST BE MY FINGERPRINT. I TOUCHED THE SAFE JUST BEFORE I WOKE YOU. BETTER TELL THEM, EH?
NO!. . .JUST LET THINGS BE!
WHAT WAS ALL THAT ABOUT?. . . HE REALLY HURT ME, TOO, SQUEEZING MY ARM LIKE THAT.
NEXT DAY, AT THE POLICE STATION. . .
MATCHED THAT PRINT FROM THE MARSHALL'S SAFE? GOOD. . .THEN WE'VE GOT THE VILLAIN.
I DON'T THINK SO, SARGE. YOU SEE, IT MATCHES UP WITH A MARGARET HAWTHORNE. AND SHE DIED A YEAR AGO IN A CAR ACCIDENT. HER AND HER WHOLE FAMILY.
I CHECKED WITH THE HOSPITAL AND EVERYTHING. THERE'S NO MISTAKE.
BUT NO TWO PEOPLE HAVE IDENTICAL FINGERPRINTS! SO WHAT'S GOING ON HERE?
NEXT PART Waking nightmare!

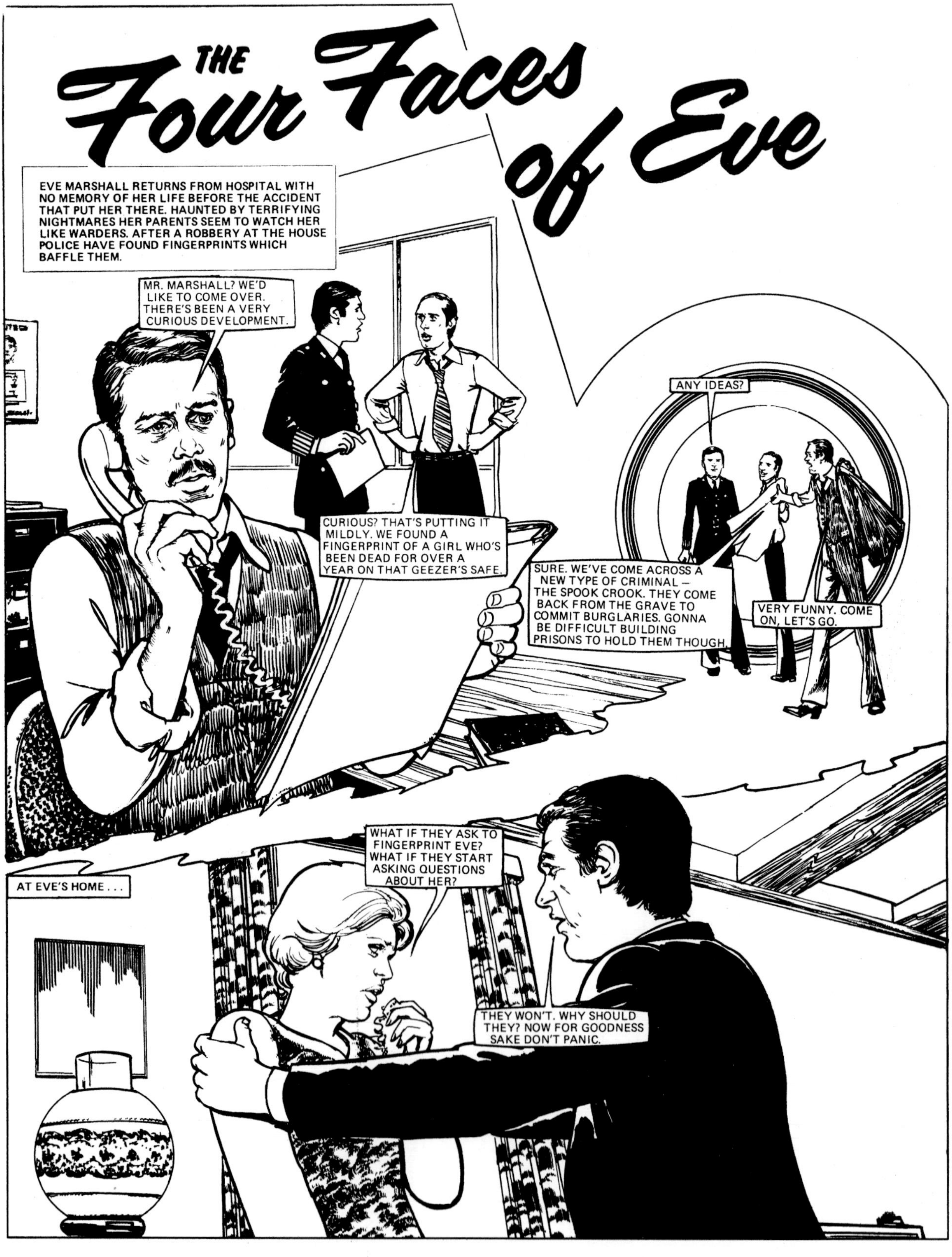
THE Four Faces of Eve
EVE MARSHALL RETURNS FROM HOSPITAL WITH NO MEMORY OF HER LIFE BEFORE THE ACCIDENT THAT PUT HER THERE. HAUNTED BY TERRIFYING NIGHTMARES HER PARENTS SEEM TO WATCH HER LIKE WARDERS. AFTER A ROBBERY AT THE HOUSE POLICE HAVE FOUND FINGERPRINTS WHICH BAFFLE THEM.
MR. MARSHALL? WE'D LIKE TO COME OVER. THERE'S BEEN A VERY CURIOUS DEVELOPMENT.
CURIOUS? THAT'S PUTTING IT MILDLY. WE FOUND A FINGERPRINT OF A GIRL WHO'S BEEN DEAD FOR OVER A YEAR ON THAT GEEZER'S SAFE.
ANY IDEAS?
SURE. WE'VE COME ACROSS A NEW TYPE OF CRIMINAL — THE SPOOK CROOK. THEY COME BACK FROM THE GRAVE TO COMMIT BURGLARIES. GONNA BE DIFFICULT BUILDING PRISONS TO HOLD THEM THOUGH.
VERY FUNNY. COME ON, LET'S GO.
AT EVE'S HOME . . .
WHAT IF THEY ASK TO FINGERPRINT EVE? WHAT IF THEY START ASKING QUESTIONS ABOUT HER?
THEY WON'T. WHY SHOULD THEY? NOW FOR GOODNESS SAKE DON'T PANIC.

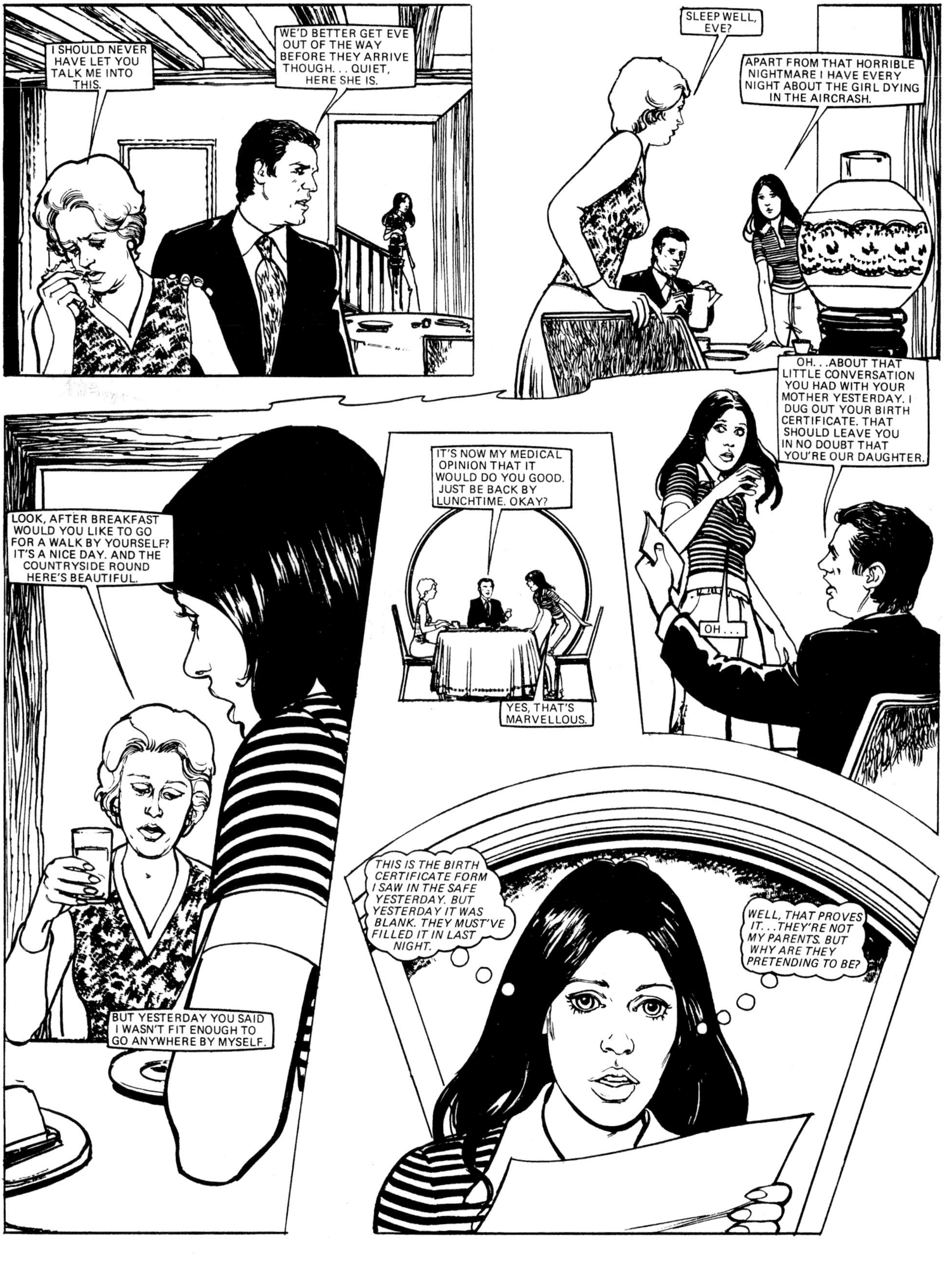
I SHOULD NEVER HAVE LET YOU TALK ME INTO THIS.
WE'D BETTER GET EVE OUT OF THE WAY BEFORE THEY ARRIVE THOUGH. . . QUIET, HERE SHE IS.
SLEEP WELL, EVE?
APART FROM THAT HORRIBLE NIGHTMARE I HAVE EVERY NIGHT ABOUT THE GIRL DYING IN THE AIRCRASH.
OH. . . ABOUT THAT LITTLE CONVERSATION YOU HAD WITH YOUR MOTHER YESTERDAY. I DUG OUT YOUR BIRTH CERTIFICATE. THAT SHOULD LEAVE YOU IN NO DOUBT THAT YOU'RE OUR DAUGHTER.
OH . . .
LOOK, AFTER BREAKFAST WOULD YOU LIKE TO GO FOR A WALK BY YOURSELF? IT'S A NICE DAY. AND THE COUNTRYSIDE ROUND HERE'S BEAUTIFUL.
BUT YESTERDAY YOU SAID I WASN'T FIT ENOUGH TO GO ANYWHERE BY MYSELF.
IT'S NOW MY MEDICAL OPINION THAT IT WOULD DO YOU GOOD. JUST BE BACK BY LUNCHTIME. OKAY?
YES, THAT'S MARVELLOUS.
THIS IS THE BIRTH CERTIFICATE FORM I SAW IN THE SAFE YESTERDAY. BUT YESTERDAY IT WAS BLANK. THEY MUST'VE FILLED IT IN LAST NIGHT.
WELL, THAT PROVES IT. . . THEY'RE NOT MY PARENTS. BUT WHY ARE THEY PRETENDING TO BE?

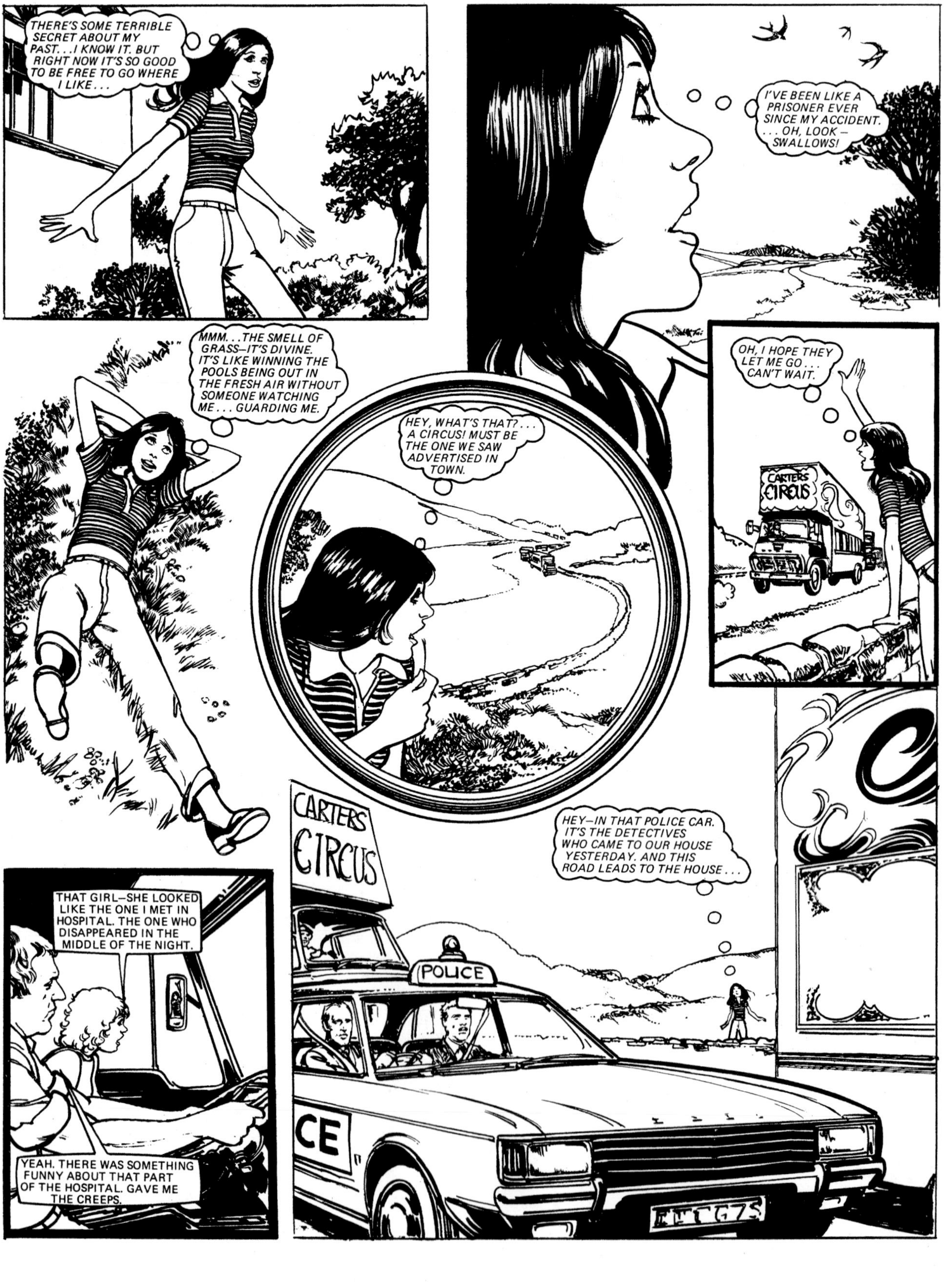
THERE'S SOME TERRIBLE SECRET ABOUT MY PAST...I KNOW IT. BUT RIGHT NOW IT'S SO GOOD TO BE FREE TO GO WHERE I LIKE...
I'VE BEEN LIKE A PRISONER EVER SINCE MY ACCIDENT. ... OH, LOOK – SWALLOWS!
MMM...THE SMELL OF GRASS–IT'S DIVINE. IT'S LIKE WINNING THE POOLS BEING OUT IN THE FRESH AIR WITHOUT SOMEONE WATCHING ME... GUARDING ME.
HEY, WHAT'S THAT?... A CIRCUS! MUST BE THE ONE WE SAW ADVERTISED IN TOWN.
OH, I HOPE THEY LET ME GO... CAN'T WAIT.
CARTERS CIRCUS
THAT GIRL–SHE LOOKED LIKE THE ONE I MET IN HOSPITAL. THE ONE WHO DISAPPEARED IN THE MIDDLE OF THE NIGHT.
YEAH. THERE WAS SOMETHING FUNNY ABOUT THAT PART OF THE HOSPITAL. GAVE ME THE CREEPS.
CARTERS CIRCUS
HEY–IN THAT POLICE CAR. IT'S THE DETECTIVES WHO CAME TO OUR HOUSE YESTERDAY. AND THIS ROAD LEADS TO THE HOUSE...
POLICE
CE

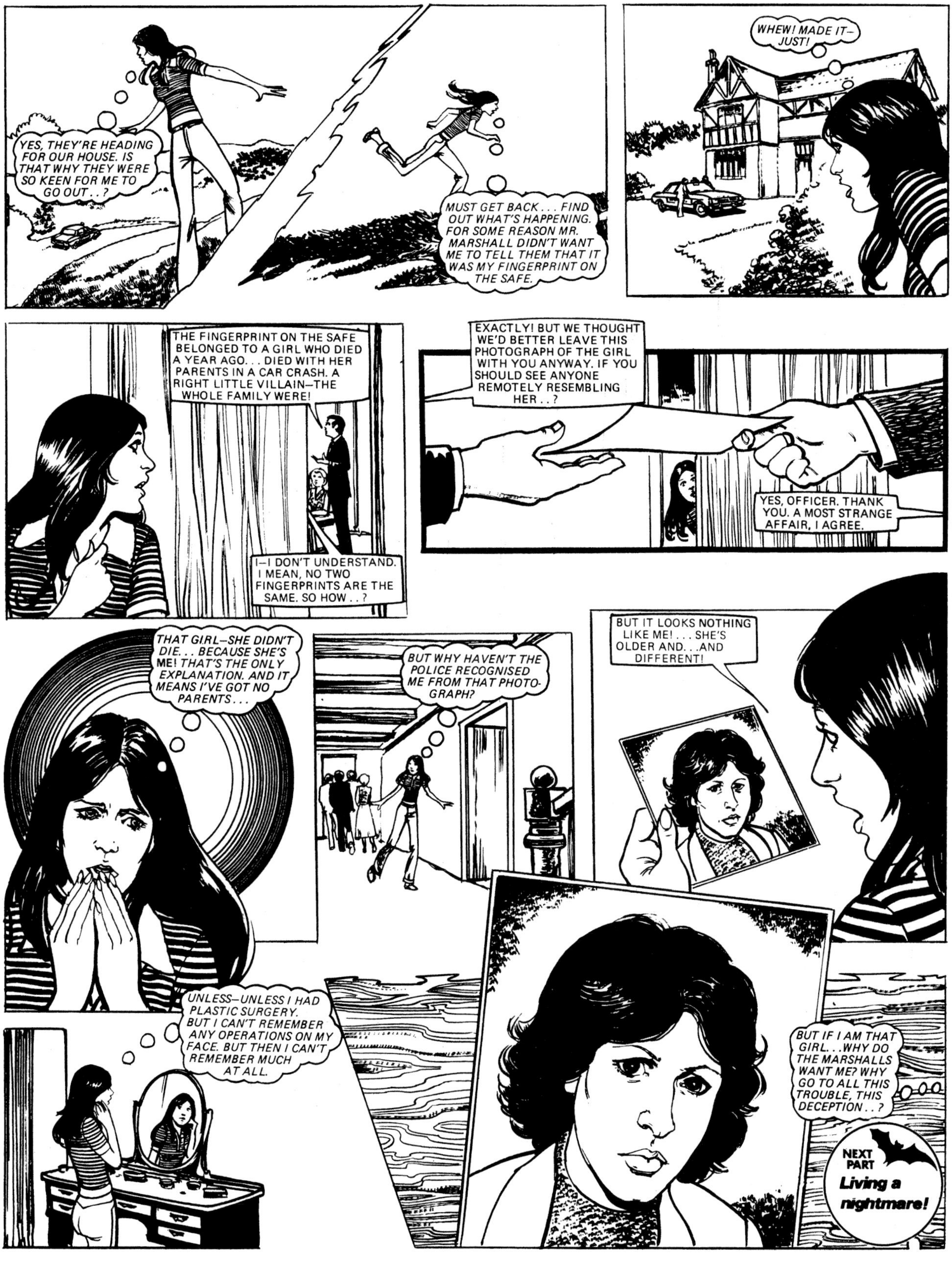

YES, THEY'RE HEADING FOR OUR HOUSE. IS THAT WHY THEY WERE SO KEEN FOR ME TO GO OUT . . ?
MUST GET BACK . . . FIND OUT WHAT'S HAPPENING. FOR SOME REASON MR. MARSHALL DIDN'T WANT ME TO TELL THEM THAT IT WAS MY FINGERPRINT ON THE SAFE.
WHEW! MADE IT— JUST!
THE FINGERPRINT ON THE SAFE BELONGED TO A GIRL WHO DIED A YEAR AGO. . . DIED WITH HER PARENTS IN A CAR CRASH. A RIGHT LITTLE VILLAIN—THE WHOLE FAMILY WERE!
I—I DON'T UNDERSTAND. I MEAN, NO TWO FINGERPRINTS ARE THE SAME. SO HOW . . ?
EXACTLY! BUT WE THOUGHT WE'D BETTER LEAVE THIS PHOTOGRAPH OF THE GIRL WITH YOU ANYWAY. IF YOU SHOULD SEE ANYONE REMOTELY RESEMBLING HER . . ?
YES, OFFICER. THANK YOU. A MOST STRANGE AFFAIR, I AGREE.
THAT GIRL—SHE DIDN'T DIE. . . BECAUSE SHE'S ME! THAT'S THE ONLY EXPLANATION. AND IT MEANS I'VE GOT NO PARENTS . . .
BUT WHY HAVEN'T THE POLICE RECOGNISED ME FROM THAT PHOTO-GRAPH?
BUT IT LOOKS NOTHING LIKE ME! . . . SHE'S OLDER AND. . .AND DIFFERENT!
UNLESS—UNLESS I HAD PLASTIC SURGERY. BUT I CAN'T REMEMBER ANY OPERATIONS ON MY FACE. BUT THEN I CAN'T REMEMBER MUCH AT ALL.
BUT IF I AM THAT GIRL. . .WHY DO THE MARSHALLS WANT ME? WHY GO TO ALL THIS TROUBLE, THIS DECEPTION . . ?
NEXT PART
Living a nightmare!

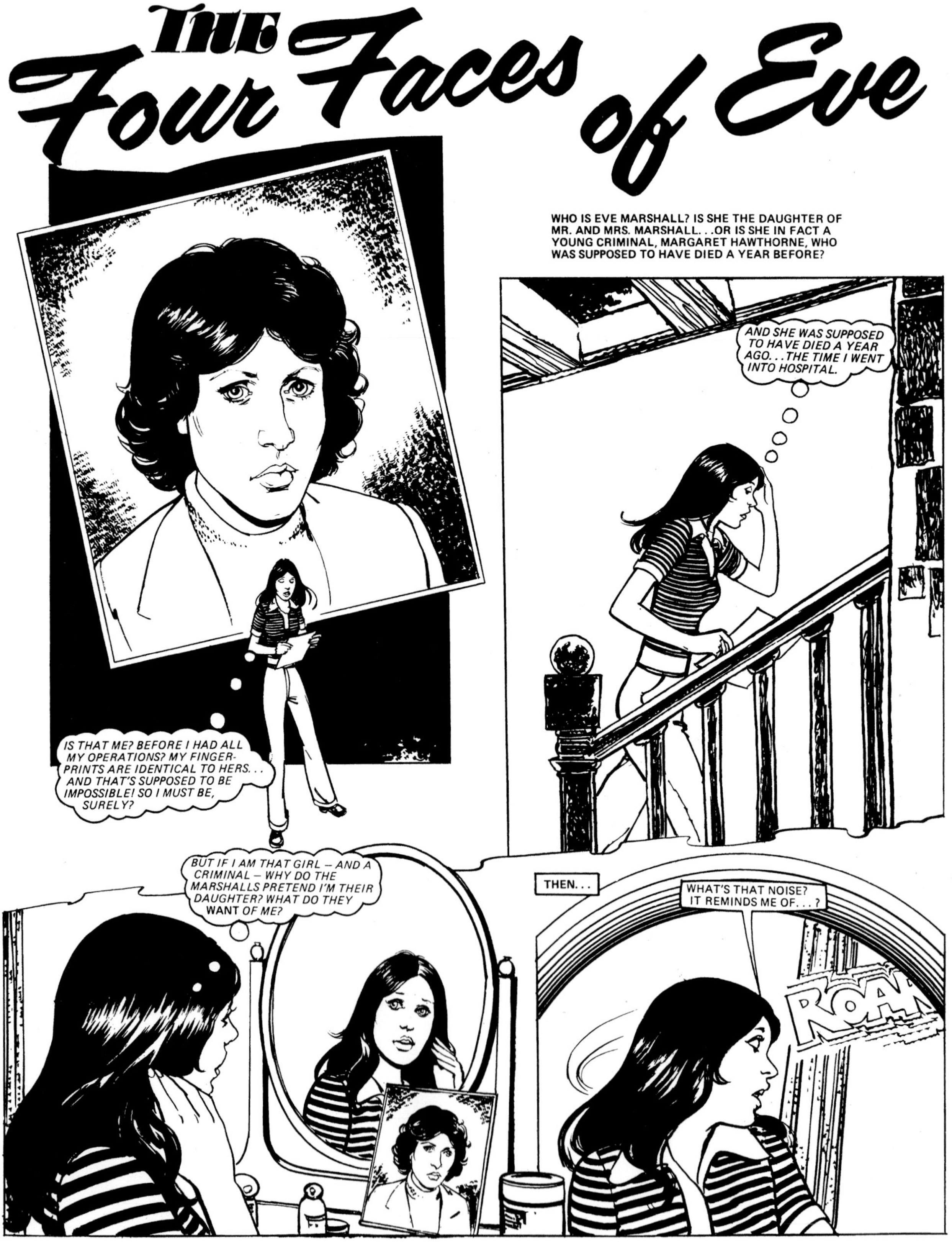
The Four Faces of Eve
WHO IS EVE MARSHALL? IS SHE THE DAUGHTER OF MR. AND MRS. MARSHALL. . .OR IS SHE IN FACT A YOUNG CRIMINAL, MARGARET HAWTHORNE, WHO WAS SUPPOSED TO HAVE DIED A YEAR BEFORE?
IS THAT ME? BEFORE I HAD ALL MY OPERATIONS? MY FINGER-PRINTS ARE IDENTICAL TO HERS. . . AND THAT'S SUPPOSED TO BE IMPOSSIBLE! SO I MUST BE, SURELY?
AND SHE WAS SUPPOSED TO HAVE DIED A YEAR AGO. . . THE TIME I WENT INTO HOSPITAL.
BUT IF I AM THAT GIRL – AND A CRIMINAL – WHY DO THE MARSHALLS PRETEND I'M THEIR DAUGHTER? WHAT DO THEY WANT OF ME?
THEN. . .
WHAT'S THAT NOISE? IT REMINDS ME OF. . .?
ROAR

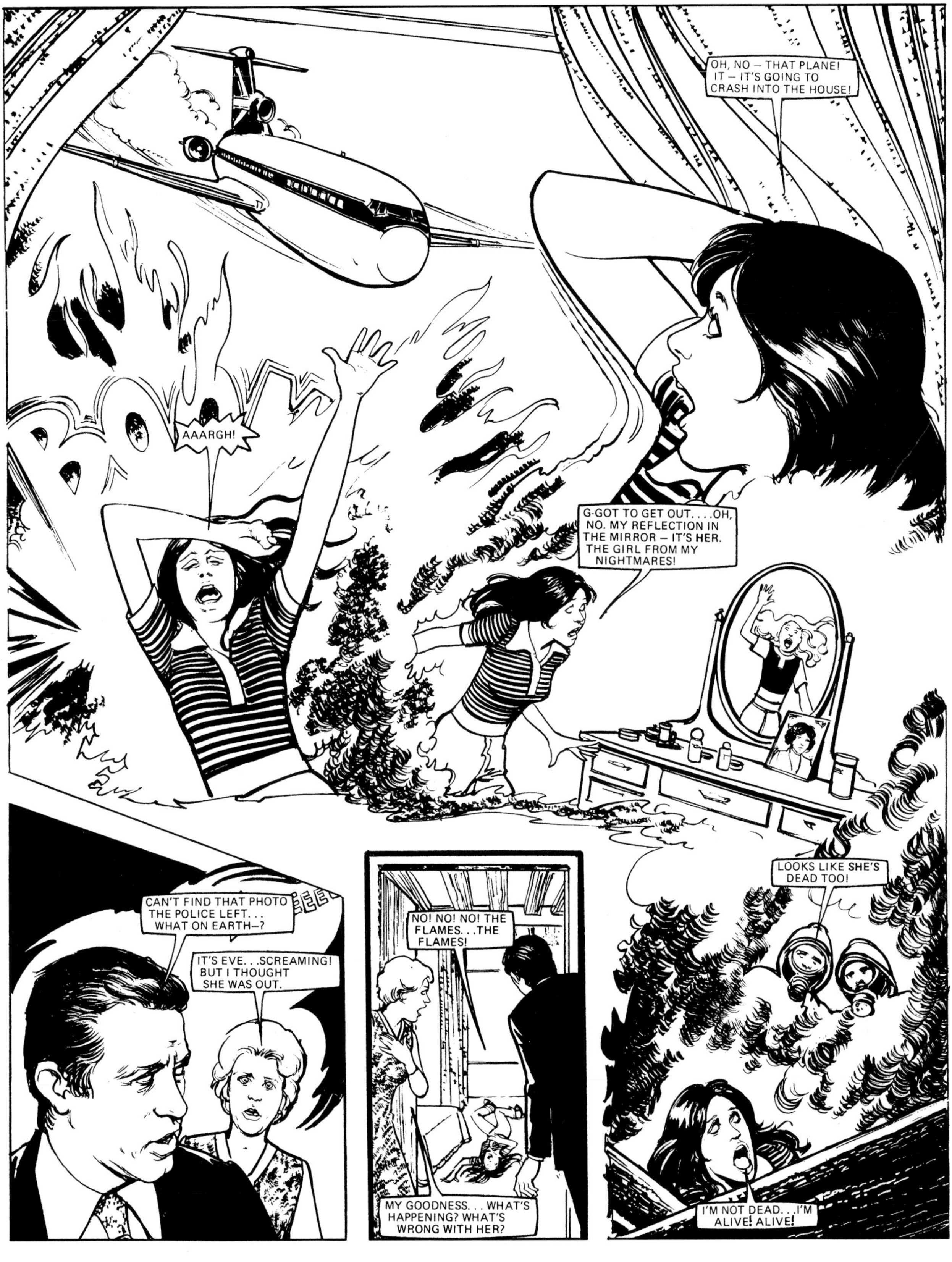
OH, NO — THAT PLANE! IT — IT'S GOING TO CRASH INTO THE HOUSE!
AAARGH!
G-GOT TO GET OUT. . . .OH, NO. MY REFLECTION IN THE MIRROR — IT'S HER. THE GIRL FROM MY NIGHTMARES!
CAN'T FIND THAT PHOTO THE POLICE LEFT. . . WHAT ON EARTH—?
IT'S EVE. . .SCREAMING! BUT I THOUGHT SHE WAS OUT.
NO! NO! NO! THE FLAMES. . .THE FLAMES!
MY GOODNESS. . . WHAT'S HAPPENING? WHAT'S WRONG WITH HER?
LOOKS LIKE SHE'S DEAD TOO!
I'M NOT DEAD. . .I'M ALIVE! ALIVE!

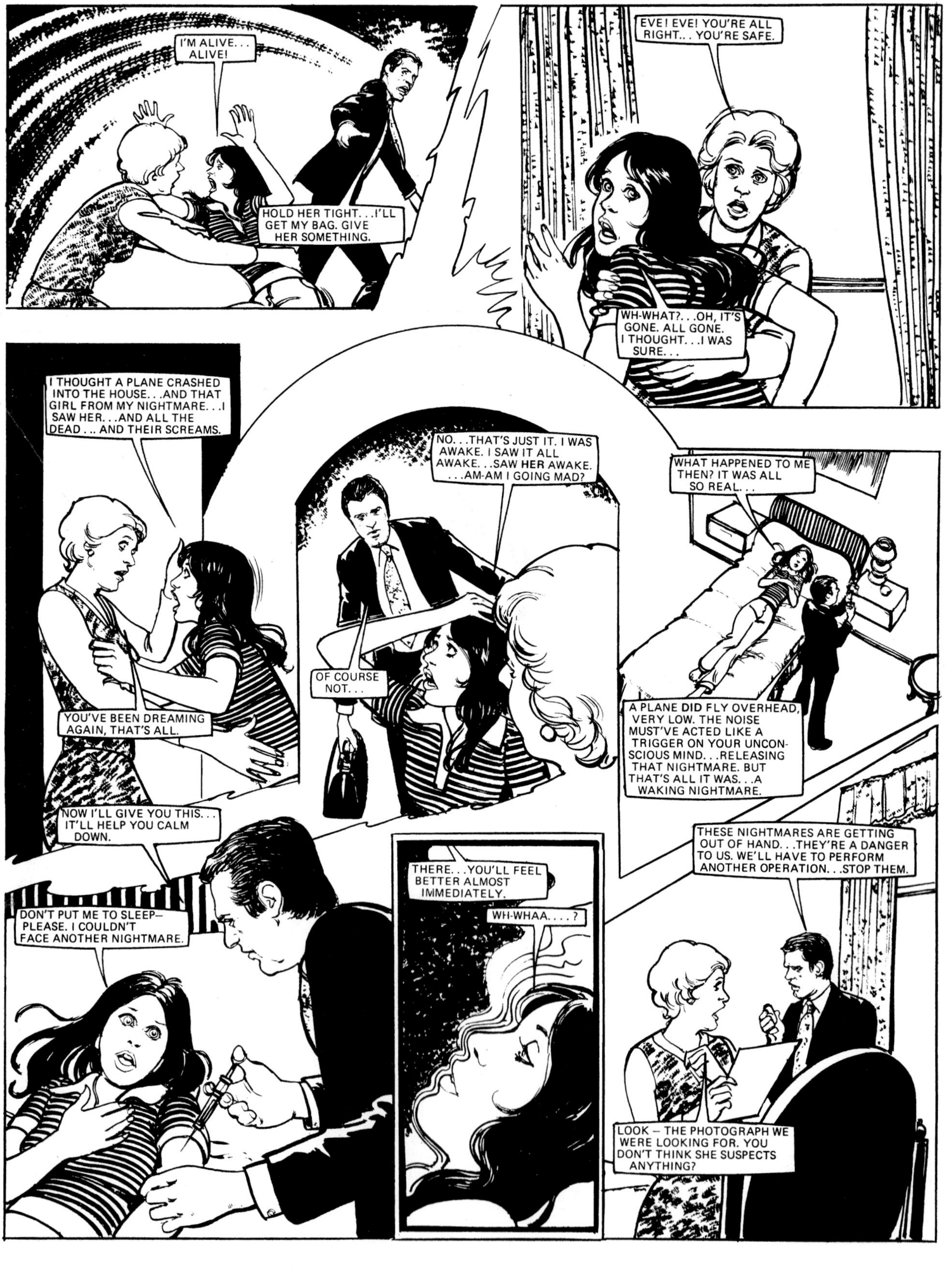
I'M ALIVE... ALIVE!
HOLD HER TIGHT...I'LL GET MY BAG. GIVE HER SOMETHING.
EVE! EVE! YOU'RE ALL RIGHT... YOU'RE SAFE.
WH-WHAT?...OH, IT'S GONE. ALL GONE. I THOUGHT...I WAS SURE...
I THOUGHT A PLANE CRASHED INTO THE HOUSE...AND THAT GIRL FROM MY NIGHTMARE...I SAW HER...AND ALL THE DEAD... AND THEIR SCREAMS.
YOU'VE BEEN DREAMING AGAIN, THAT'S ALL.
NO...THAT'S JUST IT. I WAS AWAKE. I SAW IT ALL AWAKE...SAW HER AWAKE. ...AM-AM I GOING MAD?
OF COURSE NOT...
WHAT HAPPENED TO ME THEN? IT WAS ALL SO REAL...
A PLANE DID FLY OVERHEAD, VERY LOW. THE NOISE MUST'VE ACTED LIKE A TRIGGER ON YOUR UNCONSCIOUS MIND...RELEASING THAT NIGHTMARE. BUT THAT'S ALL IT WAS...A WAKING NIGHTMARE.
NOW I'LL GIVE YOU THIS... IT'LL HELP YOU CALM DOWN.
DON'T PUT ME TO SLEEP— PLEASE. I COULDN'T FACE ANOTHER NIGHTMARE.
THERE...YOU'LL FEEL BETTER ALMOST IMMEDIATELY.
WH-WHAA....?
THESE NIGHTMARES ARE GETTING OUT OF HAND...THEY'RE A DANGER TO US. WE'LL HAVE TO PERFORM ANOTHER OPERATION...STOP THEM.
LOOK – THE PHOTOGRAPH WE WERE LOOKING FOR. YOU DON'T THINK SHE SUSPECTS ANYTHING?

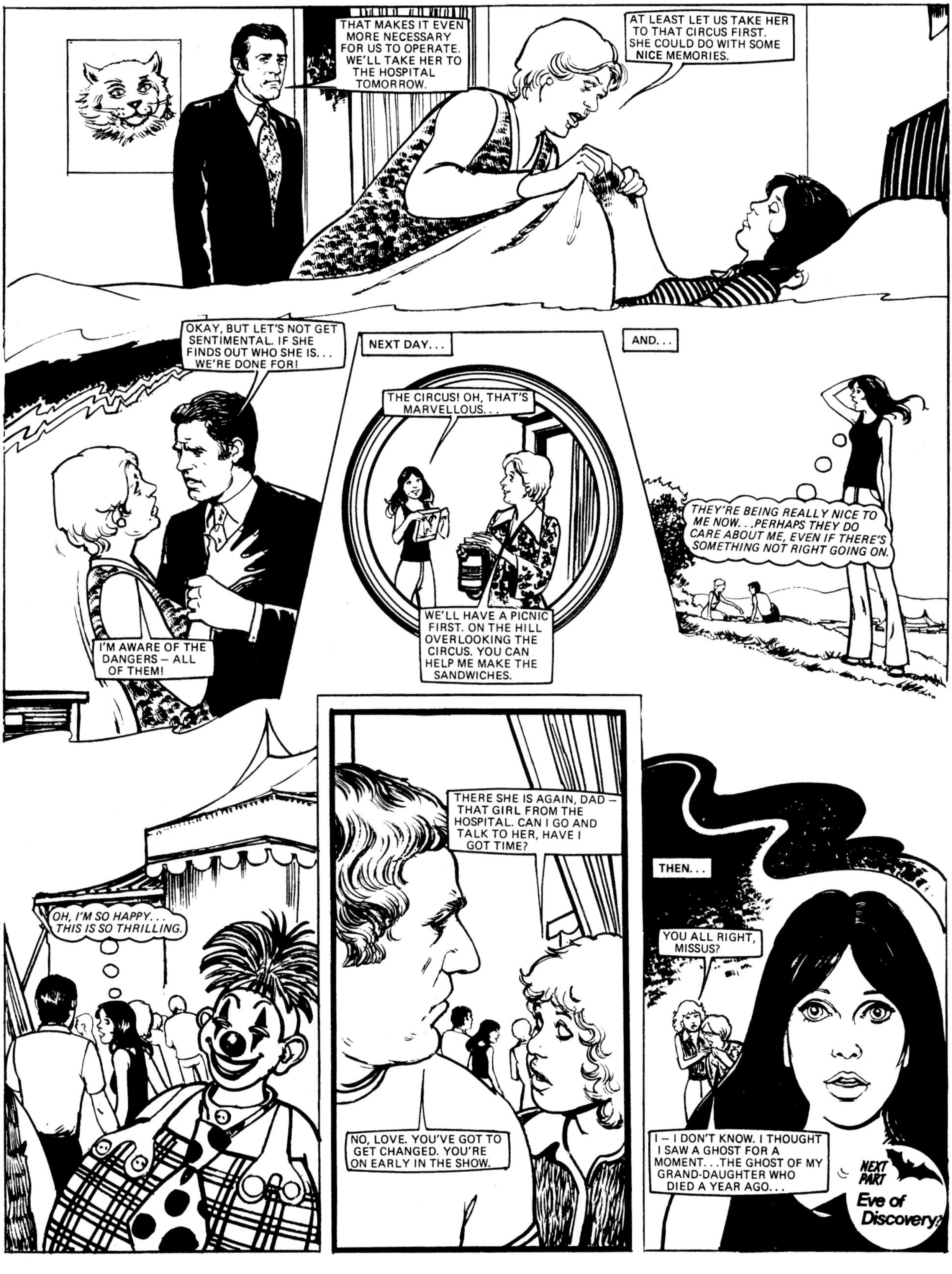
THAT MAKES IT EVEN MORE NECESSARY FOR US TO OPERATE. WE'LL TAKE HER TO THE HOSPITAL TOMORROW.
AT LEAST LET US TAKE HER TO THAT CIRCUS FIRST. SHE COULD DO WITH SOME NICE MEMORIES.
OKAY, BUT LET'S NOT GET SENTIMENTAL. IF SHE FINDS OUT WHO SHE IS... WE'RE DONE FOR!
I'M AWARE OF THE DANGERS – ALL OF THEM!
NEXT DAY...
THE CIRCUS! OH, THAT'S MARVELLOUS...
WE'LL HAVE A PICNIC FIRST. ON THE HILL OVERLOOKING THE CIRCUS. YOU CAN HELP ME MAKE THE SANDWICHES.
AND...
THEY'RE BEING REALLY NICE TO ME NOW...PERHAPS THEY DO CARE ABOUT ME, EVEN IF THERE'S SOMETHING NOT RIGHT GOING ON.
OH, I'M SO HAPPY... THIS IS SO THRILLING.
THERE SHE IS AGAIN, DAD – THAT GIRL FROM THE HOSPITAL. CAN I GO AND TALK TO HER, HAVE I GOT TIME?
NO, LOVE. YOU'VE GOT TO GET CHANGED. YOU'RE ON EARLY IN THE SHOW.
THEN...
YOU ALL RIGHT, MISSUS?
I – I DON'T KNOW. I THOUGHT I SAW A GHOST FOR A MOMENT...THE GHOST OF MY GRAND-DAUGHTER WHO DIED A YEAR AGO...
NEXT PART
Eve of Discovery?

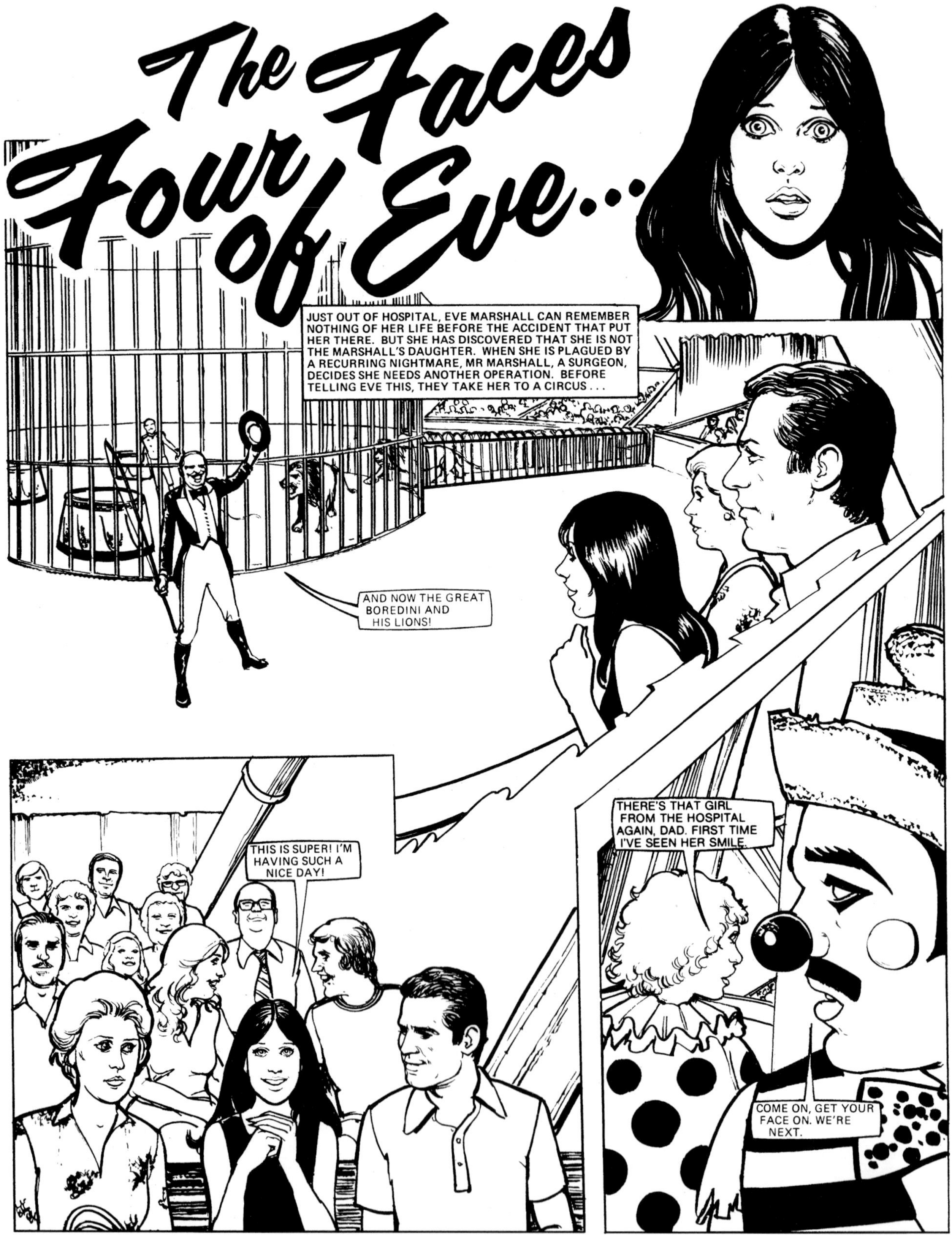
The Four Faces of Eve...
JUST OUT OF HOSPITAL, EVE MARSHALL CAN REMEMBER NOTHING OF HER LIFE BEFORE THE ACCIDENT THAT PUT HER THERE. BUT SHE HAS DISCOVERED THAT SHE IS NOT THE MARSHALL'S DAUGHTER. WHEN SHE IS PLAGUED BY A RECURRING NIGHTMARE, MR MARSHALL, A SURGEON, DECIDES SHE NEEDS ANOTHER OPERATION. BEFORE TELLING EVE THIS, THEY TAKE HER TO A CIRCUS . . .
AND NOW THE GREAT BOREDINI AND HIS LIONS!
THIS IS SUPER! I'M HAVING SUCH A NICE DAY!
THERE'S THAT GIRL FROM THE HOSPITAL AGAIN, DAD. FIRST TIME I'VE SEEN HER SMILE.
COME ON, GET YOUR FACE ON. WE'RE NEXT.

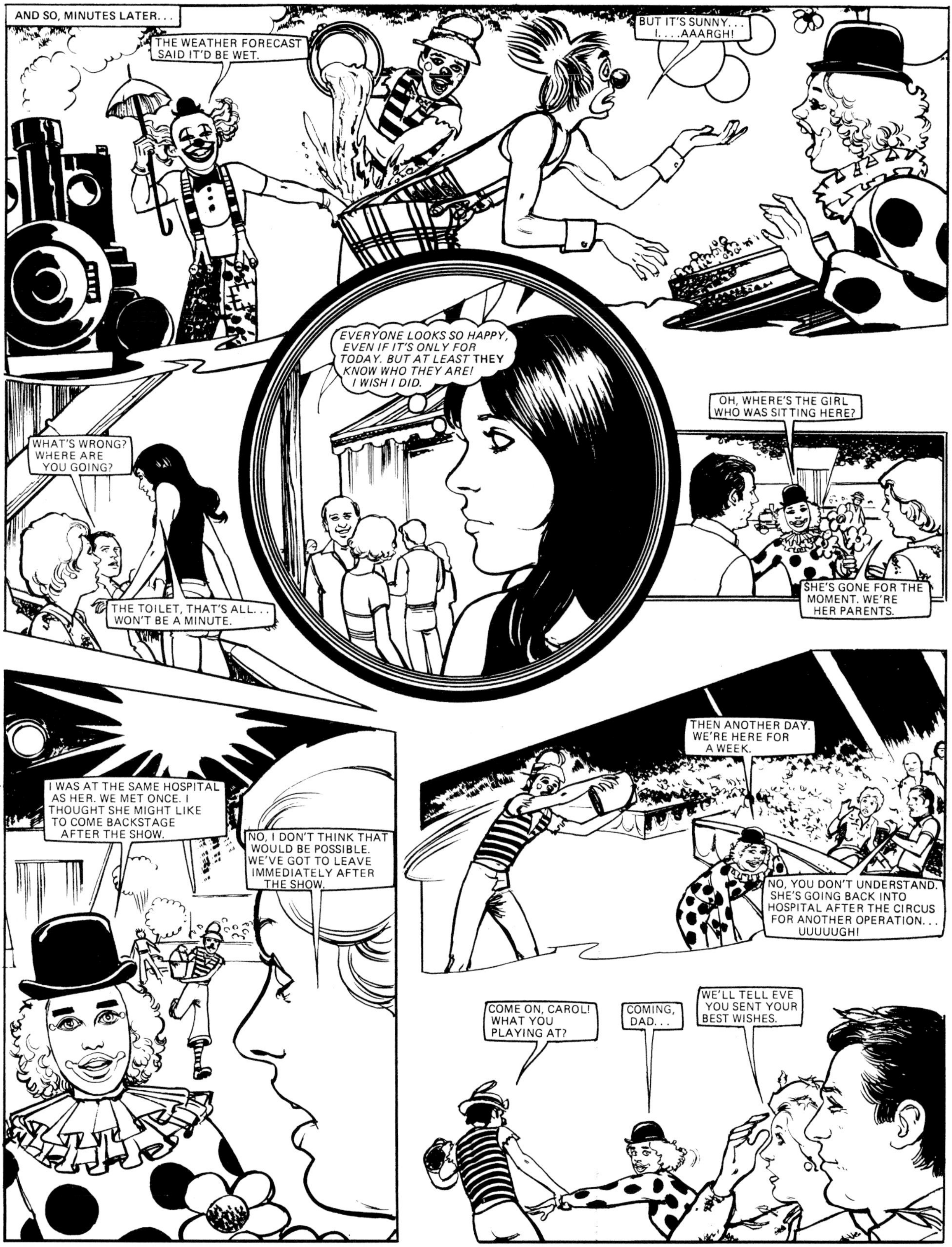
AND SO, MINUTES LATER. . .
THE WEATHER FORECAST SAID IT'D BE WET.
BUT IT'S SUNNY. . . I. . . .AAARGH!
EVERYONE LOOKS SO HAPPY, EVEN IF IT'S ONLY FOR TODAY. BUT AT LEAST THEY KNOW WHO THEY ARE! I WISH I DID.
WHAT'S WRONG? WHERE ARE YOU GOING?
THE TOILET, THAT'S ALL. . . WON'T BE A MINUTE.
OH, WHERE'S THE GIRL WHO WAS SITTING HERE?
SHE'S GONE FOR THE MOMENT. WE'RE HER PARENTS.
I WAS AT THE SAME HOSPITAL AS HER. WE MET ONCE. I THOUGHT SHE MIGHT LIKE TO COME BACKSTAGE AFTER THE SHOW.
NO, I DON'T THINK THAT WOULD BE POSSIBLE. WE'VE GOT TO LEAVE IMMEDIATELY AFTER THE SHOW.
THEN ANOTHER DAY. WE'RE HERE FOR A WEEK.
NO, YOU DON'T UNDERSTAND. SHE'S GOING BACK INTO HOSPITAL AFTER THE CIRCUS FOR ANOTHER OPERATION. . . UUUUUGH!
COME ON, CAROL! WHAT YOU PLAYING AT?
COMING, DAD. . .
WE'LL TELL EVE YOU SENT YOUR BEST WISHES.

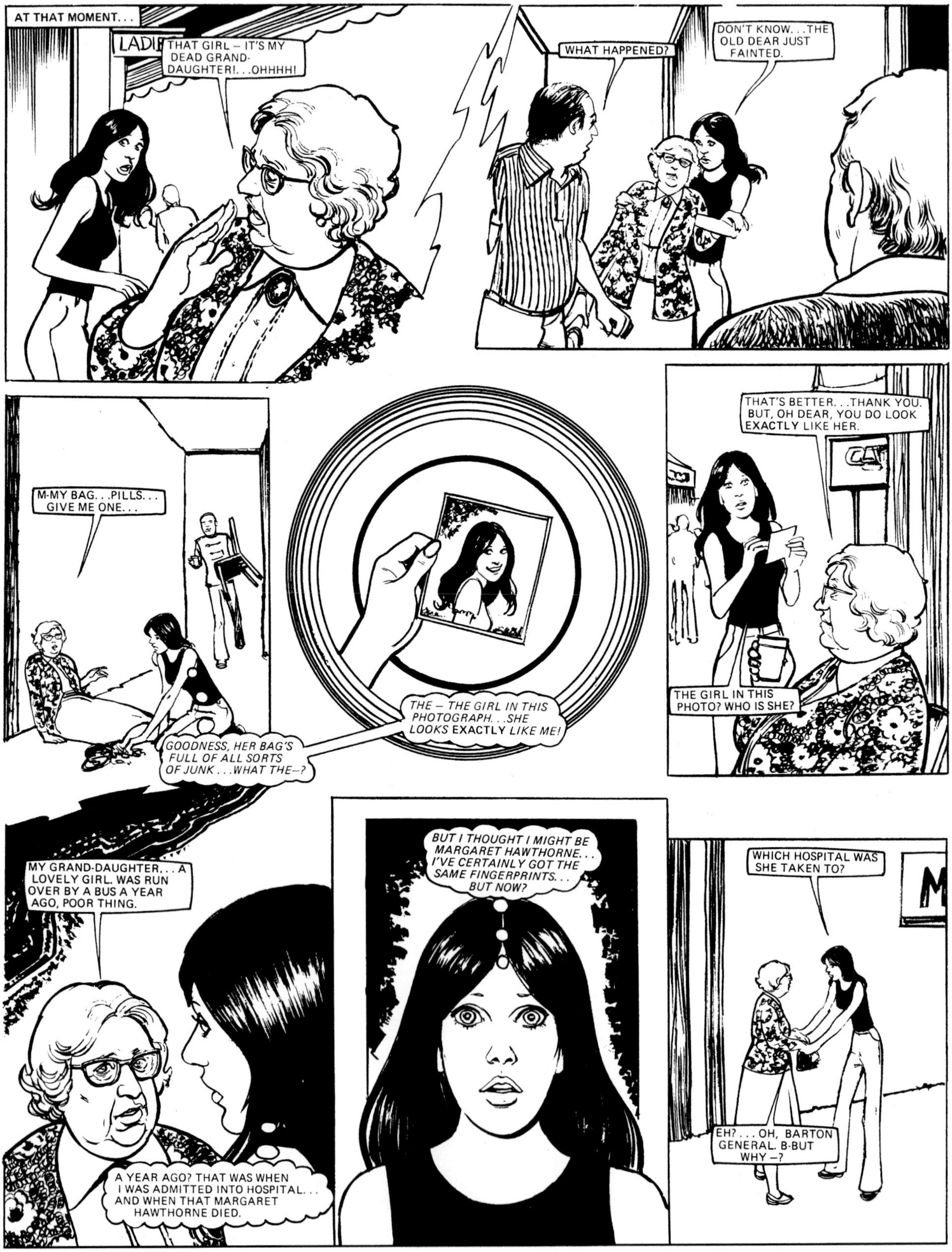
AT THAT MOMENT. . .
LADIE
THAT GIRL – IT'S MY DEAD GRAND-DAUGHTER!. . .OHHHH!
WHAT HAPPENED?
DON'T KNOW. . .THE OLD DEAR JUST FAINTED.
M-MY BAG. . .PILLS. . . GIVE ME ONE. . .
GOODNESS, HER BAG'S FULL OF ALL SORTS OF JUNK. . .WHAT THE–?
THE – THE GIRL IN THIS PHOTOGRAPH. . .SHE LOOKS EXACTLY LIKE ME!
THAT'S BETTER. . .THANK YOU. BUT, OH DEAR, YOU DO LOOK EXACTLY LIKE HER.
THE GIRL IN THIS PHOTO? WHO IS SHE?
MY GRAND-DAUGHTER. . . A LOVELY GIRL. WAS RUN OVER BY A BUS A YEAR AGO, POOR THING.
A YEAR AGO? THAT WAS WHEN I WAS ADMITTED INTO HOSPITAL. . . AND WHEN THAT MARGARET HAWTHORNE DIED.
BUT I THOUGHT I MIGHT BE MARGARET HAWTHORNE. . . I'VE CERTAINLY GOT THE SAME FINGERPRINTS. . . BUT NOW?
WHICH HOSPITAL WAS SHE TAKEN TO?
EH?. . . OH, BARTON GENERAL. B-BUT WHY –?

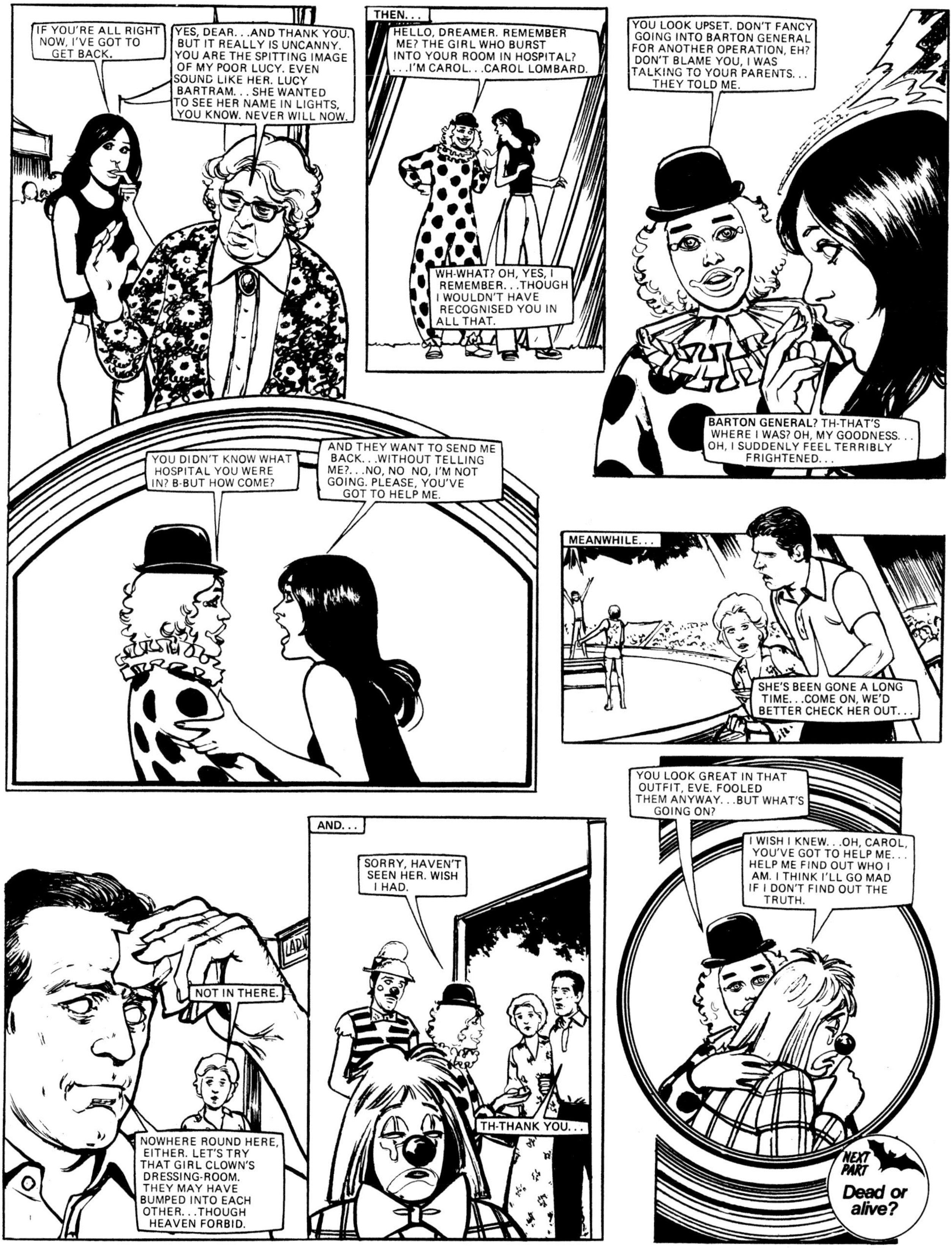

IF YOU'RE ALL RIGHT NOW, I'VE GOT TO GET BACK.
YES, DEAR...AND THANK YOU. BUT IT REALLY IS UNCANNY. YOU ARE THE SPITTING IMAGE OF MY POOR LUCY. EVEN SOUND LIKE HER. LUCY BARTRAM...SHE WANTED TO SEE HER NAME IN LIGHTS, YOU KNOW. NEVER WILL NOW.
THEN...
HELLO, DREAMER. REMEMBER ME? THE GIRL WHO BURST INTO YOUR ROOM IN HOSPITAL? ...I'M CAROL...CAROL LOMBARD.
WH-WHAT? OH, YES, I REMEMBER...THOUGH I WOULDN'T HAVE RECOGNISED YOU IN ALL THAT.
YOU LOOK UPSET. DON'T FANCY GOING INTO BARTON GENERAL FOR ANOTHER OPERATION, EH? DON'T BLAME YOU, I WAS TALKING TO YOUR PARENTS... THEY TOLD ME.
BARTON GENERAL? TH-THAT'S WHERE I WAS? OH, MY GOODNESS... OH, I SUDDENLY FEEL TERRIBLY FRIGHTENED...
YOU DIDN'T KNOW WHAT HOSPITAL YOU WERE IN? B-BUT HOW COME?
AND THEY WANT TO SEND ME BACK...WITHOUT TELLING ME?...NO, NO NO, I'M NOT GOING. PLEASE, YOU'VE GOT TO HELP ME.
MEANWHILE...
SHE'S BEEN GONE A LONG TIME...COME ON, WE'D BETTER CHECK HER OUT...
NOT IN THERE.
NOWHERE ROUND HERE, EITHER. LET'S TRY THAT GIRL CLOWN'S DRESSING-ROOM. THEY MAY HAVE BUMPED INTO EACH OTHER...THOUGH HEAVEN FORBID.
AND...
SORRY, HAVEN'T SEEN HER. WISH I HAD.
TH-THANK YOU...
YOU LOOK GREAT IN THAT OUTFIT, EVE. FOOLED THEM ANYWAY...BUT WHAT'S GOING ON?
I WISH I KNEW...OH, CAROL, YOU'VE GOT TO HELP ME... HELP ME FIND OUT WHO I AM. I THINK I'LL GO MAD IF I DON'T FIND OUT THE TRUTH.
NEXT PART
Dead or alive?

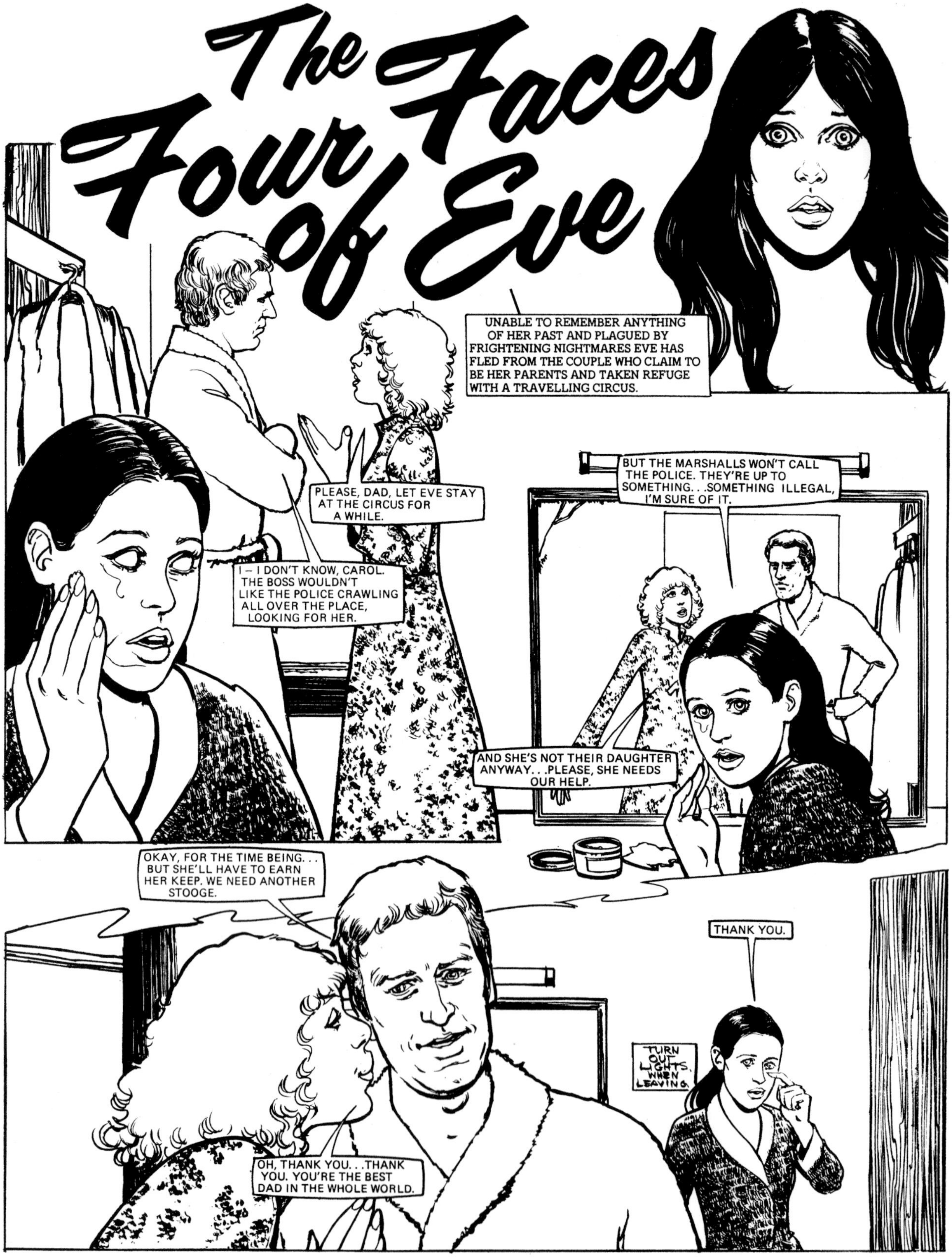
The Four Faces of Eve
UNABLE TO REMEMBER ANYTHING OF HER PAST AND PLAGUED BY FRIGHTENING NIGHTMARES EVE HAS FLED FROM THE COUPLE WHO CLAIM TO BE HER PARENTS AND TAKEN REFUGE WITH A TRAVELLING CIRCUS.
PLEASE, DAD, LET EVE STAY AT THE CIRCUS FOR A WHILE.
I — I DON'T KNOW, CAROL. THE BOSS WOULDN'T LIKE THE POLICE CRAWLING ALL OVER THE PLACE, LOOKING FOR HER.
BUT THE MARSHALLS WON'T CALL THE POLICE. THEY'RE UP TO SOMETHING. . .SOMETHING ILLEGAL, I'M SURE OF IT.
AND SHE'S NOT THEIR DAUGHTER ANYWAY. . .PLEASE, SHE NEEDS OUR HELP.
OKAY, FOR THE TIME BEING. . . BUT SHE'LL HAVE TO EARN HER KEEP. WE NEED ANOTHER STOOGE.
TURN OUT LIGHTS WHEN LEAVING.
THANK YOU.
OH, THANK YOU. . .THANK YOU. YOU'RE THE BEST DAD IN THE WHOLE WORLD.

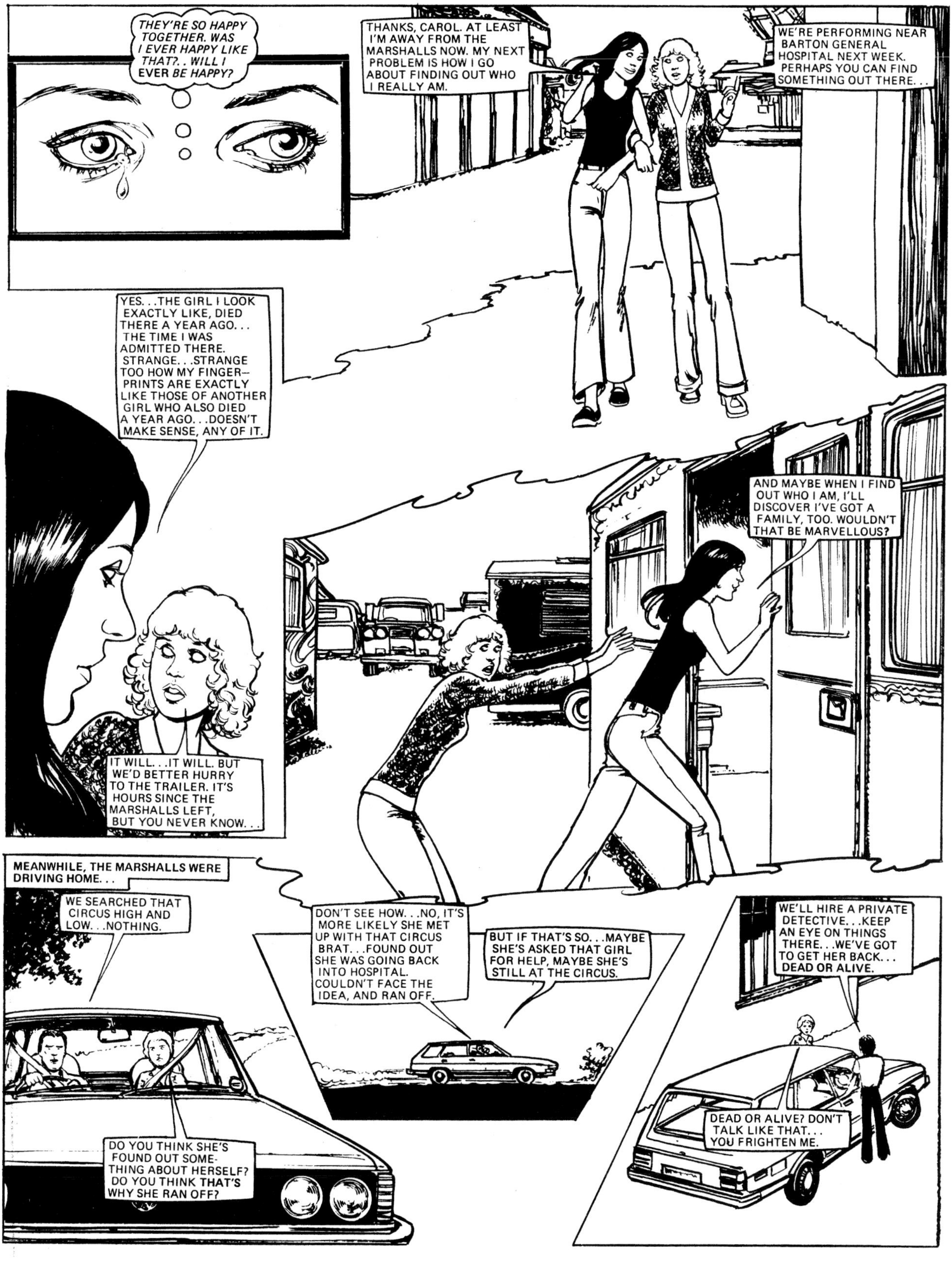
THEY'RE SO HAPPY TOGETHER. WAS I EVER HAPPY LIKE THAT?. . WILL I EVER BE HAPPY?
THANKS, CAROL. AT LEAST I'M AWAY FROM THE MARSHALLS NOW. MY NEXT PROBLEM IS HOW I GO ABOUT FINDING OUT WHO I REALLY AM.
WE'RE PERFORMING NEAR BARTON GENERAL HOSPITAL NEXT WEEK. PERHAPS YOU CAN FIND SOMETHING OUT THERE. . .
YES. . .THE GIRL I LOOK EXACTLY LIKE, DIED THERE A YEAR AGO. . . THE TIME I WAS ADMITTED THERE. STRANGE. . .STRANGE TOO HOW MY FINGER-PRINTS ARE EXACTLY LIKE THOSE OF ANOTHER GIRL WHO ALSO DIED A YEAR AGO. . .DOESN'T MAKE SENSE, ANY OF IT.
IT WILL. . .IT WILL. BUT WE'D BETTER HURRY TO THE TRAILER. IT'S HOURS SINCE THE MARSHALLS LEFT, BUT YOU NEVER KNOW. . .
AND MAYBE WHEN I FIND OUT WHO I AM, I'LL DISCOVER I'VE GOT A FAMILY, TOO. WOULDN'T THAT BE MARVELLOUS?
MEANWHILE, THE MARSHALLS WERE DRIVING HOME. . .
WE SEARCHED THAT CIRCUS HIGH AND LOW. . .NOTHING.
DO YOU THINK SHE'S FOUND OUT SOME-THING ABOUT HERSELF? DO YOU THINK THAT'S WHY SHE RAN OFF?
DON'T SEE HOW. . .NO, IT'S MORE LIKELY SHE MET UP WITH THAT CIRCUS BRAT. . .FOUND OUT SHE WAS GOING BACK INTO HOSPITAL. COULDN'T FACE THE IDEA, AND RAN OFF.
BUT IF THAT'S SO. . .MAYBE SHE'S ASKED THAT GIRL FOR HELP, MAYBE SHE'S STILL AT THE CIRCUS.
WE'LL HIRE A PRIVATE DETECTIVE. . .KEEP AN EYE ON THINGS THERE. . .WE'VE GOT TO GET HER BACK. . . DEAD OR ALIVE.
DEAD OR ALIVE? DON'T TALK LIKE THAT. . . YOU FRIGHTEN ME.

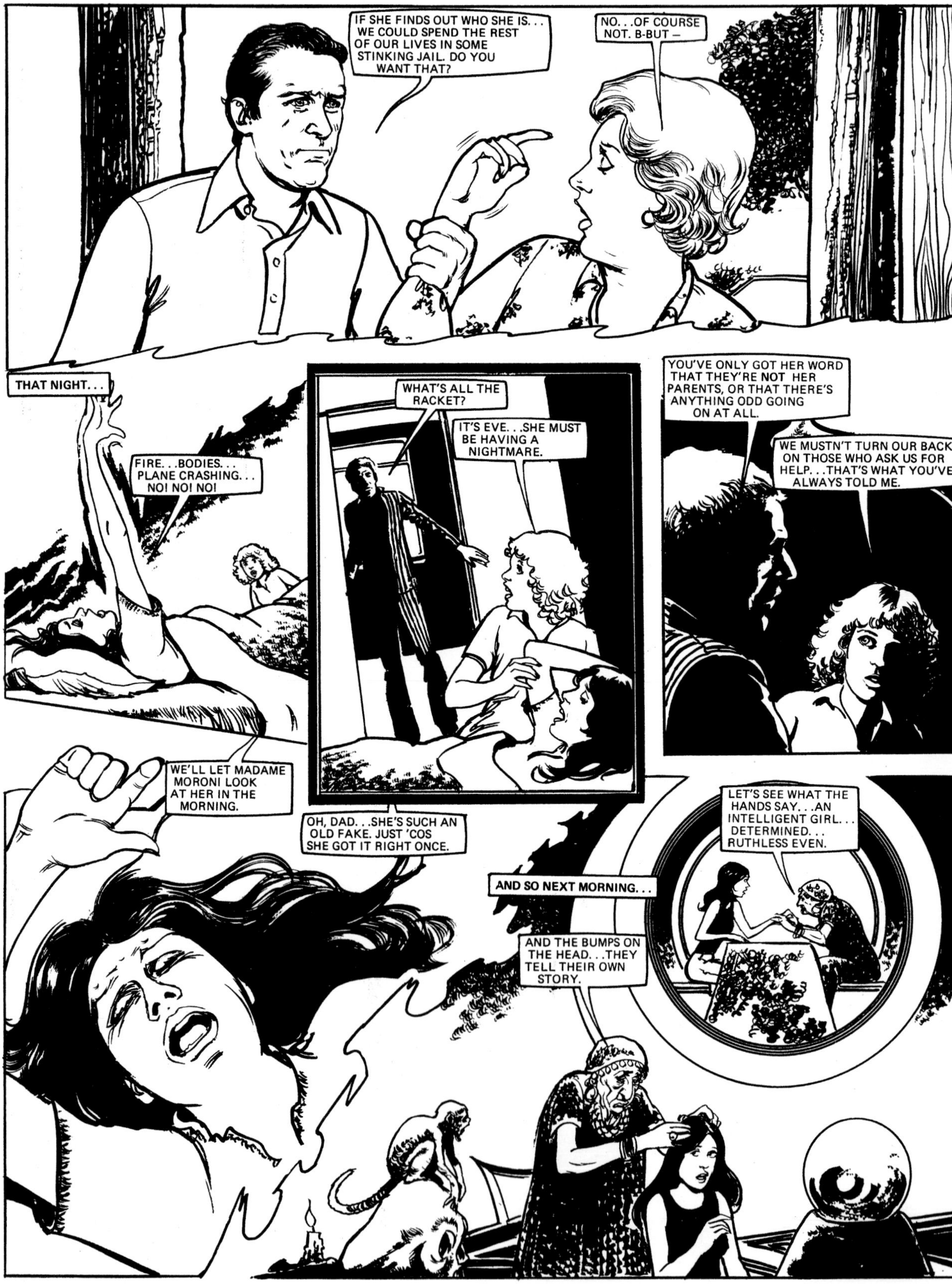
IF SHE FINDS OUT WHO SHE IS... WE COULD SPEND THE REST OF OUR LIVES IN SOME STINKING JAIL. DO YOU WANT THAT?
NO...OF COURSE NOT. B-BUT –
THAT NIGHT...
FIRE...BODIES... PLANE CRASHING... NO! NO! NO!
WHAT'S ALL THE RACKET?
IT'S EVE...SHE MUST BE HAVING A NIGHTMARE.
WE'LL LET MADAME MORONI LOOK AT HER IN THE MORNING.
OH, DAD...SHE'S SUCH AN OLD FAKE. JUST 'COS SHE GOT IT RIGHT ONCE.
YOU'VE ONLY GOT HER WORD THAT THEY'RE NOT HER PARENTS, OR THAT THERE'S ANYTHING ODD GOING ON AT ALL.
WE MUSTN'T TURN OUR BACKS ON THOSE WHO ASK US FOR HELP...THAT'S WHAT YOU'VE ALWAYS TOLD ME.
AND SO NEXT MORNING...
LET'S SEE WHAT THE HANDS SAY...AN INTELLIGENT GIRL... DETERMINED... RUTHLESS EVEN.
AND THE BUMPS ON THE HEAD...THEY TELL THEIR OWN STORY.

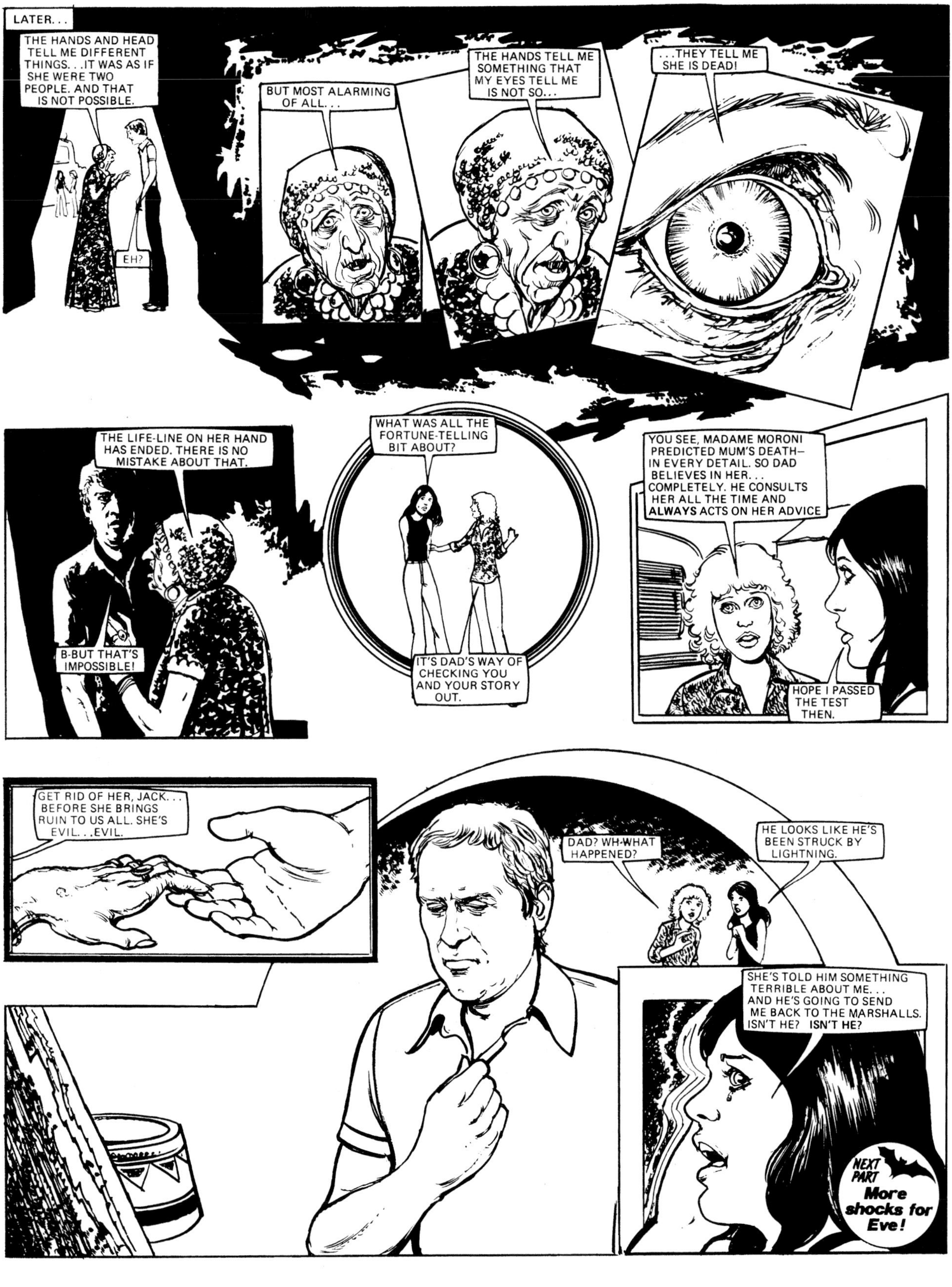
LATER...
THE HANDS AND HEAD TELL ME DIFFERENT THINGS... IT WAS AS IF SHE WERE TWO PEOPLE. AND THAT IS NOT POSSIBLE.
EH?
BUT MOST ALARMING OF ALL...
THE HANDS TELL ME SOMETHING THAT MY EYES TELL ME IS NOT SO...
...THEY TELL ME SHE IS DEAD!
THE LIFE-LINE ON HER HAND HAS ENDED. THERE IS NO MISTAKE ABOUT THAT.
B-BUT THAT'S IMPOSSIBLE!
WHAT WAS ALL THE FORTUNE-TELLING BIT ABOUT?
IT'S DAD'S WAY OF CHECKING YOU AND YOUR STORY OUT.
YOU SEE, MADAME MORONI PREDICTED MUM'S DEATH— IN EVERY DETAIL. SO DAD BELIEVES IN HER... COMPLETELY. HE CONSULTS HER ALL THE TIME AND ALWAYS ACTS ON HER ADVICE
HOPE I PASSED THE TEST THEN.
GET RID OF HER, JACK... BEFORE SHE BRINGS RUIN TO US ALL. SHE'S EVIL... EVIL.
DAD? WH-WHAT HAPPENED?
HE LOOKS LIKE HE'S BEEN STRUCK BY LIGHTNING.
SHE'S TOLD HIM SOMETHING TERRIBLE ABOUT ME... AND HE'S GOING TO SEND ME BACK TO THE MARSHALLS. ISN'T HE? ISN'T HE?
NEXT PART More shocks for Eve!

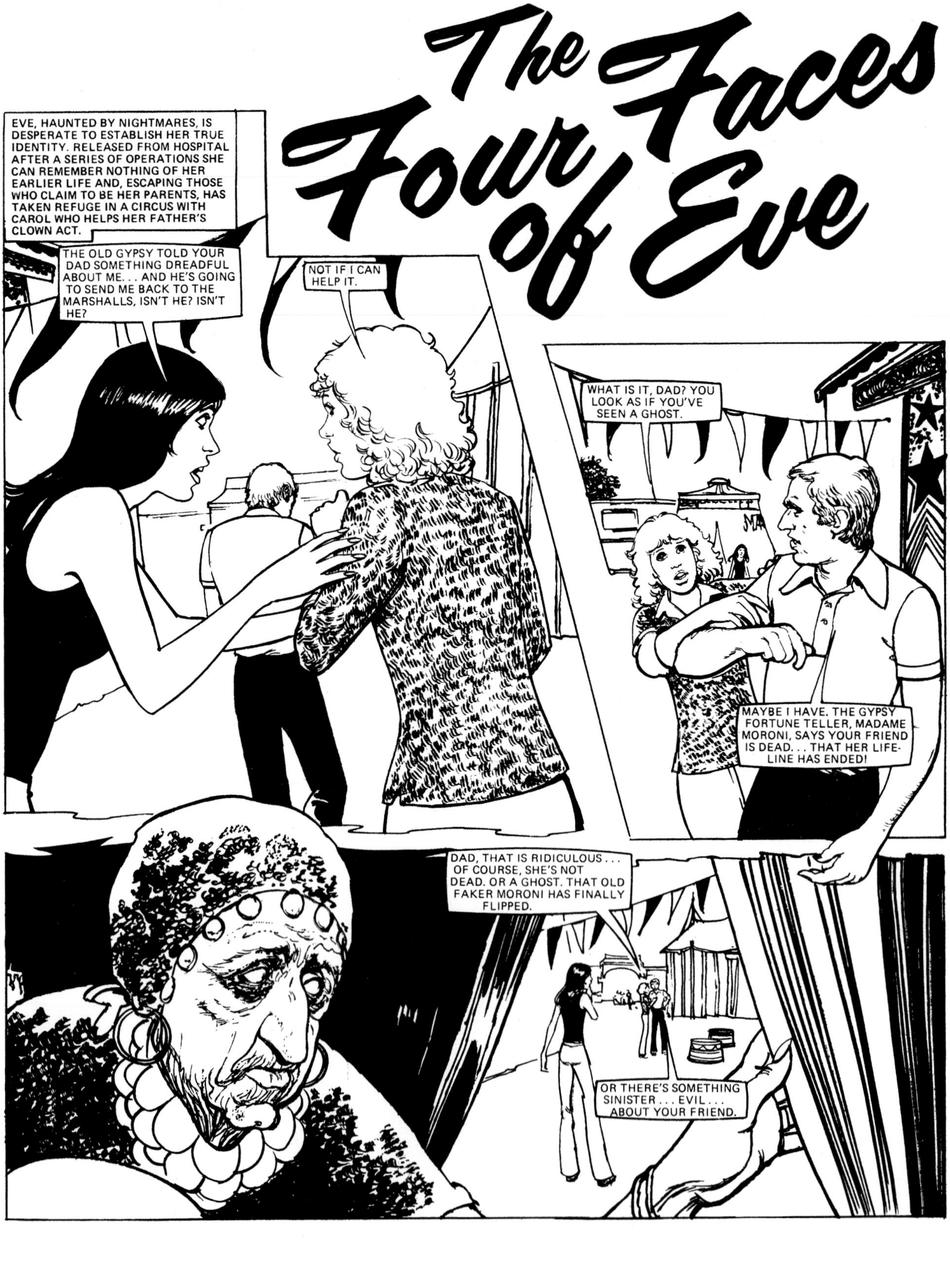

The Four Faces of Eve
EVE, HAUNTED BY NIGHTMARES, IS DESPERATE TO ESTABLISH HER TRUE IDENTITY. RELEASED FROM HOSPITAL AFTER A SERIES OF OPERATIONS SHE CAN REMEMBER NOTHING OF HER EARLIER LIFE AND, ESCAPING THOSE WHO CLAIM TO BE HER PARENTS, HAS TAKEN REFUGE IN A CIRCUS WITH CAROL WHO HELPS HER FATHER'S CLOWN ACT.
THE OLD GYPSY TOLD YOUR DAD SOMETHING DREADFUL ABOUT ME... AND HE'S GOING TO SEND ME BACK TO THE MARSHALLS, ISN'T HE? ISN'T HE?
NOT IF I CAN HELP IT.
WHAT IS IT, DAD? YOU LOOK AS IF YOU'VE SEEN A GHOST.
MAYBE I HAVE. THE GYPSY FORTUNE TELLER, MADAME MORONI, SAYS YOUR FRIEND IS DEAD... THAT HER LIFE-LINE HAS ENDED!
DAD, THAT IS RIDICULOUS... OF COURSE, SHE'S NOT DEAD. OR A GHOST. THAT OLD FAKER MORONI HAS FINALLY FLIPPED.
OR THERE'S SOMETHING SINISTER... EVIL... ABOUT YOUR FRIEND.

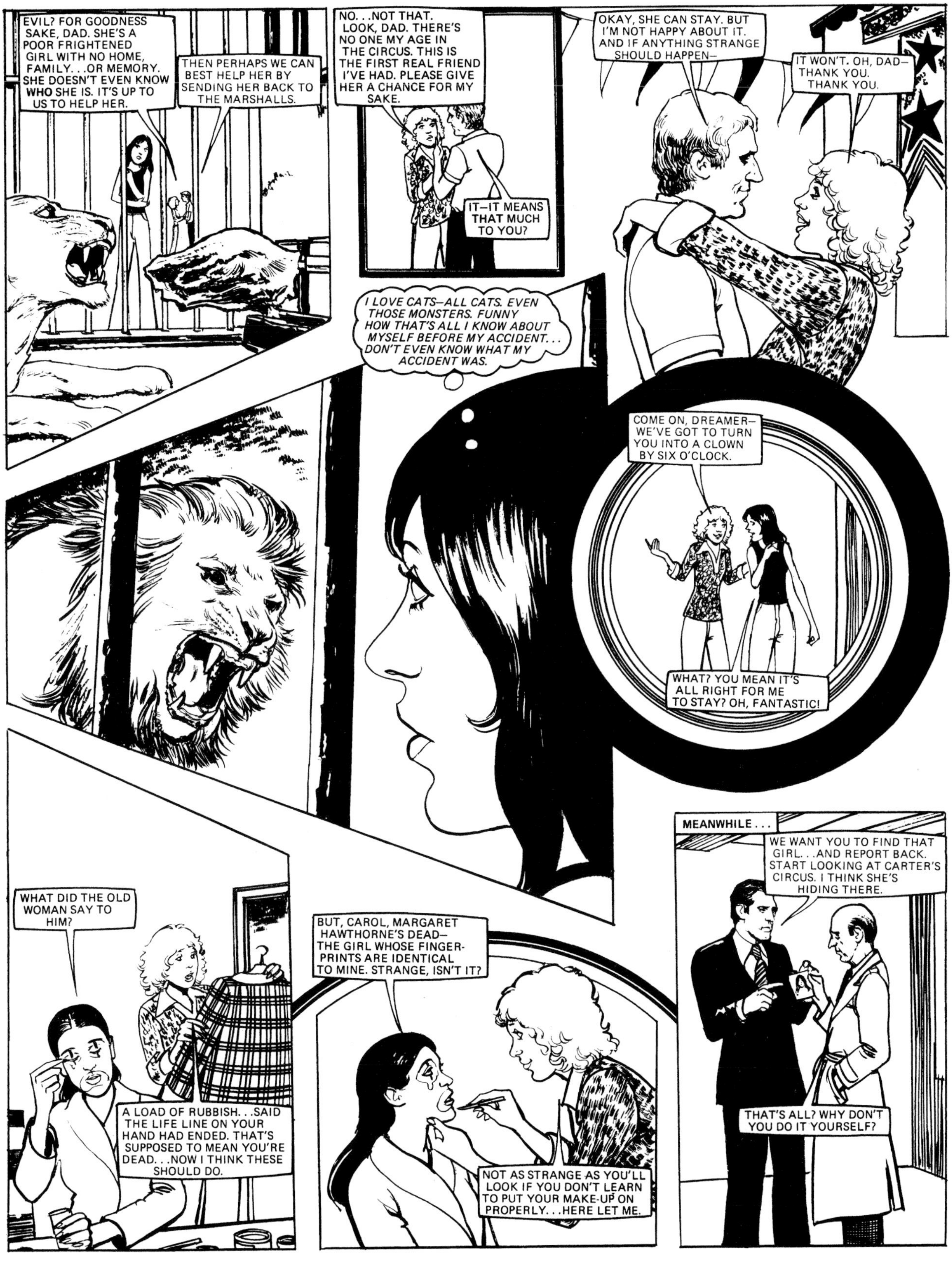
EVIL? FOR GOODNESS SAKE, DAD. SHE'S A POOR FRIGHTENED GIRL WITH NO HOME, FAMILY. . .OR MEMORY. SHE DOESN'T EVEN KNOW WHO SHE IS. IT'S UP TO US TO HELP HER.
THEN PERHAPS WE CAN BEST HELP HER BY SENDING HER BACK TO THE MARSHALLS.
NO. . .NOT THAT. LOOK, DAD. THERE'S NO ONE MY AGE IN THE CIRCUS. THIS IS THE FIRST REAL FRIEND I'VE HAD. PLEASE GIVE HER A CHANCE FOR MY SAKE.
IT—IT MEANS THAT MUCH TO YOU?
OKAY, SHE CAN STAY. BUT I'M NOT HAPPY ABOUT IT. AND IF ANYTHING STRANGE SHOULD HAPPEN—
IT WON'T. OH, DAD—THANK YOU. THANK YOU.
I LOVE CATS—ALL CATS. EVEN THOSE MONSTERS. FUNNY HOW THAT'S ALL I KNOW ABOUT MYSELF BEFORE MY ACCIDENT. . . DON'T EVEN KNOW WHAT MY ACCIDENT WAS.
COME ON, DREAMER—WE'VE GOT TO TURN YOU INTO A CLOWN BY SIX O'CLOCK.
WHAT? YOU MEAN IT'S ALL RIGHT FOR ME TO STAY? OH, FANTASTIC!
WHAT DID THE OLD WOMAN SAY TO HIM?
A LOAD OF RUBBISH. . .SAID THE LIFE LINE ON YOUR HAND HAD ENDED. THAT'S SUPPOSED TO MEAN YOU'RE DEAD. . .NOW I THINK THESE SHOULD DO.
BUT, CAROL, MARGARET HAWTHORNE'S DEAD—THE GIRL WHOSE FINGER-PRINTS ARE IDENTICAL TO MINE. STRANGE, ISN'T IT?
NOT AS STRANGE AS YOU'LL LOOK IF YOU DON'T LEARN TO PUT YOUR MAKE-UP ON PROPERLY. . .HERE LET ME.
MEANWHILE . . .
WE WANT YOU TO FIND THAT GIRL. . .AND REPORT BACK. START LOOKING AT CARTER'S CIRCUS. I THINK SHE'S HIDING THERE.
THAT'S ALL? WHY DON'T YOU DO IT YOURSELF?

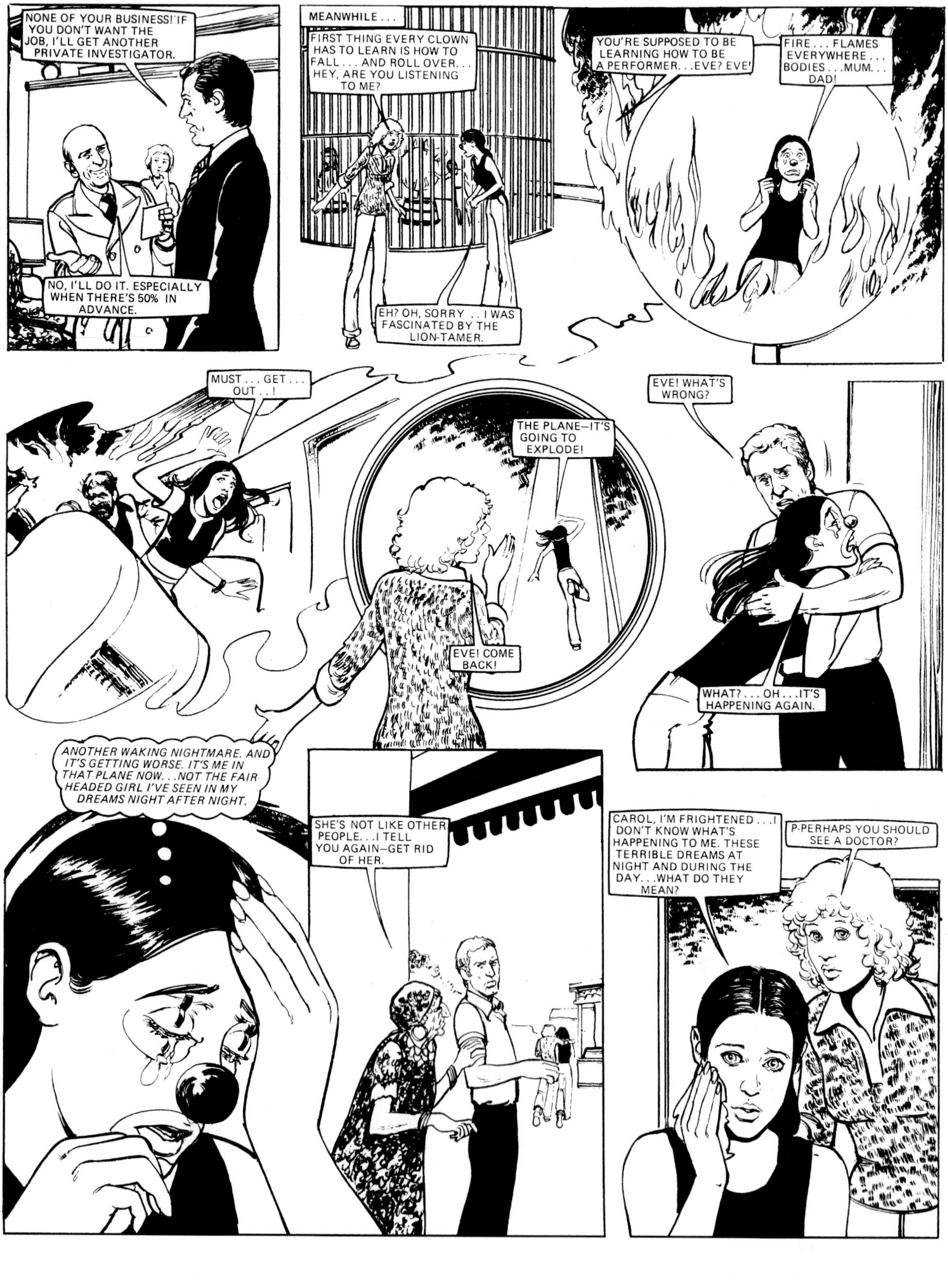
NONE OF YOUR BUSINESS! IF YOU DON'T WANT THE JOB, I'LL GET ANOTHER PRIVATE INVESTIGATOR.
NO, I'LL DO IT. ESPECIALLY WHEN THERE'S 50% IN ADVANCE.
MEANWHILE . . .
FIRST THING EVERY CLOWN HAS TO LEARN IS HOW TO FALL . . . AND ROLL OVER . . . HEY, ARE YOU LISTENING TO ME?
EH? OH, SORRY . . I WAS FASCINATED BY THE LION-TAMER.
YOU'RE SUPPOSED TO BE LEARNING HOW TO BE A PERFORMER. . . EVE? EVE!
FIRE . . . FLAMES EVERYWHERE . . . BODIES . . . MUM. . . DAD!
MUST . . . GET . . . OUT . . !
THE PLANE—IT'S GOING TO EXPLODE!
EVE! COME BACK!
EVE! WHAT'S WRONG?
WHAT? . . . OH . . . IT'S HAPPENING AGAIN.
ANOTHER WAKING NIGHTMARE. AND IT'S GETTING WORSE. IT'S ME IN THAT PLANE NOW. . . NOT THE FAIR-HEADED GIRL I'VE SEEN IN MY DREAMS NIGHT AFTER NIGHT.
SHE'S NOT LIKE OTHER PEOPLE. . . I TELL YOU AGAIN—GET RID OF HER.
CAROL, I'M FRIGHTENED . . . I DON'T KNOW WHAT'S HAPPENING TO ME. THESE TERRIBLE DREAMS AT NIGHT AND DURING THE DAY. . . WHAT DO THEY MEAN?
P-PERHAPS YOU SHOULD SEE A DOCTOR?

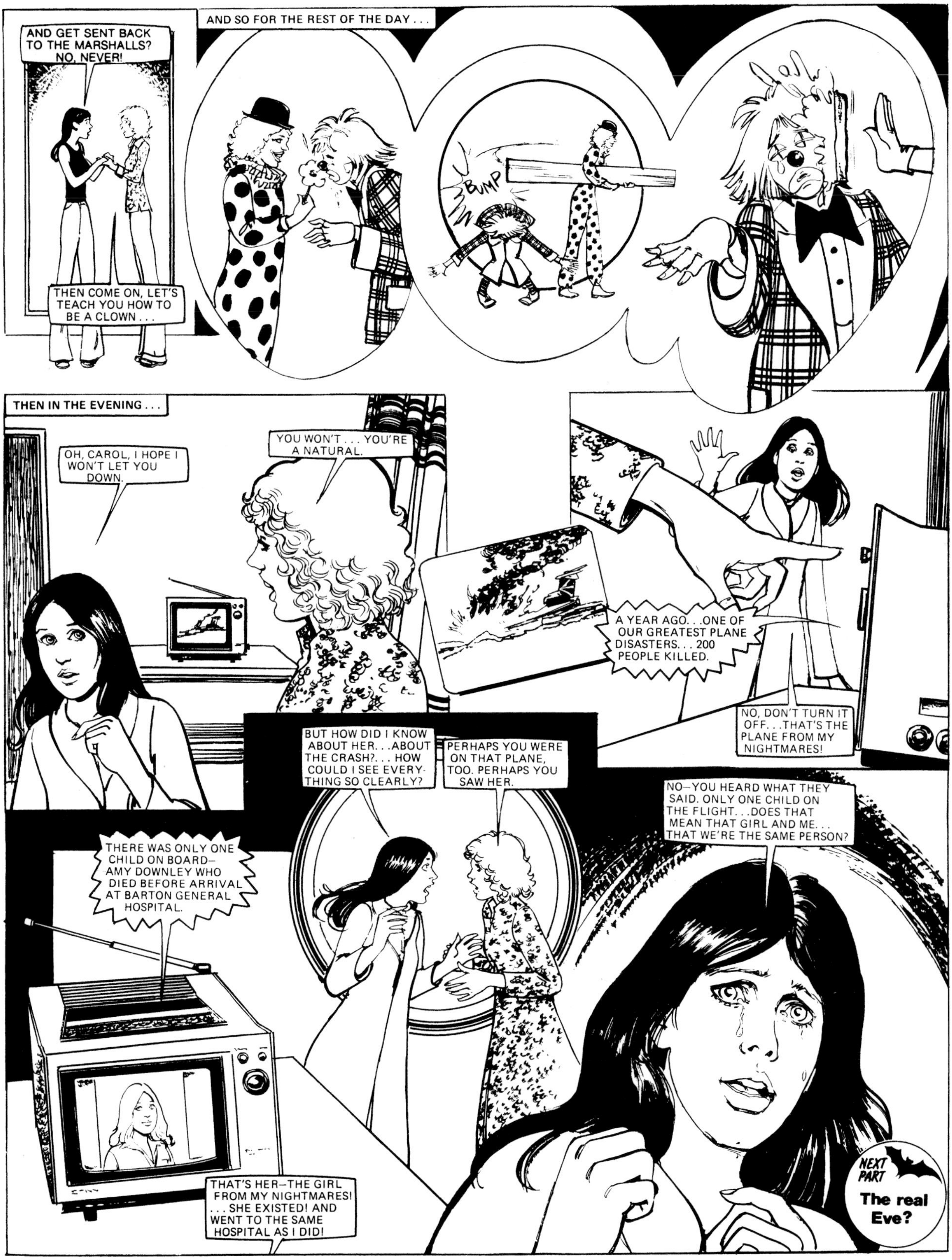

AND GET SENT BACK TO THE MARSHALLS? NO, NEVER!
THEN COME ON, LET'S TEACH YOU HOW TO BE A CLOWN . . .
AND SO FOR THE REST OF THE DAY . . .
BUMP
THEN IN THE EVENING . . .
OH, CAROL, I HOPE I WON'T LET YOU DOWN.
YOU WON'T . . . YOU'RE A NATURAL.
A YEAR AGO. . .ONE OF OUR GREATEST PLANE DISASTERS. . . 200 PEOPLE KILLED.
NO, DON'T TURN IT OFF. . .THAT'S THE PLANE FROM MY NIGHTMARES!
THERE WAS ONLY ONE CHILD ON BOARD— AMY DOWNLEY WHO DIED BEFORE ARRIVAL AT BARTON GENERAL HOSPITAL.
THAT'S HER—THE GIRL FROM MY NIGHTMARES! . . . SHE EXISTED! AND WENT TO THE SAME HOSPITAL AS I DID!
BUT HOW DID I KNOW ABOUT HER. . .ABOUT THE CRASH?. . . HOW COULD I SEE EVERY-THING SO CLEARLY?
PERHAPS YOU WERE ON THAT PLANE, TOO. PERHAPS YOU SAW HER.
NO—YOU HEARD WHAT THEY SAID. ONLY ONE CHILD ON THE FLIGHT. . .DOES THAT MEAN THAT GIRL AND ME. . . THAT WE'RE THE SAME PERSON?
NEXT PART
The real Eve?

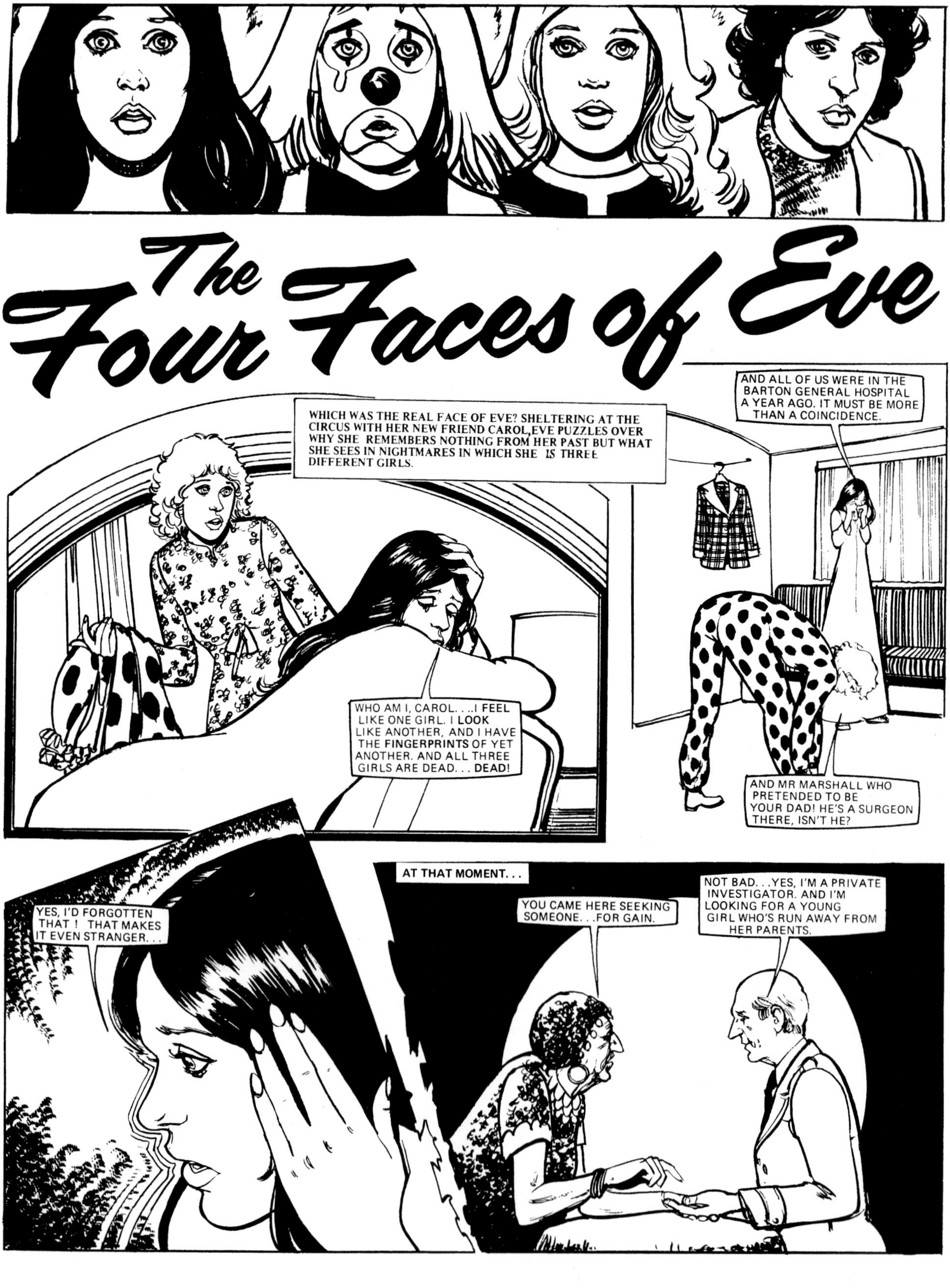

The Four Faces of Eve
WHICH WAS THE REAL FACE OF EVE? SHELTERING AT THE CIRCUS WITH HER NEW FRIEND CAROL, EVE PUZZLES OVER WHY SHE REMEMBERS NOTHING FROM HER PAST BUT WHAT SHE SEES IN NIGHTMARES IN WHICH SHE IS THREE DIFFERENT GIRLS.
WHO AM I, CAROL. . . I FEEL LIKE ONE GIRL. I LOOK LIKE ANOTHER, AND I HAVE THE FINGERPRINTS OF YET ANOTHER. AND ALL THREE GIRLS ARE DEAD. . . DEAD!
AND ALL OF US WERE IN THE BARTON GENERAL HOSPITAL A YEAR AGO. IT MUST BE MORE THAN A COINCIDENCE.
AND MR MARSHALL WHO PRETENDED TO BE YOUR DAD! HE'S A SURGEON THERE, ISN'T HE?
YES, I'D FORGOTTEN THAT ! THAT MAKES IT EVEN STRANGER. . .
AT THAT MOMENT. . .
YOU CAME HERE SEEKING SOMEONE. . . FOR GAIN.
NOT BAD. . . YES, I'M A PRIVATE INVESTIGATOR. AND I'M LOOKING FOR A YOUNG GIRL WHO'S RUN AWAY FROM HER PARENTS.

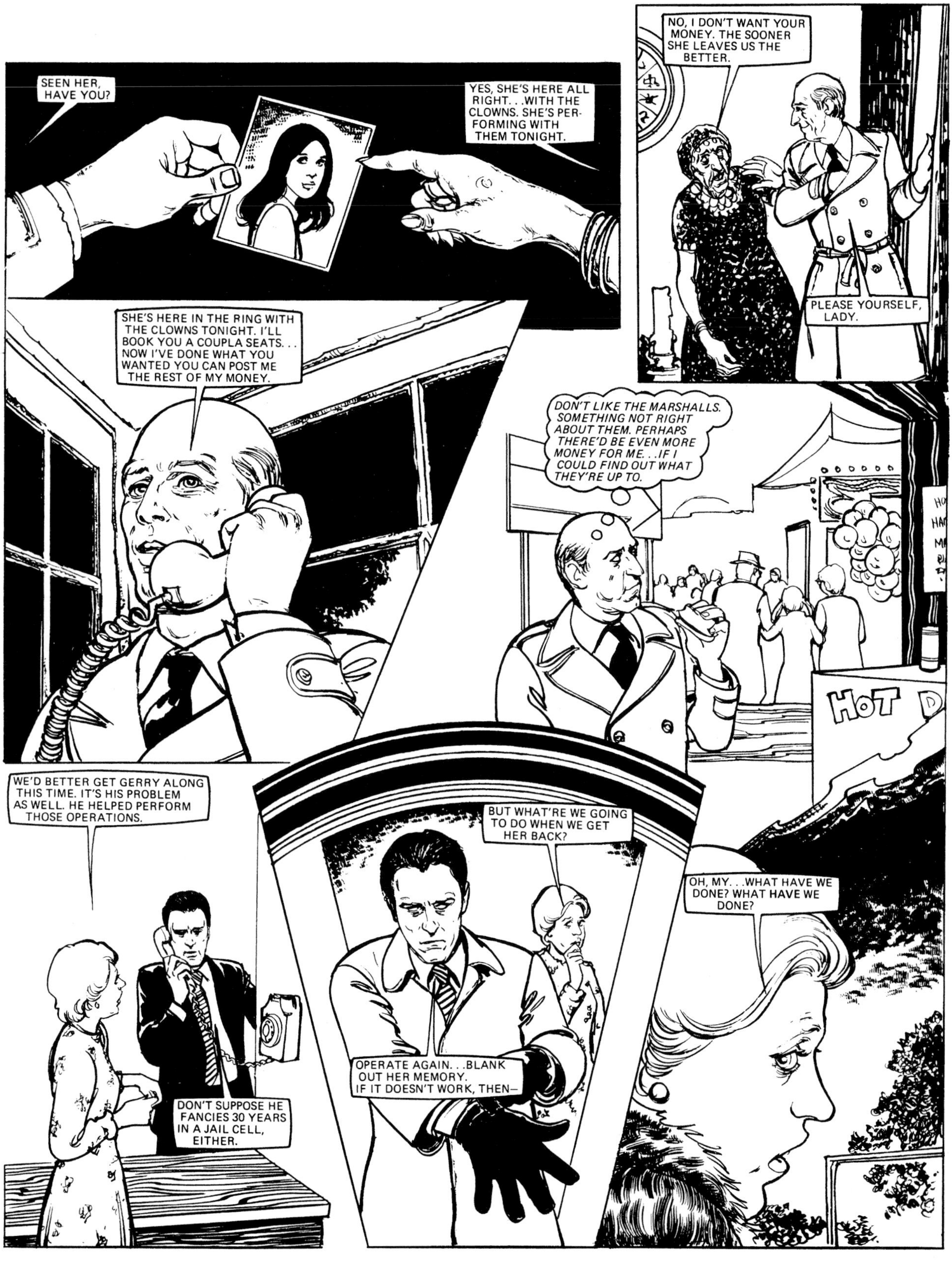

SEEN HER, HAVE YOU?
YES, SHE'S HERE ALL RIGHT. . .WITH THE CLOWNS. SHE'S PERFORMING WITH THEM TONIGHT.
NO, I DON'T WANT YOUR MONEY. THE SOONER SHE LEAVES US THE BETTER.
PLEASE YOURSELF, LADY.
SHE'S HERE IN THE RING WITH THE CLOWNS TONIGHT. I'LL BOOK YOU A COUPLA SEATS. . . NOW I'VE DONE WHAT YOU WANTED YOU CAN POST ME THE REST OF MY MONEY.
DON'T LIKE THE MARSHALLS. SOMETHING NOT RIGHT ABOUT THEM. PERHAPS THERE'D BE EVEN MORE MONEY FOR ME. . .IF I COULD FIND OUT WHAT THEY'RE UP TO.
HOT D
WE'D BETTER GET GERRY ALONG THIS TIME. IT'S HIS PROBLEM AS WELL. HE HELPED PERFORM THOSE OPERATIONS.
DON'T SUPPOSE HE FANCIES 30 YEARS IN A JAIL CELL, EITHER.
BUT WHAT'RE WE GOING TO DO WHEN WE GET HER BACK?
OPERATE AGAIN. . .BLANK OUT HER MEMORY. IF IT DOESN'T WORK, THEN–
OH, MY. . .WHAT HAVE WE DONE? WHAT **HAVE** WE DONE?

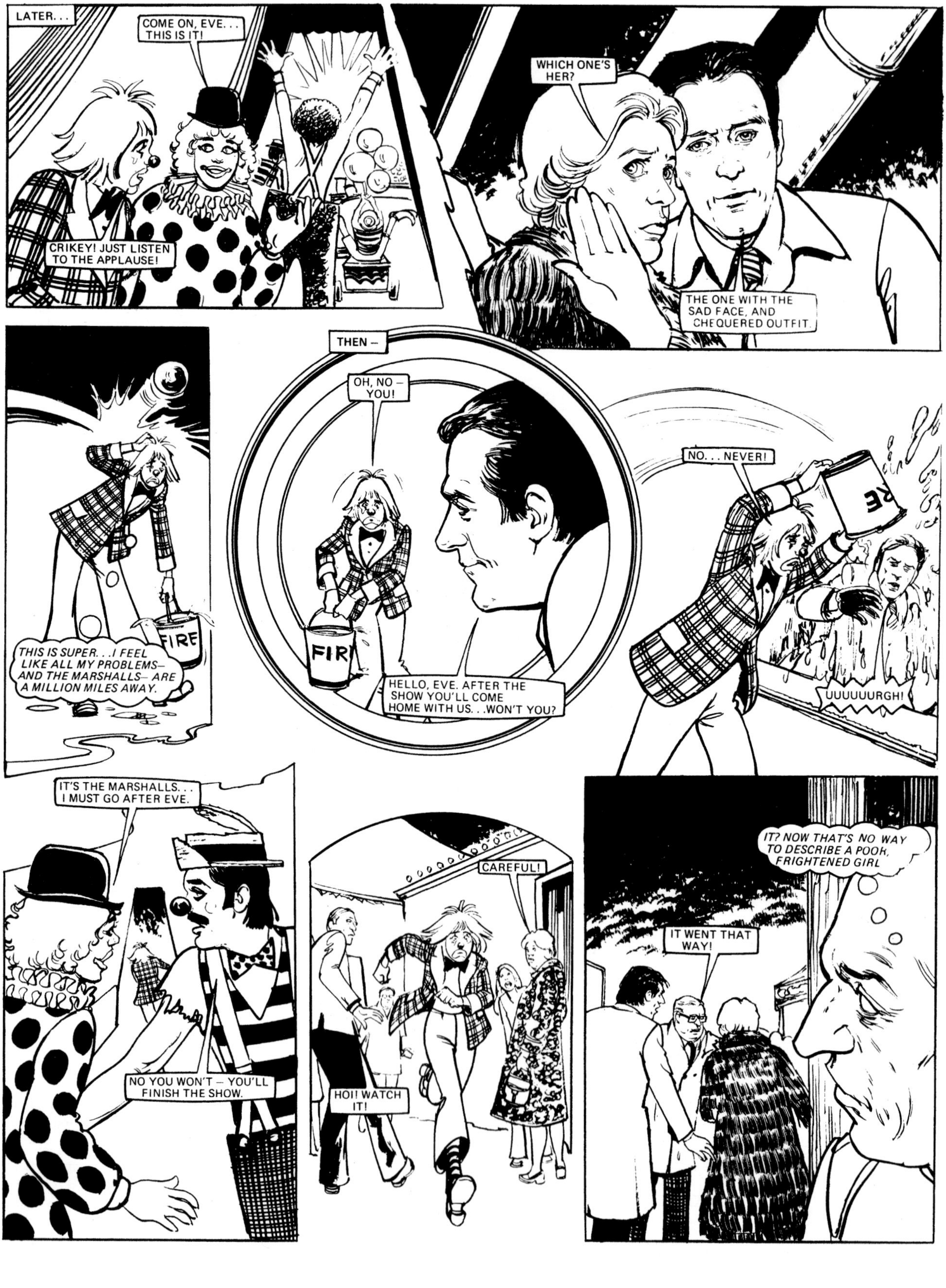

LATER...
COME ON, EVE... THIS IS IT!
CRIKEY! JUST LISTEN TO THE APPLAUSE!
WHICH ONE'S HER?
THE ONE WITH THE SAD FACE, AND CHEQUERED OUTFIT.
THIS IS SUPER... I FEEL LIKE ALL MY PROBLEMS— AND THE MARSHALLS— ARE A MILLION MILES AWAY.
FIRE
THEN —
OH, NO — YOU!
HELLO, EVE. AFTER THE SHOW YOU'LL COME HOME WITH US... WON'T YOU?
FIR
NO... NEVER!
RE
UUUUUURGH!
IT'S THE MARSHALLS... I MUST GO AFTER EVE.
NO YOU WON'T — YOU'LL FINISH THE SHOW.
CAREFUL!
HOI! WATCH IT!
IT? NOW THAT'S NO WAY TO DESCRIBE A POOR, FRIGHTENED GIRL
IT WENT THAT WAY!

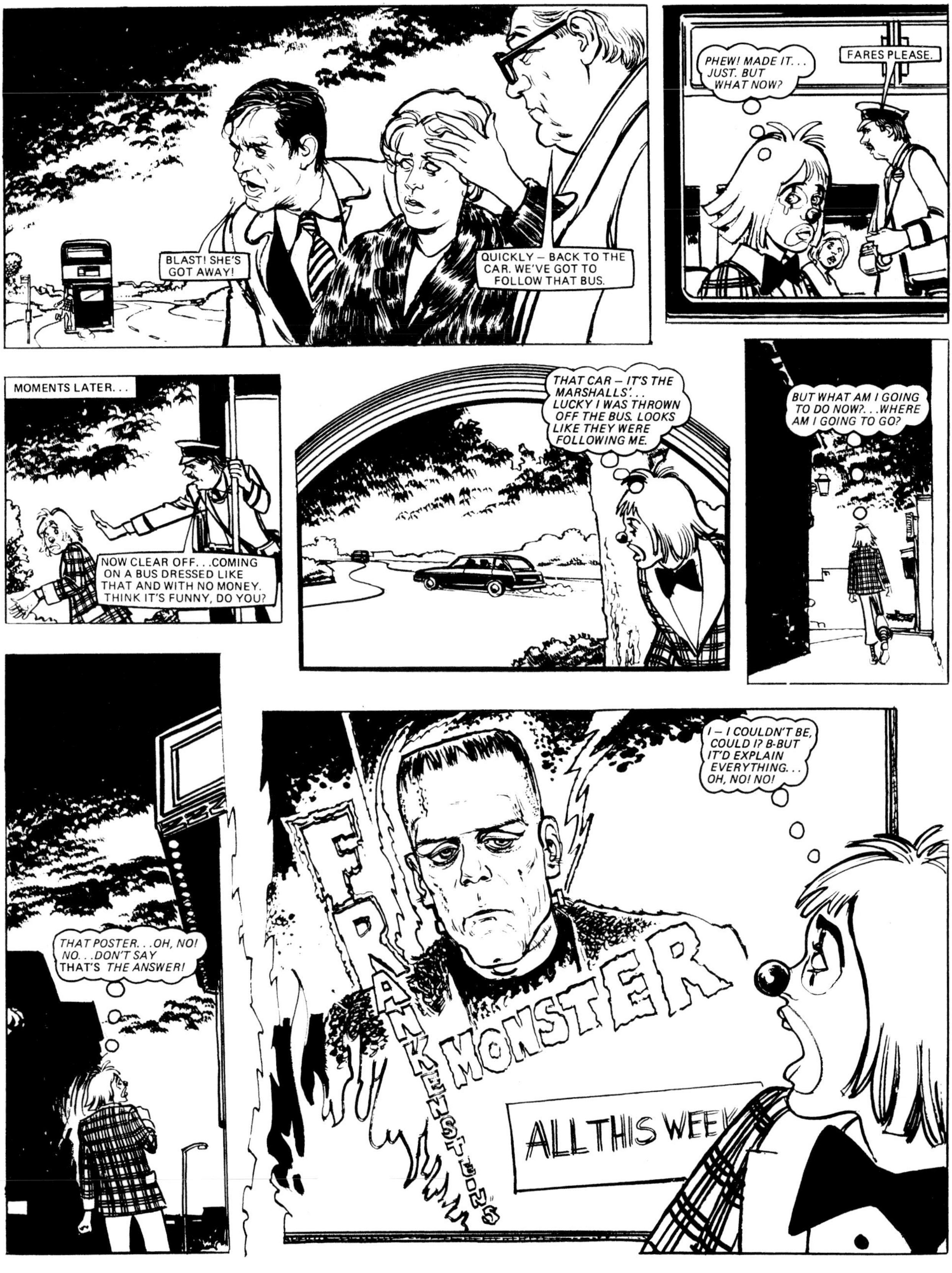
BLAST! SHE'S GOT AWAY!
QUICKLY – BACK TO THE CAR. WE'VE GOT TO FOLLOW THAT BUS.
PHEW! MADE IT... JUST. BUT WHAT NOW?
FARES PLEASE.
MOMENTS LATER...
NOW CLEAR OFF...COMING ON A BUS DRESSED LIKE THAT AND WITH NO MONEY. THINK IT'S FUNNY, DO YOU?
THAT CAR – IT'S THE MARSHALLS'... LUCKY I WAS THROWN OFF THE BUS. LOOKS LIKE THEY WERE FOLLOWING ME.
BUT WHAT AM I GOING TO DO NOW?...WHERE AM I GOING TO GO?
THAT POSTER...OH, NO! NO...DON'T SAY THAT'S THE ANSWER!
I – I COULDN'T BE, COULD I? B-BUT IT'D EXPLAIN EVERYTHING... OH, NO! NO!
FRANKENSTEIN'S MONSTER
ALL THIS WEE

# The Four Faces of Eve

WHICH WAS THE REAL EVE? WHERE HAD SHE COME FROM? SHE REMEMBERED NOTHING OF HER PAST BUT WHAT SHE SAW IN NIGHTMARES WHERE SHE SAW HERSELF AS DIFFERENT GIRLS.

COULD THAT *BE* THE ANSWER? AM I A FRANKENSTEIN-TYPE MONSTER? IT'D EXPLAIN EVERYTHING...WHY I'VE GOT ONE GIRL'S FINGERPRINTS—HER HANDS, THAT MEANS—WHY I LOOK EXACTLY LIKE ANOTHER GIRL, AND WHY I HAVE THE MEMORY, THE MIND, OF YET ANOTHER.

FRANKENSTEIN'S MONSTER

ALL THIS WEEK

THOSE THREE GIRLS DIED A YEAR AGO...DIED AT THE HOSPITAL WHERE I WAS SO MYSTERIOUSLY KEPT!

IT'S HORRIBLE—HORRIBLE!

COME ON THEN, LOVE... GET ON WITH IT!

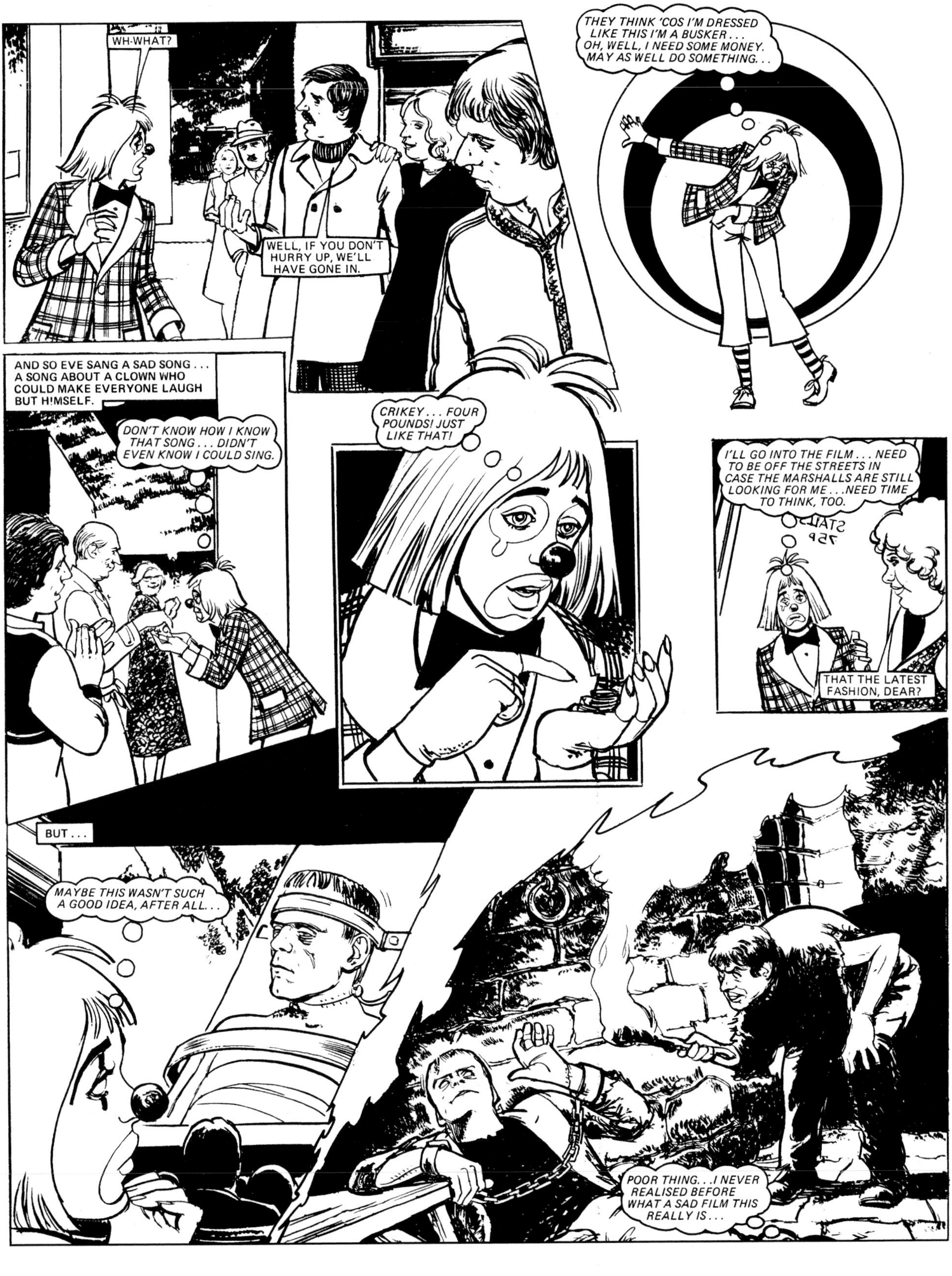
WH-WHAT?
WELL, IF YOU DON'T HURRY UP, WE'LL HAVE GONE IN.
THEY THINK 'COS I'M DRESSED LIKE THIS I'M A BUSKER . . . OH, WELL, I NEED SOME MONEY. MAY AS WELL DO SOMETHING. . .
AND SO EVE SANG A SAD SONG . . . A SONG ABOUT A CLOWN WHO COULD MAKE EVERYONE LAUGH BUT HIMSELF.
DON'T KNOW HOW I KNOW THAT SONG . . . DIDN'T EVEN KNOW I COULD SING.
CRIKEY . . . FOUR POUNDS! JUST LIKE THAT!
I'LL GO INTO THE FILM . . . NEED TO BE OFF THE STREETS IN CASE THE MARSHALLS ARE STILL LOOKING FOR ME . . . NEED TIME TO THINK, TOO.
STALLS 75P
THAT THE LATEST FASHION, DEAR?
BUT . . .
MAYBE THIS WASN'T SUCH A GOOD IDEA, AFTER ALL . . .
POOR THING. . . I NEVER REALISED BEFORE WHAT A SAD FILM THIS REALLY IS . . .

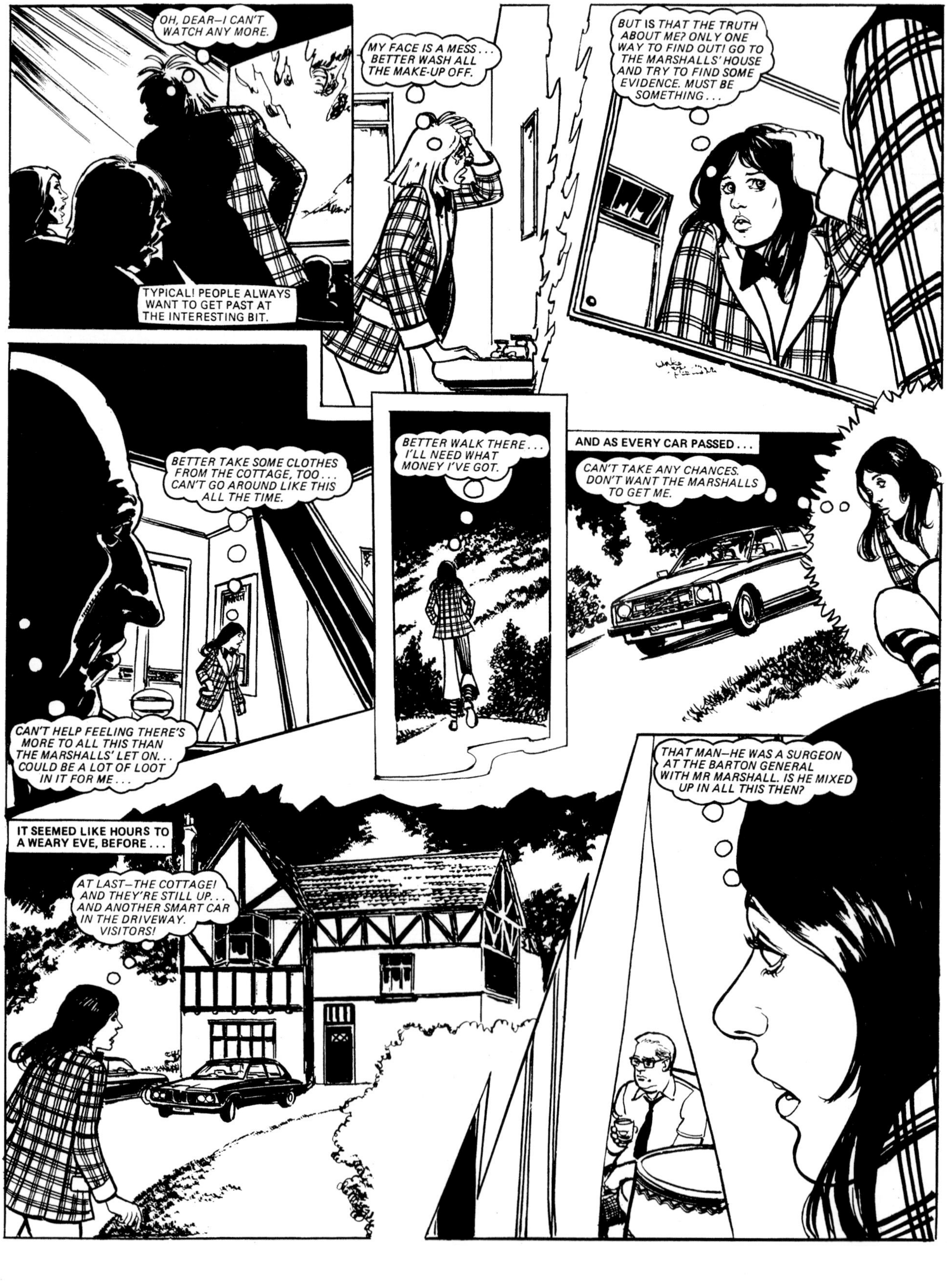

OH, DEAR—I CAN'T WATCH ANY MORE.
TYPICAL! PEOPLE ALWAYS WANT TO GET PAST AT THE INTERESTING BIT.
MY FACE IS A MESS . . . BETTER WASH ALL THE MAKE-UP OFF.
BUT IS THAT THE TRUTH ABOUT ME? ONLY ONE WAY TO FIND OUT! GO TO THE MARSHALLS' HOUSE AND TRY TO FIND SOME EVIDENCE. MUST BE SOMETHING . . .
BETTER TAKE SOME CLOTHES FROM THE COTTAGE, TOO . . . CAN'T GO AROUND LIKE THIS ALL THE TIME.
CAN'T HELP FEELING THERE'S MORE TO ALL THIS THAN THE MARSHALLS' LET ON . . . COULD BE A LOT OF LOOT IN IT FOR ME . . .
BETTER WALK THERE . . . I'LL NEED WHAT MONEY I'VE GOT.
AND AS EVERY CAR PASSED . . .
CAN'T TAKE ANY CHANCES. DON'T WANT THE MARSHALLS TO GET ME.
IT SEEMED LIKE HOURS TO A WEARY EVE, BEFORE . . .
AT LAST—THE COTTAGE! AND THEY'RE STILL UP . . . AND ANOTHER SMART CAR IN THE DRIVEWAY. VISITORS!
THAT MAN—HE WAS A SURGEON AT THE BARTON GENERAL WITH MR MARSHALL. IS HE MIXED UP IN ALL THIS THEN?

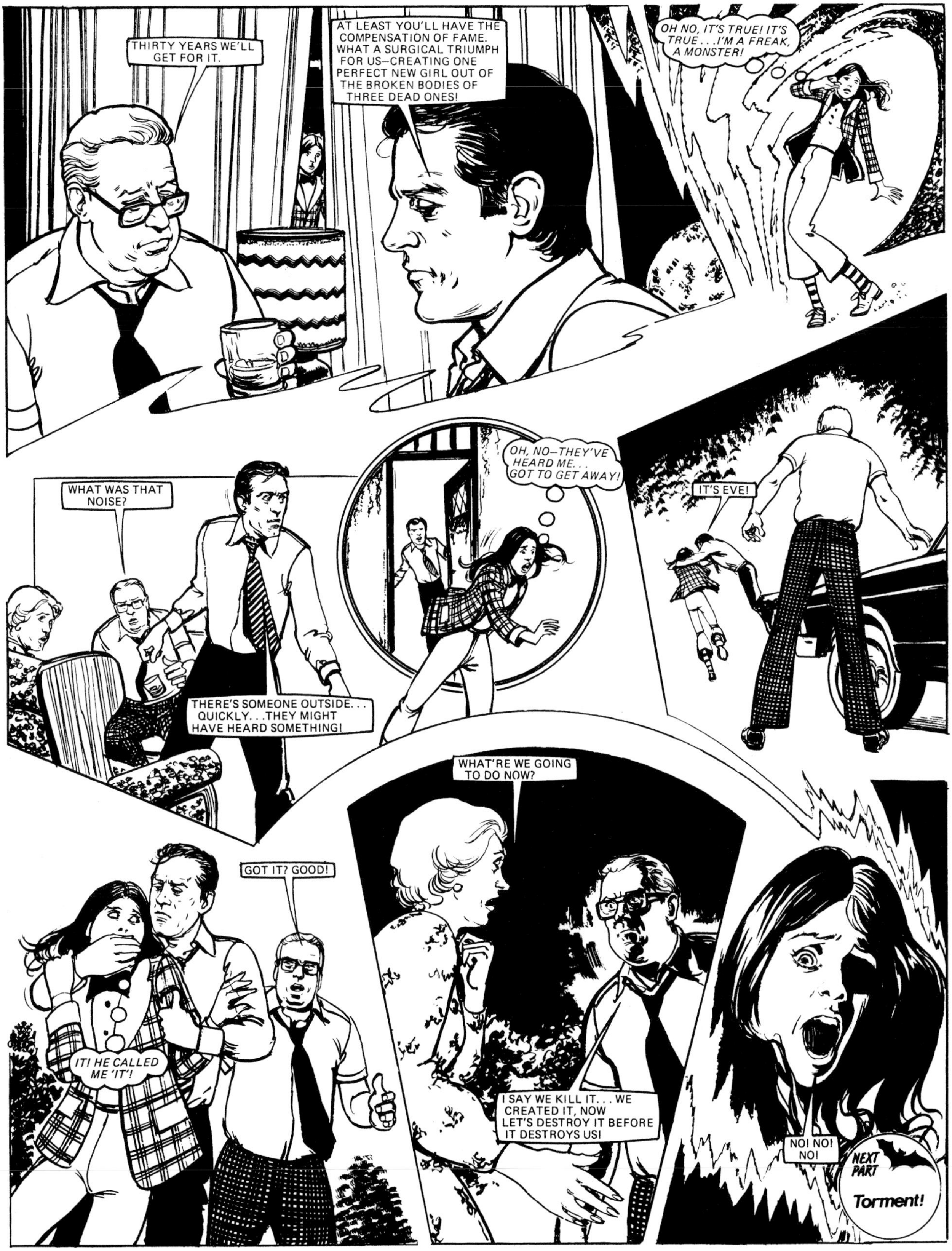
THIRTY YEARS WE'LL GET FOR IT.
AT LEAST YOU'LL HAVE THE COMPENSATION OF FAME. WHAT A SURGICAL TRIUMPH FOR US—CREATING ONE PERFECT NEW GIRL OUT OF THE BROKEN BODIES OF THREE DEAD ONES!
OH NO, IT'S TRUE! IT'S TRUE . . . I'M A FREAK, A MONSTER!
WHAT WAS THAT NOISE?
THERE'S SOMEONE OUTSIDE. . . QUICKLY. . . THEY MIGHT HAVE HEARD SOMETHING!
OH, NO—THEY'VE HEARD ME. . . GOT TO GET AWAY!
IT'S EVE!
GOT IT? GOOD!
IT! HE CALLED ME 'IT'!
WHAT'RE WE GOING TO DO NOW?
I SAY WE KILL IT. . . WE CREATED IT, NOW LET'S DESTROY IT BEFORE IT DESTROYS US!
NO! NO! NO!
NEXT PART
Torment!

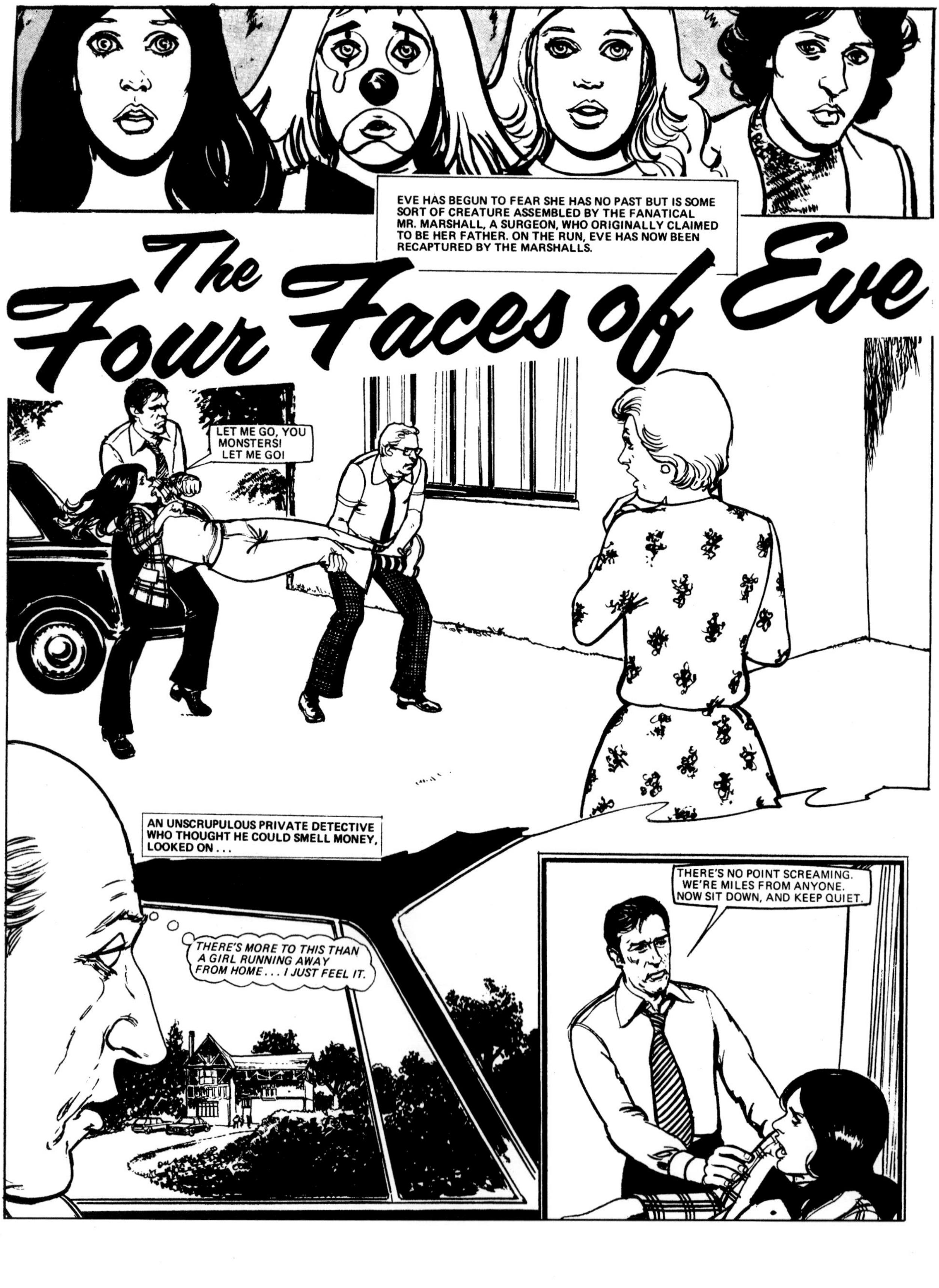
EVE HAS BEGUN TO FEAR SHE HAS NO PAST BUT IS SOME SORT OF CREATURE ASSEMBLED BY THE FANATICAL MR. MARSHALL, A SURGEON, WHO ORIGINALLY CLAIMED TO BE HER FATHER. ON THE RUN, EVE HAS NOW BEEN RECAPTURED BY THE MARSHALLS.
The Four Faces of Eve
LET ME GO, YOU MONSTERS! LET ME GO!
AN UNSCRUPULOUS PRIVATE DETECTIVE WHO THOUGHT HE COULD SMELL MONEY, LOOKED ON . . .
THERE'S MORE TO THIS THAN A GIRL RUNNING AWAY FROM HOME . . . I JUST FEEL IT.
THERE'S NO POINT SCREAMING. WE'RE MILES FROM ANYONE. NOW SIT DOWN, AND KEEP QUIET.

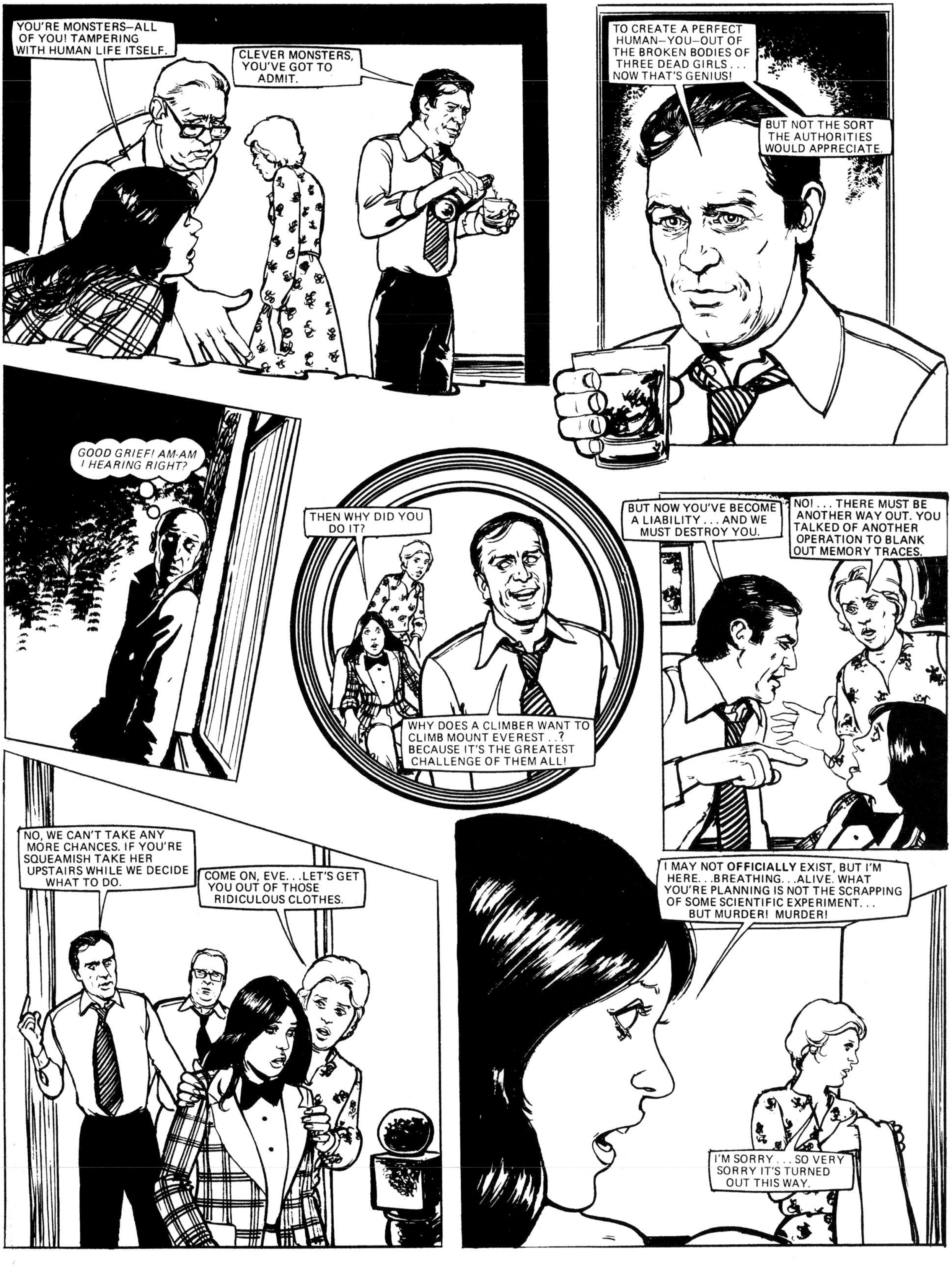
YOU'RE MONSTERS—ALL OF YOU! TAMPERING WITH HUMAN LIFE ITSELF.
CLEVER MONSTERS, YOU'VE GOT TO ADMIT.
TO CREATE A PERFECT HUMAN—YOU—OUT OF THE BROKEN BODIES OF THREE DEAD GIRLS . . . NOW THAT'S GENIUS!
BUT NOT THE SORT THE AUTHORITIES WOULD APPRECIATE.
GOOD GRIEF! AM-AM I HEARING RIGHT?
THEN WHY DID YOU DO IT?
WHY DOES A CLIMBER WANT TO CLIMB MOUNT EVEREST . .? BECAUSE IT'S THE GREATEST CHALLENGE OF THEM ALL!
BUT NOW YOU'VE BECOME A LIABILITY . . . AND WE MUST DESTROY YOU.
NO! . . . THERE MUST BE ANOTHER WAY OUT. YOU TALKED OF ANOTHER OPERATION TO BLANK OUT MEMORY TRACES.
NO, WE CAN'T TAKE ANY MORE CHANCES. IF YOU'RE SQUEAMISH TAKE HER UPSTAIRS WHILE WE DECIDE WHAT TO DO.
COME ON, EVE. . . LET'S GET YOU OUT OF THOSE RIDICULOUS CLOTHES.
I MAY NOT **OFFICIALLY** EXIST, BUT I'M HERE. . .BREATHING. . .ALIVE. WHAT YOU'RE PLANNING IS NOT THE SCRAPPING OF SOME SCIENTIFIC EXPERIMENT. . . BUT MURDER! MURDER!
I'M SORRY . . . SO VERY SORRY IT'S TURNED OUT THIS WAY.

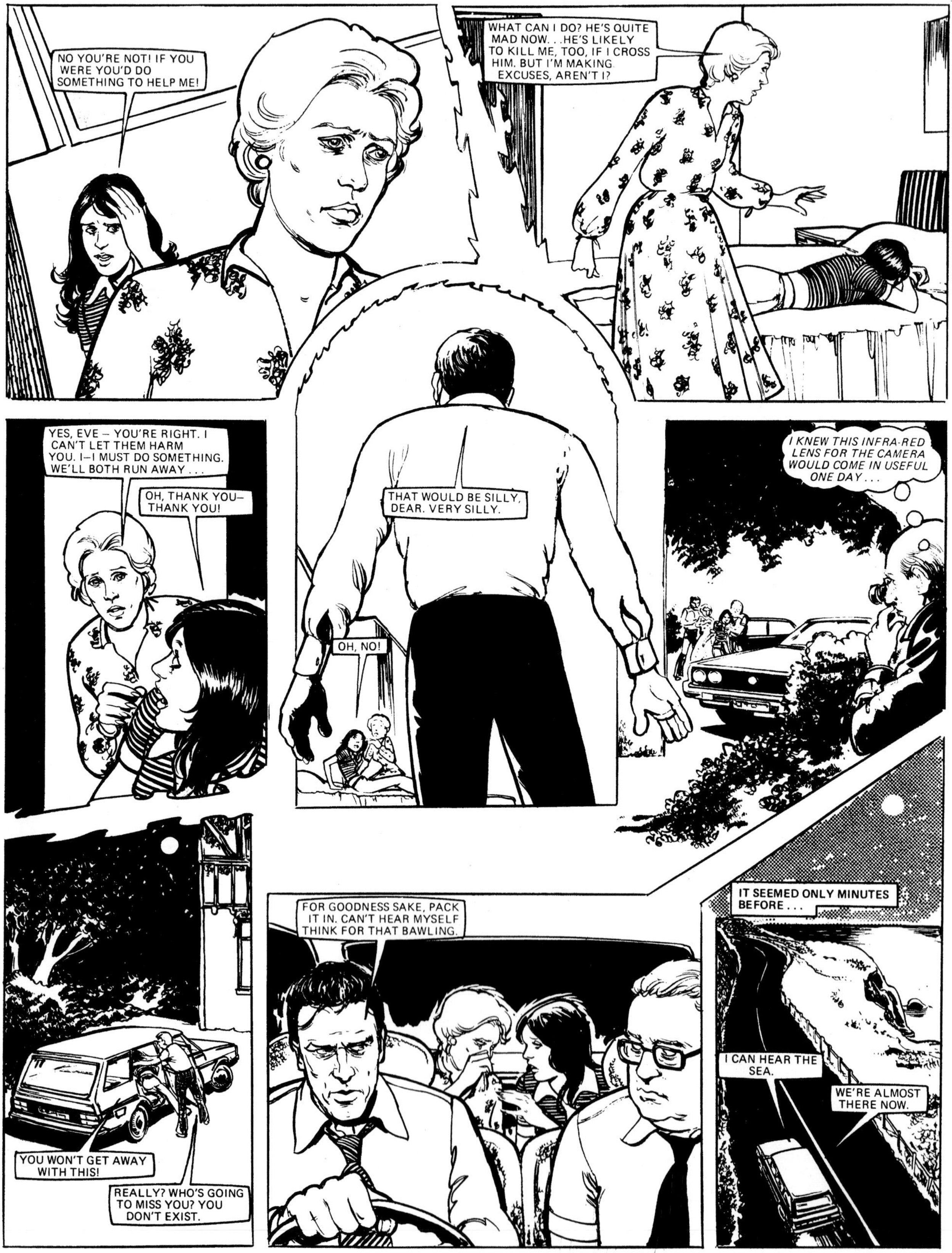
NO YOU'RE NOT! IF YOU WERE YOU'D DO SOMETHING TO HELP ME!
WHAT CAN I DO? HE'S QUITE MAD NOW. . .HE'S LIKELY TO KILL ME, TOO, IF I CROSS HIM. BUT I'M MAKING EXCUSES, AREN'T I?
YES, EVE – YOU'RE RIGHT. I CAN'T LET THEM HARM YOU. I–I MUST DO SOMETHING. WE'LL BOTH RUN AWAY . . .
OH, THANK YOU– THANK YOU!
THAT WOULD BE SILLY, DEAR. VERY SILLY.
OH, NO!
I KNEW THIS INFRA-RED LENS FOR THE CAMERA WOULD COME IN USEFUL ONE DAY . . .
YOU WON'T GET AWAY WITH THIS!
REALLY? WHO'S GOING TO MISS YOU? YOU DON'T EXIST.
FOR GOODNESS SAKE, PACK IT IN. CAN'T HEAR MYSELF THINK FOR THAT BAWLING.
IT SEEMED ONLY MINUTES BEFORE . . .
I CAN HEAR THE SEA.
WE'RE ALMOST THERE NOW.

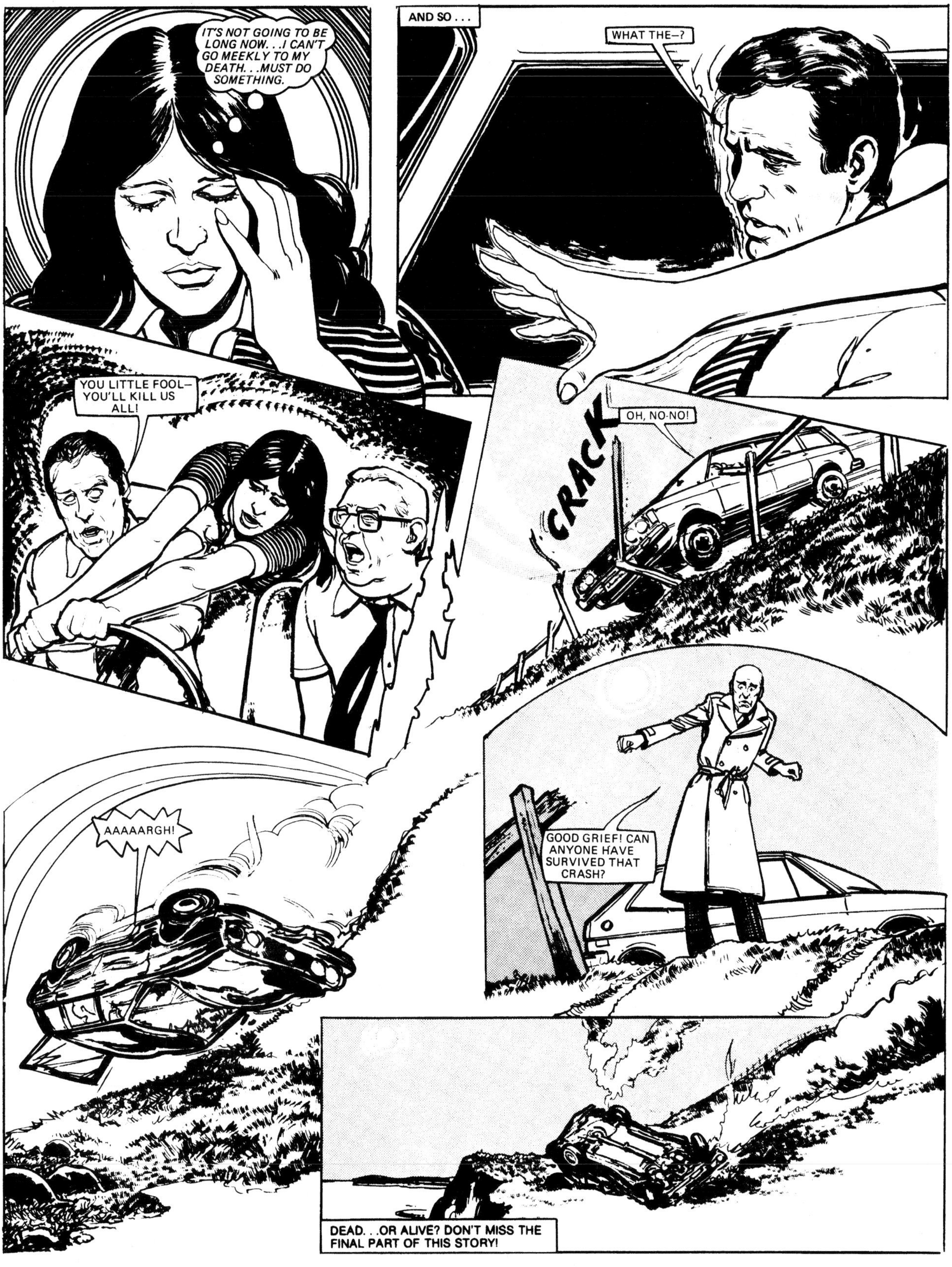

IT'S NOT GOING TO BE LONG NOW. . .I CAN'T GO MEEKLY TO MY DEATH. . .MUST DO SOMETHING.
AND SO . . .
WHAT THE–?
YOU LITTLE FOOL– YOU'LL KILL US ALL!
CRACK
OH, NO-NO!
AAAAARGH!
GOOD GRIEF! CAN ANYONE HAVE SURVIVED THAT CRASH?
DEAD. . .OR ALIVE? DON'T MISS THE FINAL PART OF THIS STORY!

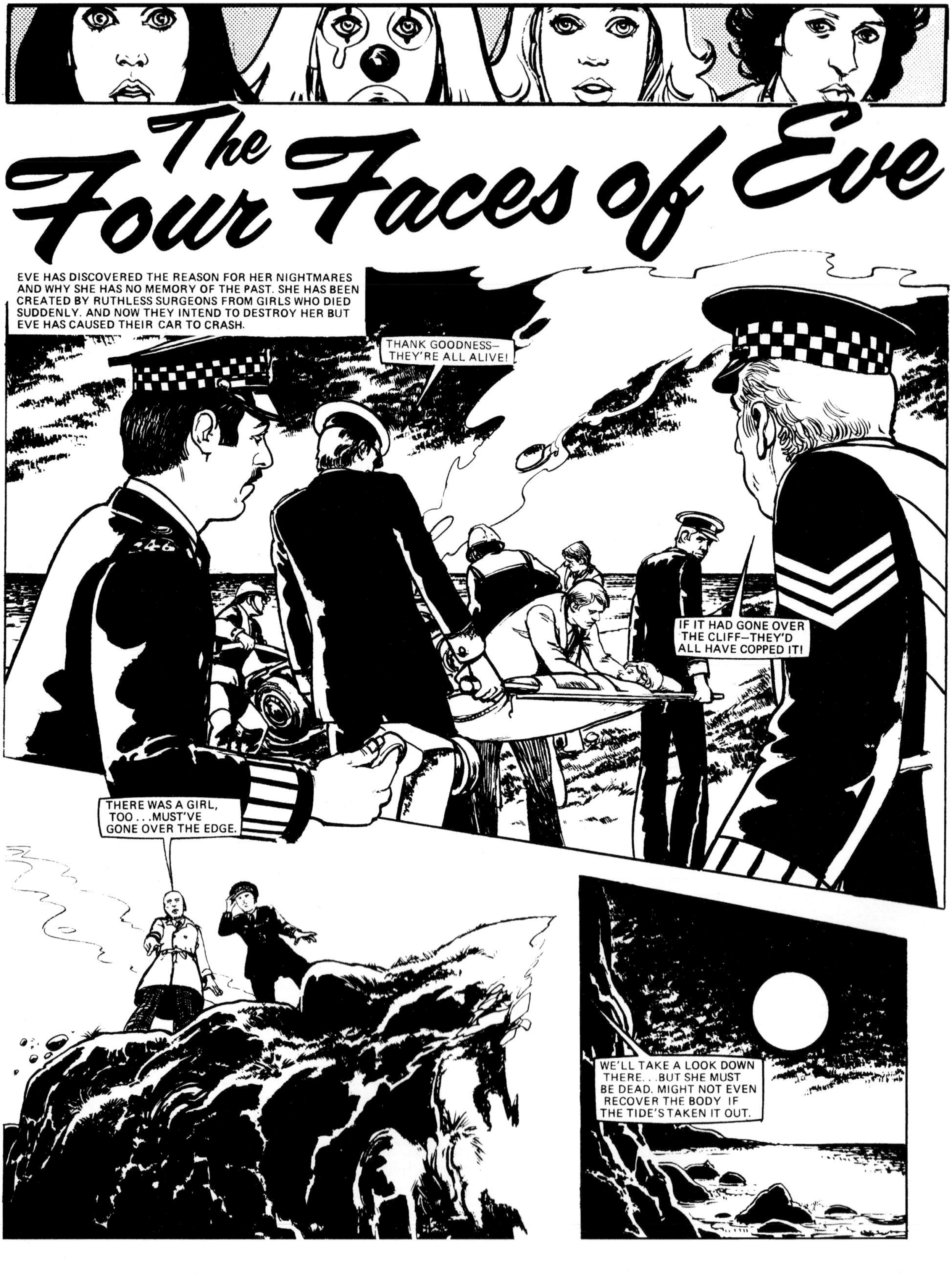
The Four Faces of Eve
EVE HAS DISCOVERED THE REASON FOR HER NIGHTMARES AND WHY SHE HAS NO MEMORY OF THE PAST. SHE HAS BEEN CREATED BY RUTHLESS SURGEONS FROM GIRLS WHO DIED SUDDENLY. AND NOW THEY INTEND TO DESTROY HER BUT EVE HAS CAUSED THEIR CAR TO CRASH.
THANK GOODNESS— THEY'RE ALL ALIVE!
IF IT HAD GONE OVER THE CLIFF—THEY'D ALL HAVE COPPED IT!
THERE WAS A GIRL, TOO . . . MUST'VE GONE OVER THE EDGE.
WE'LL TAKE A LOOK DOWN THERE. . .BUT SHE MUST BE DEAD. MIGHT NOT EVEN RECOVER THE BODY IF THE TIDE'S TAKEN IT OUT.

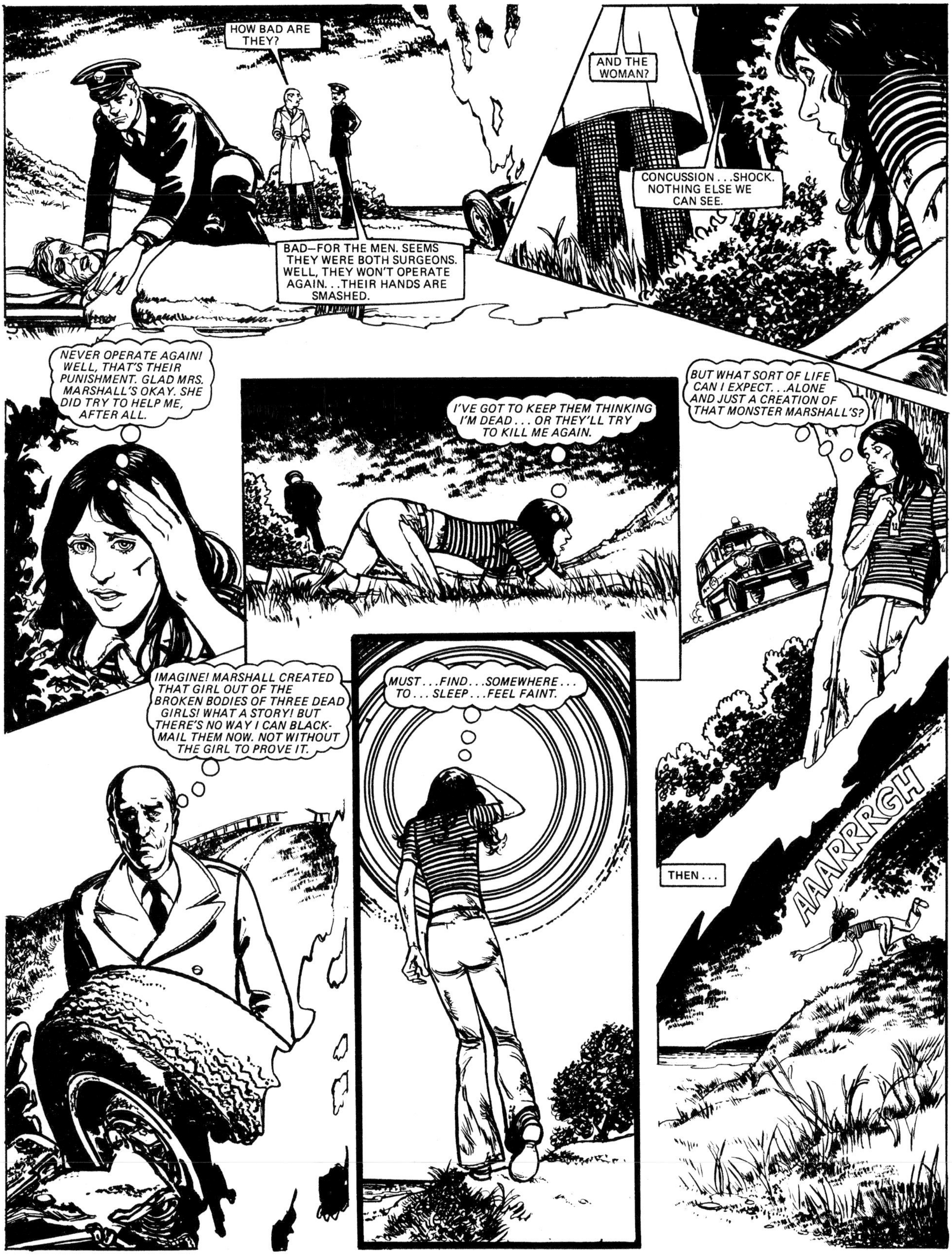
HOW BAD ARE THEY?
BAD—FOR THE MEN. SEEMS THEY WERE BOTH SURGEONS. WELL, THEY WON'T OPERATE AGAIN. . .THEIR HANDS ARE SMASHED.
AND THE WOMAN?
CONCUSSION . . .SHOCK. NOTHING ELSE WE CAN SEE.
NEVER OPERATE AGAIN! WELL, THAT'S THEIR PUNISHMENT. GLAD MRS. MARSHALL'S OKAY. SHE DID TRY TO HELP ME, AFTER ALL.
I'VE GOT TO KEEP THEM THINKING I'M DEAD . . . OR THEY'LL TRY TO KILL ME AGAIN.
BUT WHAT SORT OF LIFE CAN I EXPECT. . .ALONE AND JUST A CREATION OF THAT MONSTER MARSHALL'S?
IMAGINE! MARSHALL CREATED THAT GIRL OUT OF THE BROKEN BODIES OF THREE DEAD GIRLS! WHAT A STORY! BUT THERE'S NO WAY I CAN BLACK-MAIL THEM NOW. NOT WITHOUT THE GIRL TO PROVE IT.
MUST . . .FIND. . .SOMEWHERE . . . TO . . . SLEEP . . .FEEL FAINT.
THEN . . .
AAARRRGH

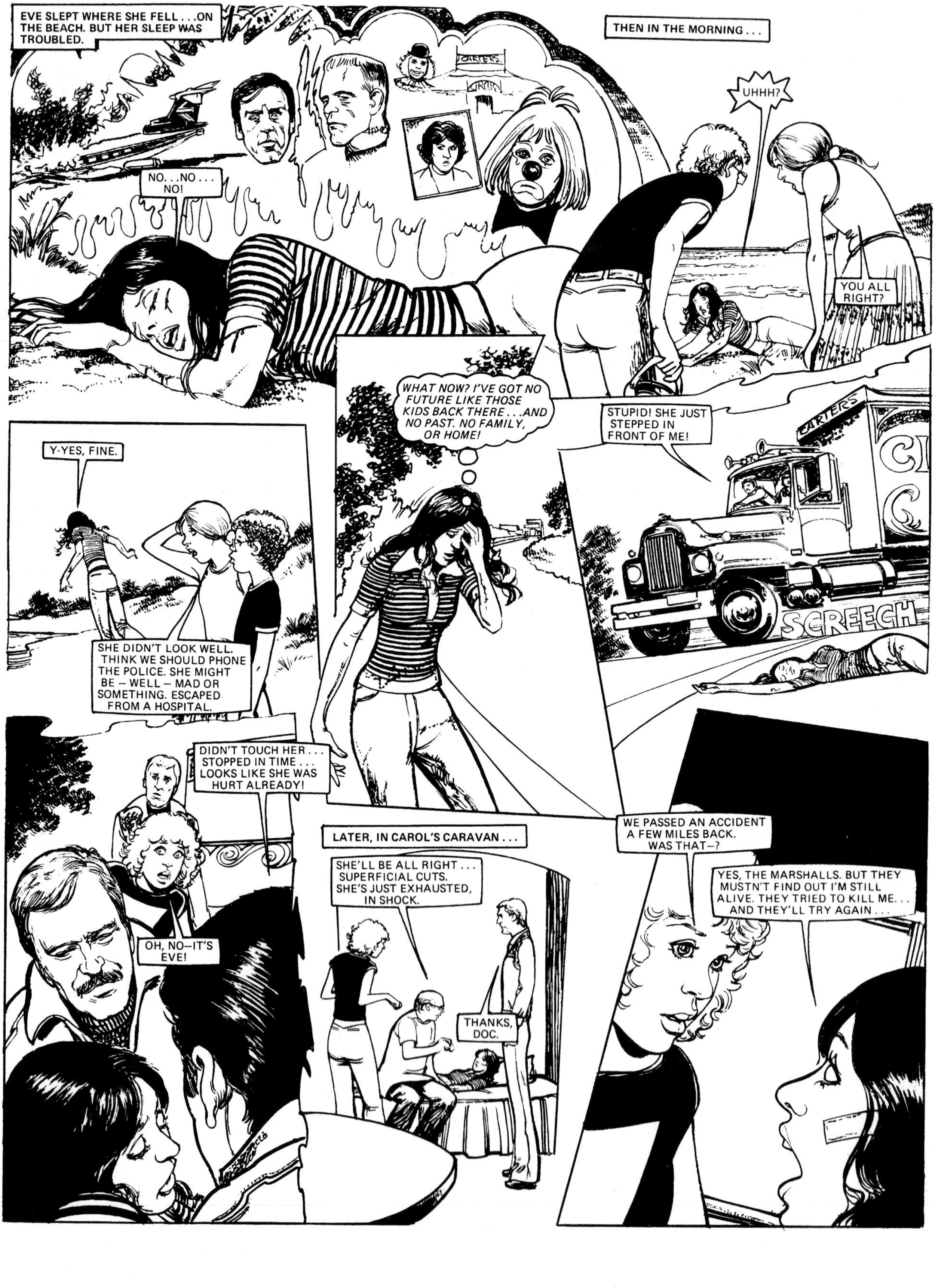
EVE SLEPT WHERE SHE FELL . . . ON THE BEACH. BUT HER SLEEP WAS TROUBLED.
CARTERS
NO. . . NO . . . NO!
THEN IN THE MORNING . . .
UHHH?
YOU ALL RIGHT?
Y-YES, FINE.
SHE DIDN'T LOOK WELL. THINK WE SHOULD PHONE THE POLICE. SHE MIGHT BE – WELL – MAD OR SOMETHING. ESCAPED FROM A HOSPITAL.
WHAT NOW? I'VE GOT NO FUTURE LIKE THOSE KIDS BACK THERE . . . AND NO PAST. NO FAMILY, OR HOME!
STUPID! SHE JUST STEPPED IN FRONT OF ME!
CARTERS
SCREECH
DIDN'T TOUCH HER . . . STOPPED IN TIME . . . LOOKS LIKE SHE WAS HURT ALREADY!
OH, NO–IT'S EVE!
LATER, IN CAROL'S CARAVAN . . .
SHE'LL BE ALL RIGHT . . . SUPERFICIAL CUTS. SHE'S JUST EXHAUSTED, IN SHOCK.
THANKS, DOC.
WE PASSED AN ACCIDENT A FEW MILES BACK. WAS THAT–?
YES, THE MARSHALLS. BUT THEY MUSTN'T FIND OUT I'M STILL ALIVE. THEY TRIED TO KILL ME. . . AND THEY'LL TRY AGAIN . . .

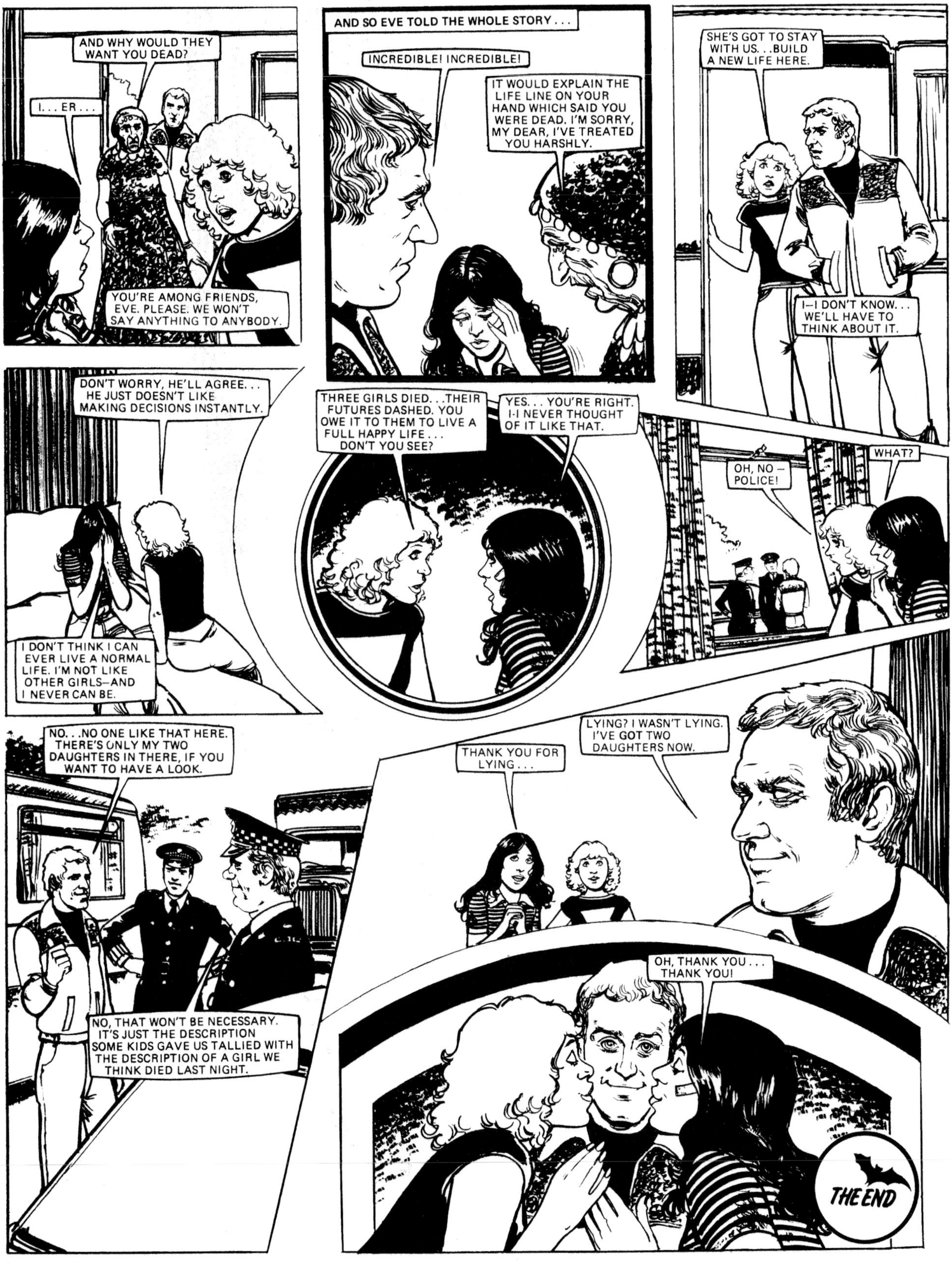
AND WHY WOULD THEY WANT YOU DEAD?
I... ER...
YOU'RE AMONG FRIENDS, EVE. PLEASE. WE WON'T SAY ANYTHING TO ANYBODY.
AND SO EVE TOLD THE WHOLE STORY...
INCREDIBLE! INCREDIBLE!
IT WOULD EXPLAIN THE LIFE LINE ON YOUR HAND WHICH SAID YOU WERE DEAD. I'M SORRY, MY DEAR, I'VE TREATED YOU HARSHLY.
SHE'S GOT TO STAY WITH US... BUILD A NEW LIFE HERE.
I—I DON'T KNOW... WE'LL HAVE TO THINK ABOUT IT.
DON'T WORRY, HE'LL AGREE... HE JUST DOESN'T LIKE MAKING DECISIONS INSTANTLY.
I DON'T THINK I CAN EVER LIVE A NORMAL LIFE. I'M NOT LIKE OTHER GIRLS—AND I NEVER CAN BE.
THREE GIRLS DIED... THEIR FUTURES DASHED. YOU OWE IT TO THEM TO LIVE A FULL HAPPY LIFE... DON'T YOU SEE?
YES... YOU'RE RIGHT. I-I NEVER THOUGHT OF IT LIKE THAT.
OH, NO — POLICE!
WHAT?
NO... NO ONE LIKE THAT HERE. THERE'S ONLY MY TWO DAUGHTERS IN THERE, IF YOU WANT TO HAVE A LOOK.
NO, THAT WON'T BE NECESSARY. IT'S JUST THE DESCRIPTION SOME KIDS GAVE US TALLIED WITH THE DESCRIPTION OF A GIRL WE THINK DIED LAST NIGHT.
THANK YOU FOR LYING...
LYING? I WASN'T LYING. I'VE GOT TWO DAUGHTERS NOW.
OH, THANK YOU... THANK YOU!
THE END

# SHIRLEY BELLWOOD
## AN UNSUNG HEROINE
## OF BRITISH COMICS

**SHIRLEY BELLWOOD** began working on comics in the 1950s, with her first work believed to be on C Arthur Pearson's *Glamour Library*. She would go on to draw story pages for titles such as *Mirabelle*, *Romeo*, *Roxy* and *Valentine*. Unusually, her name sometimes appeared on this early work, indicating the esteem in which she was held. From the 1970s onwards she drew for the new wave of girls comics such as *Sally*, *Jinty* and – of course – *Misty*. She created the character of Misty and drew her throughout the comic's run.

Misty herself was based on Shirley as a young woman, and her cat Habibi based on her own pet cat. Shirley drew all of the covers featuring Misty and several full colour paintings (like the cover of this collection) that were used as pull-out posters or calendars. She also produced delicate line drawings of Misty that were used on the inside cover of each issue along with a greeting. Misty's dramatic features, seductive stare and ethereal appearance set the tone for each issue and welcomed readers to her realm.

Outside of comics, Shirley was a highly respected portrait painter who took commissions from MPs, lords and celebrities. She provided illustrations for a large number of children's books, as well as several books for the Folio Society. She trained at Leeds College of Art and held major exhibitions with the Royal Portrait Society. Shirley's portraits contain a real sense of character and she was particularly skilled at painting children and animals, which she pursued further when she moved out of London in later life.

Shirley died on 1 February 2016 in hospital in Worcester, aged 84. She never appeared at any conventions and perhaps saw her comics work as a commercial necessity. Yet she gave *Misty* to a generation – and beyond.

**JULIA ROUND**

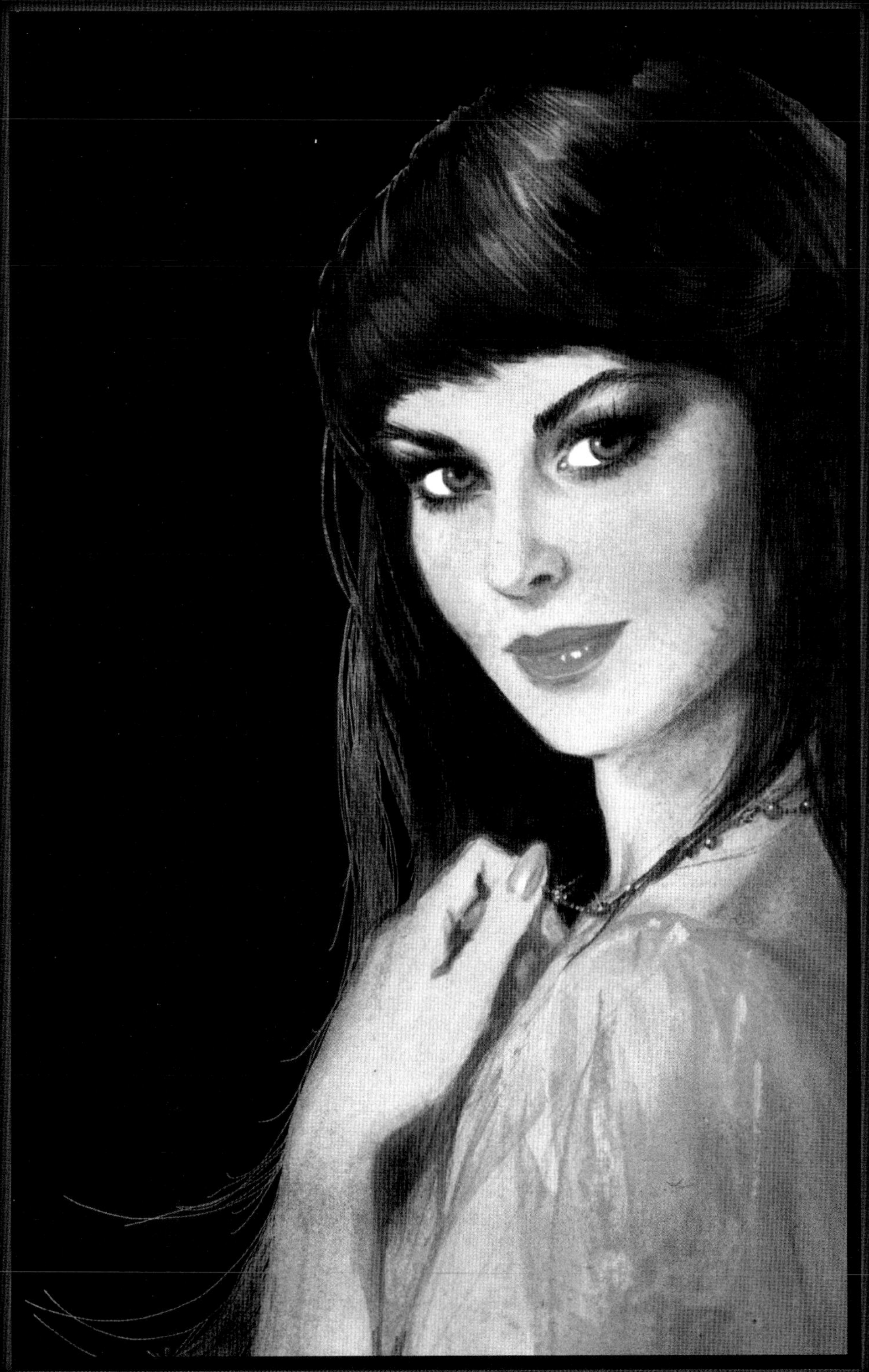

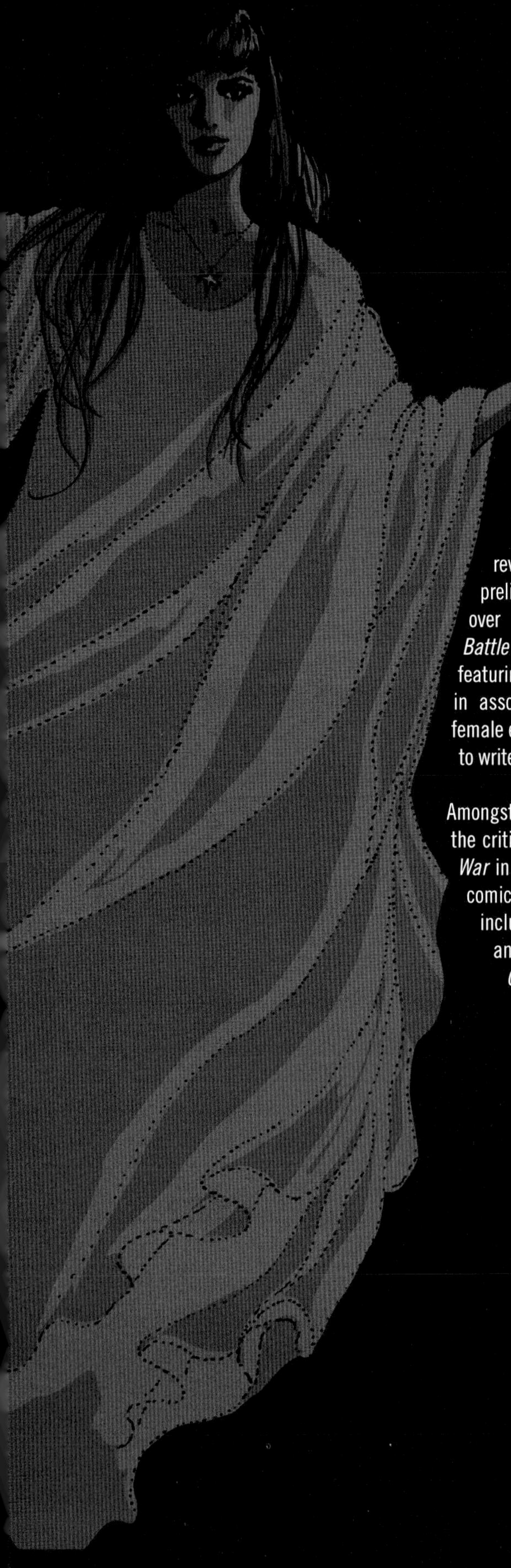

# PAT MILLS

**Pat Mills**' writing and editorial career started in Dundee, working for D.C. Thomson on the teenage romance magazine *Romeo.* Later Pat went freelance and started a long relationship with IPC Magazines, initially writing for girls titles like *Tammy*, *Pink* and *Sandy.* He was an assistant editor on *Tammy*, the publication which began the comics revolution. Then, with Malcolm Shaw, he did some preliminary work devising *Jinty* before moving over to rejuvenate boys comics. He created *Battle* (with John Wagner), *Action* and *2000 AD*, featuring *Judge Dredd.* Pat then devised *Misty*, in association with Wilf Prigmore, as the female equivalent of *2000 AD.* He continued to write for *Jinty* and later *Girl* magazine.

Amongst his most well known stories is the critically acclaimed series *Charley's War* in *Battle* which has a strong girls comic influence. Other notable works include *Marshal Law* (for *Marvel* and *DC Comics*) *Third World War* in *Crisis*, the title series for *Doctor Who Weekly* and *Dan Dare* in *2000 AD* and the *New Eagle*.

Currently Pat writes for the French market a best-selling Goth series *Requiem Vampire Knight* with art by Olivier Ledroit which is available in the UK through Pat's new digital-comic publishing imprint *Millsverse* (http://www.millsverse.com/) and on *Comixology*.

# MALCOLM SHAW

**Malcolm Shaw** began his career in journalism with D C Thomson, Dundee, in the mid 60s. He became chief sub editor on *Red Star Weekly* before he left in 1968 to work in London. For the next four years he worked at City Magazines on *Men Only*, *Parade*, *Go Girl* and *Provincial Press* Features as a features writer. He also wrote comedy sketches for an agency. He went for a job as editor of *Romance* and *My Story* and the interviewer asked him to spell "mantelpiece." He spelt it correctly and was given the job.

In 1972 he joined the Girls' Adventure Group at IPC Magazines, subbing and writing on various comics and *Mates*, teenage romantic fiction. He became editor of the revamped *Mirabelle* in 1977 and stayed with the paper until it folded. In 1979 he became freelance working on *Girl*, *Tammy*, *2000 AD*, *Princess*, *Tina* (Holland), *Saint* (Sweden), *Jackie*, *Blue Jeans* and *Misty*. He was probably best remembered as editor of *Misty* — a popular girls' mystery comic which proved popular with all the family. Malcolm wrote many *Misty* stories.

In 1980 he moved to Barcelona for a year with his partner and two sons. Many of the artists who worked for the girls' comics e.g. Blas Gallego, Jose Canovas, Santiago Hernandez, Rafael Busom, lived in Barcelona and they became firm friends. He returned to London in 1981 and shortly before his death he was helping develop *BEEB* — a new children's magazine based on BBC TV programmes — for Polystyle Publications.

He died the day before his 38th birthday.

# JOHN ARMSTRONG

**John Armstrong** worked extensively on girl's comics throughout the seventies and eighties, including *Misty*, *Bunty*, *Tammy* and *Girl's Crystal*. Having learnt his craft while serving in the British army overseas, he returned to art school at Constantine College in Middlesbrough where he graduated in Intermediate Arts & Craft.

Best known for illustrating the gymnastics-based strip, *Bella* in *Tammy*, Armstrong also drew a comic based on the popular children's school drama *Grange Hill* for Beeb magazine.

# BRIAN DELANEY

**Brian Delaney** was a regular contributor to D. C. Thomson titles including *(Buddy)*. *Hart to Hart*, *Grange Hill* (Fleetway) 80's annuals, *TV Tops* and *The Professionals*.

# Misty says...

# BE A DEVIL

## and here's how...

PEEP HOLES

TOILET ROLL CYLINDERS

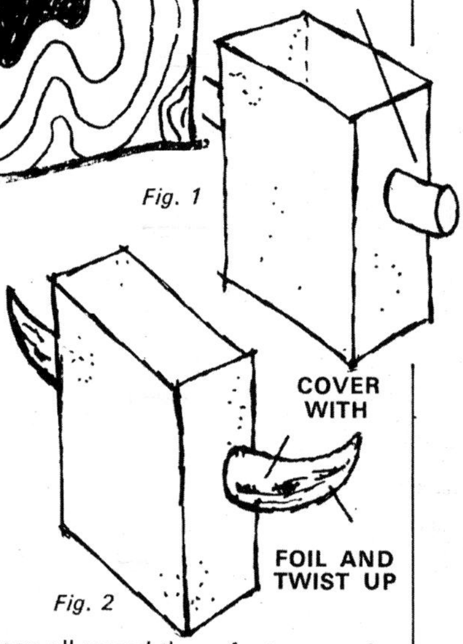

*Fig. 1*

COVER WITH

FOIL AND TWIST UP

*Fig. 2*

**I**'M SURE you've often noticed that trees appear to have faces, especially if you happen to be lost in the middle of a dark wood. Some have twisted, evil expressions while others look homely and lumpy, but kind. No wonder our ancient Briton ancestors believed in tree spirits and worshipped them in strange ceremonies in the forests.

☆

YOU too can turn yourself into a tree-devil with one of these masks. You will need:

*A large, empty breakfast cereal packet. Two cardboard cylinders from toilet rolls. Two egg-holders cut from an empty egg-box. Some green crepe paper. A sheet of silver foil. Two thin twigs for hands. A short, thick twig for the nose. Some thick paint. Gum or paste. Paint and paste brushes.*

☆

CUT OFF the top and bottom end flaps of the cereal packet, then use your toilet-roll cylinders to make the horns. Trace round the ends with a pencil on the sides of the packet, then cut out the circles and insert the cylinders (fig. 1).

Then cover them with silver foil, twisting them up into curved points, as in fig. 2.

Make the bulbous eyes with the egg-holders; cut little slits about half a centimetre long all round the edges, then bend back to form tabs (fig. 3).

Use these tabs to glue or paste them onto the mask.

In the centre of the face make two slits in the form of a cross, then push a thick bit of wood for the nose into the centre of the cross. Then paint the mask all over — sides and back too — with thick, brown paint.

### TO MAKE THE EYES

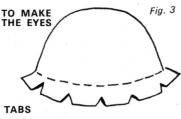

*Fig. 3*

TABS

Wait for it to dry, and paint on black, irregular circles for eyes and mouth. Using black, or different shades of brown or yellow, paint irregular, "woody" rings all round these features and between.

Cut strips from the green crepe paper, then cut one edge of each strip into a fringe.

Gum or paste the unfringed edges inside the top of the mask and bend the strips over to form leafy fronds.

Then stick twigs for hands in the sides, below the horns. Finally, try the mask on, find out where your eyes will come, then take it off and cut two tiny peepholes.

☆

**Now you're all set to be a devil and scare the family!**